Tony La Russa

Man on a Mission

Tony La Russa

Man on a Mission

Rob Rains

TRIUMPH
BOOKS

Triumph Books and colophon are registered trademarks of Random House, Inc.

Library of Congress Cataloging-in-Publication Data

This book is available in quantity at special discounts for your group or organization. For further information, contact:

Triumph Books
542 South Dearborn Street
Suite 750
Chicago, Illinois 60605
(312) 939-3330
Fax (312) 663-3557

Printed in U.S.A.
ISBN 10: 1-60078-169-1
ISBN 13: 978-1-60078-169-8
Design by Patricia Frey

"I have the fire that burns inside me, and it tells me I want to win any way that I can."

—*Tony La Russa*

Contents

Acknowledgments

The author would like to thank the following people for granting interview requests for this book: Sparky Anderson, Harold Baines, Dusty Baker, the late Ed Brinkman, Roy Carrasco, Bobby Cox, Bobby Cueto, Richard Dotson, Dave Van Dyke, Dennis Eckersley, Ed Farmer, Eva and Victor Fojaco, Gene Gieselmann, Joe Goddard, Derrick Goold, Roland Hemond, Dave Henderson, Tom Kelly, Rusty Kuntz, Art Kusnyer, Carney Lansford, Rene Lachemann, Mike Lefkow, Jim Leyland, Greg Luzinski, Charlie Miranda, Mickey Morabito, Jim Morrison, Joe Nossek, Ken Oberkfell, Tom Pagnozzi, Dave Phillips, Jim Riggleman, Jerry Reinsdorf, Kerry Robinson, Tony Saladino, Tom Spencer, Mike Squires, Terry Steinbach, Kit Stier, Ken Suarez, Marc Topkin, Greg Walker, and Walt Weiss.

The author also thanks all of the reporters and columnists who have covered Tony La Russa over the years for the *Tampa Tribune*, *St. Petersburg Times*, *Kansas City Star*, *Chicago Sun-Times*, *Chicago Tribune*, *New York Times*, *San Jose Mercury-News*, *San Francisco Chronicle*, *Oakland Tribune*, *Contra Costa Times*, *St. Louis Post-Dispatch*, *Belleville News-Democrat*, *The Sporting News*, *Sports Illustrated*, and *USA Today*.

Thanks also to the research staff of the public libraries in Knoxville, New Orleans, Des Moines, Chicago, and Oakland, who were very helpful, as were Scott Reifort and the public relations staff of the Chicago White Sox, and Bob Rose and Debbie Gallas of the Oakland Athletics.

Finally, thank you to Tony La Russa for his contributions and assistance.

Foreword

You don't know Tony La Russa. You think you do, but you don't. Unless you are a friend of his I guarantee you that what you think you know about this man is not accurate.

It does not matter if you are in the game of baseball or not. If you have been in another dugout watching from a distance, formulating opinions about him, or if you have seen him in the corner of the dugout from your seat or your television set, your picture is incomplete. Never have I met a man in sports or life who is more misunderstood.

If you owned a team, and maybe not just a baseball team, this would be a person you would want running your multimillion-dollar investment. If you ran a Fortune 500 company, he would be the one you would want to make the daily decisions. If you put together a military strategy to win a battle, he would be the guy to carry it out. But you have to know him. From a distance some think he seems arrogant. From a distance he appears to think he is better at what he does than you are at what you do. You know what? He probably is.

I don't know about you, but few things in this world bug me more than laziness. Tony La Russa is lazy's enemy. He will not be outworked. He won't always win, but it will not be from a lack of preparation or effort. If his players played the game as hard as he managed it, the other teams would be playing for second place. Before you think this is a load, that the author of this foreword must owe Tony money, and that you should skip to chapter one, stop! Don't do it! It was not always puppy dogs and rainbows with us.

My relationship with Tony La Russa began in 1996. I was in my sixth season as a Cardinals radio announcer, and he was in his first year as manager with St. Louis. Tony brought with him a résumé that included a world championship with the A's in 1989 and a reputation of not suffering fools in the media. I was 26, and I was a member of the media, unsure of whether I qualified for the "fools" part. Rumor was that Tony did his own daily "manager's show" at the end of his run in Oakland because he did not want to always answer someone else's questions about what happened the night before.

By 1995 the A's were on the way down and the questions about their futility were probably not fun to answer day after day. Guess what my job was in those days? That's right, the Cardinals' manager's show. I had done it with Joe Torre previously, and now it was day one of the La Russa era. We opened in New York against the Mets, and I was armed with my microphone and recorder, sitting in the dugout, waiting for Tony to get off the field.

After waving Tony down and reminding him that it was time to do his bit, I had to ask the question that was as awkward as it was important. "Tony, am I going to ask you questions and do an interview, or will you do this show by yourself?" was what I came up with. His answer was short and sweet: "You can ask me questions—unless I don't think you can handle it—and then we'll see."

So, nervously, away I went, and fortunately I continued to do the show throughout the season. I guess I passed the test. As it turns out Tony is the easiest interview I have ever had. Nobody I have ever met in sports puts more thought and research into every decision he makes, and he is always ready to talk about it. He is a thinking man's leader, and he is so secure in what he does, no matter what you ask him, he never gets defensive, and he always has a reason.

As I wrapped up that first visit I exhaled, not knowing how much I would come to respect No. 10 and how much he would teach me about the game we all love.

Believe it or not, for Tony, life is much more than baseball—I think. There are times during the course of any season where the game seems to overwhelm him. He carries it all on his sleeve. An innocuous greeting like "Hey, Tony, how ya doin?" is met with an icy glare and the response, "I'll let you know at 10:00 tonight." His mood, like any Cardinals fan's, is determined by the goings-on between 7:00 and 10:00 PM. However, he manages from a standpoint of strength, never fear. As Tony likes to say, "These are men, not machines." At some point a manager is only as good as the players who are asked to carry out the plan.

There is another side to Tony that some see, and others would be hard-pressed to believe it exists. He is a romantic, and someone who would give you the shirt off his back if you needed it. I am not even convinced that his players see this side. His charitable efforts are many. Some we all know about, like the Animal Rescue Foundation, and some are not so public. Tony rarely says no when he is asked for a favor. Whether it is me asking for Children's Hospital or someone he runs into who is sick or down and would get a lift from a visit to the dugout, Tony is there to help.

Tony asks for respect from his players year after year, roster after roster. Respect for him and respect for the game they play. Tony respects the game and its history more than anyone I have run across. I am convinced that Tony has stayed in St. Louis all these years because he loves the uniform he is wearing. He genuinely gets excited to put on the same uniform worn with dignity by Stan the Man, Red Schoendienst, Bob Gibson, and Lou Brock. He is a historian of the game, and when Yankee Stadium was in its final week, Tony flew there on his off day to see it one last time. His relationships in the game are far-reaching. He loves those who played the game before him and those from whom he can learn. He was mentored by Paul Richards of the White Sox, he deferred to George Kissell of the Cardinals. He stays close to the guys he played with and to those who played for him, both stars and part-timers.

It is not just baseballers, by the way. Tony is way too well-rounded to surround himself with just one group. Spring training is a who's who of luminaries from the world of politics, sports, and entertainment. At his dinner table after a game or in his office before it, you can find Bill Belichick, John Havlicek, Bob Knight, General Hal Moore, or Bruce Springsteen. He loves being able to meet interesting people while he winds his way through the seasons, pulling the strings of a big-league baseball team.

The romantic part I referred to earlier is pretty personal. I loved watching Tony around my dad Jack. There was a great relationship between the two men who loved baseball but were well-rounded, charitable people. My father was a tough nut to crack. He had a solid inner circle, and for the average person it was tough to get in there. Tony did immediately.

By the end of his life, my father would have considered Tony one of his best friends. Their relationship meant a lot to my father. They loved to talk about the game and its history. They talked politics and told jokes to each other. Tony loved having my dad around him because he respected his 50 years in the game and his sense of humor. Tony's nickname for him was "the Legendary Jack." I think my dad liked that as much as he laughed it off.

For Tony it wasn't just about my father, but my mom as well. They were a package deal. Carole Buck is an important part of Tony's life, too. After my dad died in 2002, our family, and my mom in particular, learned something about human nature. Once my dad was gone, a lot of their "friends" were off to other things and other people. Tony has never forgotten my mom. Nobody has made her feel more welcome in the Cardinals family than Tony La Russa. He does it not just because she is fun to be with, but because my dad would appreciate Tony looking after her. That's why I love this man. He is the best at what he does, and he does it the right way. There are a thousand examples that demonstrate why Tony is so unique. I know my dad would be proud of how he has continued to live his life in and out of the dugout.

That year was one I will never forget. Four days after my father passed away Darryl Kile died in his hotel room in Chicago. At no time has a professional baseball team leaned more upon its manager. A death on a team usually sinks a club. Tony gathered up that group of young men, let them grieve, and then got them focused on the game again. It turned into another trip to the postseason for the manager with the third-most wins of all time.

This is not to suggest that he is an old softy. He is a passionate and fiery manager. He gets hot when he has to. One summer night he followed Steve

Kline into the showers, still wearing his uniform, for a confrontation after Kline gave him an obscene gesture when he wasn't brought into a game. I am sure there are many stories like this. There has to be an element of fear with players, and I am sure his guys have it.

Someday, when Tony decides he has had enough, the clock will start, and the countdown to his enshrinement at Cooperstown will begin. I do not know the other managers in the Hall like I know Tony. I don't know how they worked or what they were really like as men. All I know is that when that day comes, the Hall of Fame will open its doors to someone who gave everything he had on the field, and was a world-class human being off of it.

—Joe Buck

Prologue

On the final day of the 2008 regular season, the St. Louis Cardinals and the Cincinnati Reds are playing a game at Busch Stadium that means virtually nothing. A playoff spot will not be waiting for the winner. Nobody will be fired because of a loss. In three hours or so, the year will be over, the final results ready for the archives.

The mood seems relaxed and jovial, almost like the first game of spring training. Players from both teams mingle and talk about their plans for the winter. Best wishes are exchanged, with promises to call or "see you next year."

This scene is being played out in stadiums all across the country, where 20 of the 30 major-league teams already know that they are 27 outs away from the top of the winter. In his 29 full seasons managing in the major leagues, this is the 17th time Tony La Russa has found himself in this position.

Experience does not make him hate the feeling any less.

To La Russa, who has managed the Cardinals for the last 13 of those 29 years, there is no such thing as a meaningless game. If a game is being played and a winner and loser will be determined by the outcome, he wants to win. He had that mentality growing up in Tampa, Florida. He had it as a player in the minor leagues, and, for a brief time, in the majors. Most important, he has had it since August 2, 1979, the day Bill Veeck hired him as the manager of the Chicago White Sox.

"We missed the playoffs, and I don't like it," La Russa would say after this game. "October baseball is the best. I'm not a happy camper. October is why you go to spring training."

This is the 4,610[th] regular-season game that La Russa has managed in the major leagues. The only two managers ahead of him on the all-time list are Connie Mack and John McGraw. If La Russa completes the 2009 season, he will move past McGraw into second place on the all-time list of games managed.

When La Russa broke into the fraternity of managers at the age of 34, Sparky Anderson, Gene Mauch, Billy Martin, Earl Weaver, and Whitey Herzog were in opposing dugouts. He talked to them, he listened, and he learned. Over the 29-plus years he has managed, 156 other men have come and gone as managers in the major leagues, alphabetically running from Manny Acta all the way to Don Zimmer—and that doesn't count interim replacements.

"What tells you how good a manager is, is length of time," Anderson said when talking about La Russa. "Owners don't keep you around if you don't have a lot of good things going for you."

In 2006 La Russa became the second manager in history to win a World Series in each league, joining Anderson. In addition to winning two world championships, La Russa's teams in Chicago, Oakland, and St. Louis have won five league pennants and 10 division titles and made two wild-card appearances.

Part of what has made La Russa so successful, if you listen to his former players, is the attitude that the only thing that matters is the game today. If you win, great, let's try to win again tomorrow. If you lose, try to figure out why and don't let it happen again.

"He takes it personally when his team loses," said his former player and coach, Carney Lansford. "What has made him so good is he is so competitive. If he loses, he is the first one to look in the mirror and ask what he could have done differently to help win the game. Sometimes it is not a good thing because he is so hard on himself."

The only factor that will determine La Russa's mood following a game is whether his team has won or lost. He has canceled postgame dinner plans with opposing managers after a loss. He does not call his wife Elaine at home after losses. In the minor leagues, he often spent the night in the clubhouse if his team lost, thinking about what he could do differently in the next game.

Nobody who has spent any time with La Russa fails to appreciate his work ethic. Nobody prepares more for a game, devotes more hours to studying charts and data when putting a starting lineup together, or tries harder to find even the slightest statistical advantage. He could well make a move during a game that doesn't work, or that critics disagree with, but one fact is certain—he will have a reason, and an explanation, ready at the end of the game.

"I came into the league as a baby," La Russa once said. "There were giants in the league, guys so big you knew them by their first name—Billy and Whitey and Sparky and Earl. My club had to look at who we were playing and think [the opponent] had the best of it. To narrow that difference, I got as much information as I could—my own notes, reports from scouts.

"When I watch the game, there's no script. I have all that information, but I have to trust my gut."

La Russa never likes to use the word *surprise*. If you ask him if he is surprised by a player's success, he thinks a yes answer could be interpreted that he didn't believe the player would be successful. If he is surprised by something that happens during a game, it means he was not adequately prepared—a notion that is totally unacceptable.

The word most of his former players use to describe La Russa during a game is *intense*. He is focused on one thing and one thing only, winning the game that his team is playing that day.

La Russa is often credited with developing the closer, who does nothing but pitch the ninth inning when his team is in a save situation. He makes more pitching changes than a lot of managers and almost always prefers to have a left-handed pitcher work against a left-handed batter, even if it means he will go through three or more relievers in an inning.

Once, in Oakland, La Russa even had a backup catcher warming up in the bullpen during a game because he knew that if a couple of fast runners reached base, he would change catchers to better guard against stealing.

He is not afraid to make unconventional decisions, such as putting his starting pitcher eighth in the batting order. Does it really make any difference in determining whether his team wins or loses? Perhaps in some games, not in others, but if La Russa thinks it gives his team an advantage, he will do it.

At least today, the final game of the 2008 regular seasons, it helps. The pitcher's first at-bat comes up in the second inning, with the Cardinals leading 2–1 thanks to a Ryan Ludwick home run in the first. With two outs and nobody on base, Brad Thompson drops a bloop single behind first base. Brendan Ryan, batting ninth, also singles, as does leadoff hitter Cesar Izturis. When Felipe Lopez follows with a double, the Cardinals have stretched their lead to 5–1.

A six-run third inning blows the game open and the Cardinals go on to win 11–4. Along the way La Russa has honored his team's best player, Albert Pujols, by lifting him from the game after his third-inning double so he can receive one final standing ovation for the season and a curtain call from the fans.

Ludwick also comes out of the game early and gets his own cheers, but afterward La Russa realizes one more hit would have raised Ludwick's batting average to .300 instead of finishing at .299. He purposely did not start Aaron Miles and Skip Schumaker so they could finish the year above .300 and he feels bad about not giving Ludwick a chance to get to that level too.

"I was focusing on a bunch of stuff and I missed it completely," La Russa said. "It will take me a while to get over it. His neck's been stiff and I wanted to get him out of there on a high note. I didn't even think about him having another at-bat with a chance to hit .300. I was really sick to my stomach about it.

"I remember from when I first started managing. I was told you can never have a great day completely. There will always be something that bothers you. I cost Ryan a chance to hit .300, and that's not a good thought."

Part of the reason for that reaction is that La Russa himself had been in that position once, in the minor leagues. In 1966, playing at Double-A Mobile, La Russa saw his average drop from .300 to .294 on the final day of the season.

La Russa's reaction demonstrated not only the loyalty and respect that he gives his players, but the respect that he has for the game. He knows that one hit in 539 at-bats would have made the difference between hitting .300 and hitting .299, a difference far greater than a single percentage point.

La Russa was aware that relief pitcher Russ Springer was considering retirement, so he made certain that he called on him to come in and get the final out of the game, just in case he does not return in 2009.

It was another sign of respect. "Springer deserved to get the last out," La Russa said.

Only two seasons in La Russa's long career have truly ended the way he hopes every season could end: with his team as the world champions. Falling short of that goal makes for a long winter, waiting for next year to begin.

Before this game, La Russa called Joe Maddon, the manager of the Tampa Bay Rays, to congratulate him on his team's success and to wish the team well in their first trip to the playoffs. La Russa knows what it is like to be playing deep into October, as well as what it is like to finish in last place.

Only three players in the Cardinals' lineup for this game—Ludwick, Troy Glaus, and Jason LaRue—were alive when La Russa managed his first game in the major leagues. As much as the game has changed three decades later, some things have remained the same. La Russa asks for the same commitment from his players today as he did the first day he managed. He wants them to be totally dedicated to their job, to play the game hard, to play the game right, and to do whatever it takes to try to win the game. Nothing more, nothing less.

He has not wavered on his promise to his players, either. "A manager's job is to stand in front of a team and say, 'Trust in me, because I can help make you a team that can win,'" La Russa said many years ago.

La Russa's passion for the game has not diminished over time. Neither has his commitment to winning.

Says Detroit Tigers manager and longtime friend Jim Leyland, "He loves the game, he respects it. He loves the players. He is relentless in competing, even in golf. He won't let up, no matter what. The rest of us are just out there to have a good time, and he won't let up. He doesn't always count accurately either. If he hits a bad shot, he drops another ball and sometimes has a tendency not to count it."

The opposing manager in this game, Dusty Baker, has played with La Russa, for La Russa, and managed against him.

"I like managing and competing against Tony," Baker said. "It's fun."

Baker even made an appearance to help another of La Russa's passions, raising money for his Animal Rescue Foundation.

"I had been duck hunting, and I stopped at a gas station to change out of my fatigues," Baker said. "When I got to the fund-raiser, I was in the back, laughing with Rickey Henderson. I raised my hand because I was laughing so hard, and they said, 'Sold to the man in the blue shirt.' It was me. I didn't know if it was $500 or $5,000 or what I had bid on. The lady came up to me and I had to ask her what I had just bought and how much it had cost me. I bought an autographed Patrick Ewing shoe and it only cost me $100."

Friends such as Leyland, White Sox owner Jerry Reinsdorf, basketball coach Bobby Knight, football coach Bill Parcells, and other high-profile celebrities have seen La Russa when he is smiling, laughing, and having a good time. That side of La Russa is often kept in private, revealed only to those he considers close friends. When the public only sees him standing near the steps of the Cardinals' dugout, they see someone who is a hundred percent serious, focused, and dedicated. It is the reason he earned the nickname "Dr. Jekyll and Mr. Tony" when he managed the A's.

Leyland, who is two months younger than La Russa, has a prediction about how long La Russa will continue to manage.

"He will stick around as long as the fire is burning to manage," Leyland said. "If the fire is not there, he won't do it. He won't stick around just to get a record. I know him too well. The day he thinks he is cheating somebody out of a day's pay he will move on."

Make no mistake, the fire that began a long time ago, when La Russa was a young boy, is still burning as brightly as ever. Next year can't begin soon enough.

CHAPTER

Early Years

The clothes had been carefully selected and laid out on the six-year-old's bed. All of the first-graders at V.M. Ybor Elementary School in Tampa, Florida, were expected to dress nicely for the school's annual picture day. When Tony La Russa walked into his bedroom, however, he knew something was wrong. His mother's choice of a shirt, slacks, and his good shoes was not going to work.

"No, Mama," he said in a respectful voice. "I can't wear that. I'm wearing my baseball uniform."

Oliva La Russa started to protest. "Baseball uniform?" she said. "Oh no you're not."

The discussion did not last long, and had a predictable outcome—predictable to anyone who has ever dealt with a determined Tony La Russa. "You know Tony," his mother said many years later, in an interview with the *Tampa Tribune*. "He talked me into it. When Tony puts his mind to something, there is just no convincing him otherwise."

Even at that early age, the son of Oliva and Tony La Russa Sr. had fallen in love with baseball. The elder La Russa had played sandlot baseball as a youth growing up in the Ybor City section of Tampa. He was a catcher, but he never had the chance to pursue his favorite sport as a career. In the years before World War II, finding a job that paid well was more important.

1

"You had to make a living," said La Russa Sr., whose family had emigrated from Italy to Tampa. "There weren't many guys who had the chance to make a career in baseball."

He found a job at the Perfecto-Garcia cigar factory in Ybor City. That was where he met his future wife, Oliva, who also was working there. In 1942, their first child, a daughter they named Eva, was born. Two years later, Oliva became pregnant again.

"We didn't know if it was a boy or a girl, but my husband was telling everyone, 'I'm going to have a junior baseball player in the family,'" Mrs. La Russa said.

On October 4, 1944, Anthony La Russa Jr. was born. His first instructions in baseball soon followed, almost before he could walk or talk.

La Russa Sr. recalled those days in a 1990 interview with the *Tampa Tribune*. "I would throw him little tennis balls, soft ones so he wouldn't get hurt, and teach him how to swing the bat," he said. "He loved it. It got to be where he would be waiting in the door for me when I got home from work. He always wanted to play ball."

The family lived in Oliva's mother's house for a few years until her death. Home then became an apartment above a service station. Luckily for La Russa the apartment was near Cuscaden Park, a gathering place for the boys in the Ybor City area, which included perhaps the best baseball diamond in the city.

Whenever he wasn't in school, La Russa was at the park. He wasn't the only boy in the area who liked baseball, so there always was a pickup game of some sort going on, depending on how many kids were there. Games of corkball, three-man ball, and pepper filled his days. La Russa even brought a couple of sandwiches with him so he would not have to interrupt his day of baseball by going home to eat.

While other kids would come and go, combining baseball with other activities such as going to the swimming pool or the beach or fishing, La Russa was a fixture at the park. On the rare occasions when La Russa had no one else to play with, he even enlisted the services of his mother, who went out into the alley with her son and either pitched to him or threw him groundballs so he could practice his fielding.

La Russa also knew as a young boy that he liked animals, but the family never had a pet because of some frightening moments for La Russa's mother and sister.

"Before we were born, our mother got bit by a cat that had rabies," said Eva (La Russa) Fojaco. "She had to get all of the shots and got very sick. She had been walking to work and the cat just jumped her one day."

Then, when Eva was four years old, the family was visiting her aunt and uncle's house when a dog jumped up and bit her in the face. The cuts required stitches, but luckily Eva did not have to undergo rabies shots.

"Our mother loved animals but she just could not be around them after that," Fojaco said. "She always felt bad that we couldn't have a pet but Tony and I told her it was not a big deal. She never wanted harm to come to any animal."

By age six, La Russa was playing organized baseball in the park league, where he was often the youngest and smallest boy on the field. His already developing skill made up for the difference in age and size, however. If anyone tried to take advantage of him, he quickly learned he had made a mistake.

"We were both at the park one day, but I was in a different group of older kids," said La Russa's cousin, Bobby Cueto, who is six years older. "I saw a kid push Tony. The kid was bigger than him, and I went over and told Tony he could not let that kid push him around. The next thing I knew Tony had knocked him down. He didn't look very tough, but he was."

The reputation that was building throughout the community, however, was about La Russa's skills on the baseball field. Even Cueto's friends would walk or ride their bicycles to watch when they knew La Russa had a game to play.

"They weren't going because he was my cousin, they were going because of the amazing things he could do as a little kid," Cueto said. "He would be running toward a base, and would throw his slide away from the base, and after the fielder missed the tag, he would reach back and touch the base with his hand. A lot of major leaguers don't slide any better than that."

Perhaps one of the few places in the world where baseball was more popular in the early 1950s than Tampa was the island of Cuba. In 1954, a coach at Cuscaden Park, Andrew Espolita, organized an All-Star team and raised enough money to take 12 young players to Cuba for a week-long series of games. It would be five years before Fidel Castro became president of Cuba and seven years before the U.S. trade embargo with Cuba began. The youngest player selected for the team was the shortstop, La Russa, age 10. Most of the other players were 12 or 13 years old.

"He was like a vacuum cleaner," said Charlie Miranda, another player selected for the traveling team. "Not only could he catch everything but his release to first was very quick."

La Russa's parents were nervous about letting their son make the trip, which was not only his first time on an airplane but his first time away from home. The same was true for most of the other boys as well, and they knew they had to let him go.

Miranda recalled the start of the trip as being the most nerve-wracking moment of his life. "I remember when the engines started, there was all this black smoke and flames," Miranda said. "I think I said out loud, 'Holy hell, what is this?' I almost went to the bathroom in my pants." Luckily, the plane took off safely and there were no problems en route to Havana.

Because La Russa had been raised in a home where Spanish, the native language of his mother and grandmother, had been spoken before English, he was chosen to be the captain of the team, along with Miranda.

"That first night we didn't stay with the rest of the team," Miranda said. "We stayed in the house of the president of the Optimist Club, which sponsored the trip. I had never seen a house like that. It had marble floors and was absolutely gorgeous."

Miranda and La Russa were interviewed on the Cuban national radio and television stations about the upcoming games, and huge crowds turned out to watch. The Tampa team played different teams from throughout Cuba, and for the final game they were scheduled to play what was billed as the best youth team in the country.

The stands were packed, and some of the more vocal fans were chanting "Yankee go home" as Tampa's starting pitcher began to warm up on the mound. Miranda had pitched an earlier game and was playing in left field when he saw the team's coach motioning for him to come to the mound. The Tampa team's starting pitcher had literally thrown up on the mound, and there was nobody else who could pitch, the coach said.

"The Cuba kids were supposed to be the same age as us, but as the first batter came to the plate, I swore he had a moustache and a beard," Miranda said. "He had to be at least 15 or 16 years old. I saw why our other pitcher had thrown up."

Miranda got ahead in the count with two curveballs for strikes, but then he threw a fastball. "I think they are still looking for the ball," Miranda said.

It probably was better for international relations that Cuba won the game 4–2, although La Russa's teammates learned that, from an early age, he never wanted to lose any game or competition of any kind.

By the time La Russa was set to leave grade school and begin junior high, his father had left the cigar factory and, after delivering ice, began a new job driving a delivery truck for Florida Dairy. The family also had bought their first home, in West Tampa, about 15 minutes away from Ybor City.

"Tony didn't want to go and I didn't want to go," said his sister. "All our friends were there. But my parents told Tony there was another park right by the house and that things would work out."

The new house was directly behind Macfarlane Park and, like Cuscaden Park, quickly became La Russa's home away from home. "He could walk down the alley and be at the park in a couple of minutes," said his new friend, Roy Carrasco, who coincidentally had also moved from Ybor City to West Tampa in the summer of 1956, before the boys began at West Tampa Junior High as seventh graders. "We played all day long," Carrasco recalled. "We would be there until 8:00 or 9:00 at night. His mother would yell a couple of times for us to come in, but as soon as his dad yelled once, we knew we had to get going. He had super parents, the best parents any kid could have. They were just super people."

As La Russa's parents had predicted, the move did not interrupt La Russa's ability to play baseball or attract friends. "From the first day we moved and he went to the park to check it out, he had friends," said La Russa's sister, Eva.

La Russa also was now old enough to be assigned chores around the new house, such as mowing the lawn. It was not unusual, however, for Eva or her parents to look outside and find one of La Russa's new friends doing the work for him. "I don't know how he got his friends to do stuff like that for him," Eva Fojaco said. She suspects that it had something to do with their mother's cooking.

"Tony always came in the house and asked Mom if she baked any cookies or anything that he could give to his friends," she said. "Our house was always full of people, his friends and my friends, and our mother enjoyed cooking for them."

One day a friend showed up at La Russa's house with a BB gun. Since his father was not a hunter, the young La Russa had no experience with guns. "There was a sparrow sitting on the chain-link fence, maybe six or seven yards away," La Russa said. "I can't believe I hit it, but I did and I killed it. It traumatized the hell out of me. It was the last time I ever shot at an animal." It was a moment that had a huge impact on him.

Carrasco had heard of La Russa's reputation as a baseball player, but he did not meet La Russa until their families both moved to West Tampa. Their love of baseball instantly bonded them together. The boys sometimes attempted to sneak into the Cincinnati Reds' spring-training games at Al Lopez Field. More often than not, they went to those games and waited outside the stadium in hopes that a baseball would come flying over the wall.

"When we ran out of baseballs for our games, we didn't have any money to buy one," Carrasco said. "We'd go to Al Lopez Field, which wasn't too far away, and chase balls that came over the wall. It really was a game because they had a security guard named Manny DeCastro who used to chase kids, trying to get the balls back. Manny's favorite saying was, 'Hey, son, stop. I know your mother and I know your father.' After the person stopped and returned the ball to Manny he would ask them their name. Tony and I knew all about Manny's tactics. We also knew we could outrun him.

"One day we had just gotten to the park and a ball came over the wall and landed right at my feet. Manny was already on the move, headed right for us, when another ball came over the wall and landed right at Tony's feet. He picked it up and we both took off. Manny had a good start on us, but we ran through the cars and got to a dead end. We split up and each went one way and Manny finally stopped chasing us. That's how we got our baseballs."

The boys were at Macfarlane Park one day playing when an older gentleman approached them. "He asked us if we wanted to play Pony League ball," Carrasco said. "We said yes, but where would we play?" He said the games would be in south Tampa, at Grady Field, behind Christ the King Church.

Carrasco and La Russa said there was no way they could do that, because they were not old enough to drive and with their parents working, they had no way to get to and from the games. The man was persistent, however. He said there was a tryout scheduled for the league for the next Saturday, and said if the boys came and tried out, and he was able to pick both of them for his team, he would speak to their parents and arrange to pick them up and bring them home for every game.

"How do you think you can get both of us on your team?" Carrasco asked.

"He said, 'You guys have to do one thing…you guys have to look terrible at the tryouts.'" When the boys asked the man what he meant, he continued, "The only way I will be able to pick both of you is if you both look bad at the tryouts. That's the only shot I have of getting you both." Carrasco, who was a pitcher and outfielder, and La Russa, still a shortstop, talked it over and decided to take the chance.

"It was hilarious," Carrasco said. "Tony was the type of kid who never missed a ground ball. The coaches were hitting him ground balls and he was letting them go right through his legs. I was playing the outfield and would let fly balls land behind my head. When we came in to hit we were hacking at the ball. We were terrible. We were secretly laughing at each other because we knew we were not that kind of players."

The strategy worked. The draft came, and both La Russa and Carrasco ended up on the same team. The surprise was on the rest of the league as the two ended up on the All-Star team and led their squad to consecutive undefeated seasons.

The team was sponsored by Rock-a-Bye Diapers, the company that also gave La Russa his first paying job.

"On Saturday mornings, Roy and I would go there and work several hours, taking dirty diapers and putting them in the washing machines, then the dryers," La Russa said. "They were hot as hell and we burned our hands."

After starring at that level, both La Russa and Carrasco were selected to play on a Colt League All-Star team representing Tampa. Carrasco was not able to play because he was attending summer school. La Russa and the rest of the team, however, advanced to the Colt League World Series, played in Ontario, California It was on that team that the 15-year-old La Russa first came into contact with a boy who would be a teammate and rival for the rest of his life, Lou Piniella.

Like La Russa, Piniella had been a fixture at the local baseball parks in Tampa. He was a year older than La Russa, and was primarily a pitcher and outfielder. La Russa's new home in West Tampa was only a couple of miles from Piniella's home.

"There were times I had to drag him off the field," Piniella's mother once said of her young son, a comment that could have also been made by La Russa's mother. "He would come home from school, do his homework, and then go to the playground and play baseball. He always wanted to be a baseball player."

Piniella's dream, and his life, almost ended on that Colt League trip to California. Another player on the team, Paul Ferlita, recalled what happened in an interview with the *St. Petersburg Times*.

"We had taken a trip up to one of the mountains and we were walking along a ledge toward a waterfall," Ferlita said. "Piniella and La Russa rolled a log down the side and my father held them back from the group and lectured them while the rest of us walked ahead. They tried to catch up and ran along the edge of the mountain and Lou fell and tumbled for quite a while before he hit a big boulder. It was the only thing between him and a 2,000-foot drop. If he hadn't hit the boulder, he'd probably have been killed."

Piniella was injured seriously enough that he did not start either of the final two games of the tournament. He had severe cuts on his head and a badly swollen ankle, which limited him to pinch-hitting appearances. The Tampa team had been undefeated up to that point in the tournament, but lost both of the final games and finished second. If Piniella, the team's best pitcher, had been healthy they may well have won the national championship.

Piniella's now-famous temper came out when the winning team gathered on the pitcher's mound after the final out, saying a team prayer. "All of a sudden, Lou gets up out of the dugout and throws a ball at them," Ferlita said. "It landed right in the middle of their prayer meeting."

Piniella had not bothered to call home to tell his parents about his accident. When he got back to Tampa, a trip to the doctor's office revealed he had suffered a broken ankle.

La Russa was at his best in those games, observers said. "One of the players on the team told me that they did not give an MVP award, but if they did, Tony would have won it easily," Cueto said. "He said that when they introduced players to start the game, Tony received a standing ovation because of the plays he made."

Professional scouts had now taken notice of both La Russa, who was attending Jefferson High School, and Piniella, who was at nearby Jesuit High, a Catholic school. That attention would not diminish.

The first time Tony La Russa knew a professional scout was watching one of his games, by his own estimation, he threw five balls over the first baseman's head and let three balls go between his legs.

It was understandable that his nerves had gotten the best of him, at least for that one day, and luckily the scouts returned. As La Russa became accustomed to scouts scrutinizing his every move, he quickly began impress to them the way he had impressed everybody who had watched him play baseball since he was a young boy.

One veteran scout who came to watch him play was George Zuraw, then with the Pittsburgh Pirates. "He came up to Tony before the game and introduced himself and said he could not stay for the entire game because he had another appointment, but that he wanted to let him know the Pirates were interested in him and they would be back in touch," Cueto said. "The game started and Tony didn't think any more about it. At the end of the game the first man onto the field was George Zuraw. He had stayed for the entire game after all.

"He told Tony, 'You made plays today that Dick Groat can't make.' That's the kind of player he was." Groat had won the National League's MVP award in 1960 as the shortstop for the world champion Pirates.

Another baseball man who took notice of La Russa was from the neighborhood, Al Lopez, the manager of the 1959 AL champion Chicago White Sox the baseball patriarch of Tampa and lived only a few blocks from La Russa. Lopez and La Russa's father often played cards together. Lopez even gave some pointers to La Russa about how to play shortstop.

"Al made a great impression on me because he never changed," La Russa once said. "Ten days after managing in the World Series, he'd be back playing cards and flipping dominos at the local Cuban club."

Lopez's success served as an inspiration to La Russa, Piniella, and the other youths playing baseball in Tampa. He had made it from the playgrounds to the major leagues and eventually to the Hall of Fame.

La Russa's relatives and friends had no doubts about his future in baseball and persuaded him not to continue to play either football or basketball after his sophomore year in high school.

"He was just a natural athlete," Cueto said, "but he worked at it too. When he was little we were playing football in the street and he came for a visit. He had never played football before and soon he was running routes and catching balls like it was nothing. He could have been good at any sport."

La Russa was the quarterback of the Jefferson High football team as a sophomore, and also played junior varsity basketball. After dropping those sports, La Russa did continue to play golf, and one day found himself on a par-3 course, Lockraven, with his friend Roy Carrasco. "We were on about the second or third hole and you had to hit the ball over a pond to get to the green," Carrasco said. "I hit my shot and it went over the water. Tony hit his shot, and it went about a mile up in the air. Both of us lost sight of it. We didn't know if it had gone in the water or not.

"We walked around to the green and saw one ball. It was mine. We didn't see Tony's ball, so we figured it must have gone in the water. He started looking and looking because he didn't want to have to give up a stroke. Finally he spotted the ball sitting on top of what appeared to be a small island."

La Russa sized up the situation and thought if he got a running start, he could jump over the approximate 10 feet of water that separated the land from the island. He was going to get his ball and jump back to the land.

"You had to be there to see it," Carrasco said. "He jumped and his legs were churning as he tried to clear the water. He got there and went straight down and that's when I realized that what appeared to look like an island was really a marsh of lily pads. I knew Tony didn't know how to swim so I was taking my shoes off and getting ready to dive in when I saw these mud bubbles coming up to the surface. He came up, and had a lily pad sitting right on top of his head. When I saw he was OK, I started laughing so hard my stomach hurt. I was rolling on the ground. There were a lot of golf balls lying there, and he started picking them up and firing them at me because I was making fun of him."

La Russa had to jump back into the water to get back to the green, and when he rejoined Carrasco he was wet and covered with mud. Carrasco suggested they go home so he could change clothes, but La Russa's competitiveness took over.

"He said, 'Hell no, I'm going to whip your ass.' He played the rest of the 18 holes covered with mud and he *did* kick my butt."

La Russa was also competitive in all of his school activities. He made good grades and was popular with his classmates. Jefferson High's 1962 yearbook, the Monticello, noted that La Russa had been voted the "Most Dignified" boy in the senior class. He was a member of the Student Council for three years, junior director for Key Club, and team captain, All-City, and All-Conference as a baseball player.

While he was concerned with his own activities, he also looked out for his older sister. "She was a senior and Tony was a sophomore," cousin Bobby Cueto remembered. "She was having trouble in one class and was worried that if she did not pass the class she would not be able to graduate. The family had discussed it, and Tony knew what was happening.

"Without anyone saying anything to him, or asking for his help, Tony, on his own, went to Eva's teacher and told the teacher how upset his sister was, and how she was worried about the class. He asked if there was anything he or his parents could do to help her. That's the kind of kid he was." Whether it was because of La Russa's intervention or not will never be known, but his sister did pass the class and graduate on time.

Other than school and family, La Russa's life was mostly consumed by baseball.

"You just knew if he wasn't going to make it as a player he was going to find some other way," Carrasco said. "He was smart. He would always come up to me on the mound and tell me things to calm me down and remind me what I was supposed to do if the ball was hit back to me. He was always one step ahead of everybody else. It was like he was just born that way."

When he didn't have to worry about school in the summer, La Russa often awoke in the middle of the night so he could accompany his father on his route delivering milk. "His dad was a great influence on Tony," Carrasco said. "His dad never missed a game, and he would talk to Tony after the games about what had happened. I know Tony learned a lot from his dad."

Other friends of La Russa's were aware that he was working in the middle of the night, helping his father.

Buck DelaTorre played with La Russa from childhood to high school and later married a girl who had been one of La Russa's neighbors. "There was always something about him," Esther DelaTorre said once. "You just knew he was going to be something someday. When I had slumber parties, girls would come so they could see Tony deliver milk in the morning."

It was while Tony Sr. and Jr. were on one of those early-morning delivery runs that they had a father-to-son heart-to-heart talk, said La Russa's sister. "My dad told him, 'I don't want you doing this. You can do better than this.'"

Buck DelaTorre told the *Tampa Tribune*, "He was always so smooth and fast and sharp. He wasn't an ordinary old fat kid like the rest of us. He was going places. There was something very studious and meticulous about the way he played and practiced. It was something to see."

La Russa's competitive fire helped him to hit .333 as a junior at Jefferson High School and lead his team to the city and conference championship and into the state tournament.

As the team celebrated on the field after winning the city championship, La Russa suggested that they grab their coach, Nello Rimaldi, and dump him in the swimming pool across the street. Four or five of the players picked up Rimaldi, and the rest of the players and about 150 fans followed.

"When we dumped the coach into the deep end of the pool Tony accidentally fell in at the same time," Carrasco said. "Everybody was still in our uniforms. We all looked at each other for a second, then all of us jumped in the pool. I noticed Tony didn't get very far from the edge."

The summer between his junior and senior years, La Russa again teamed with Piniella, along with another future major leaguer, catcher Ken Suarez, to form the heart of the American Legion Post 248 team.

"Lou and I were the same age, one year ahead of Tony," Suarez said. "We were similar in the sense that we just loved to play. All of us hated to lose, but we expressed it in different ways. Lou yelled a lot more."

La Russa had been reminded of that a year earlier when his Jefferson team had been playing Jesuit in an important game and Piniella was on the mound. He walked the bases loaded before finally striking out one of the Dragons players to end the threat.

Walking off the mound, Piniella stopped and hurled his glove—over the plate, over the head of the umpire, and over the backstop. The umpire threw Piniella out of the game.

"He was really a hot-tempered, great athlete," La Russa said. "He was a great basketball player, a great baseball player. He was a really good, competitive player, I thought. A terrific winning player."

After Piniella got into a dispute with Jesuit's coach, it was no surprise that he didn't play his senior year. The coach had reportedly wanted Piniella to pitch a game one day after the school's basketball season ended—Piniella was also a star in that sport. Piniella refused. He was such a good basketball player that he was offered and accepted a basketball scholarship to the University of Tampa.

Piniella still wanted to play baseball, and returned to the American Legion team for the summer of 1961. Since Piniella and Suarez had already graduated from high school, La Russa knew it would be their final chance to play together—at least in amateur ball—and the team's goal was to win the national championship.

La Russa was the team's leadoff hitter and shortstop, posting a .385 average for the season as Post 248 captured its first goal, qualifying for the state tournament by winning its second area championship in three years.

The team reached the finals of the state tournament against West Palm Beach and was just one out away from a victory—and a spot in the national tournament—when it all fell apart. Post 248 was leading 4–2 with two outs in the bottom of the ninth and two runners on base, when Piniella and center fielder Paul Aldridge misplayed a fly ball. Both runs scored to tie the game, and after a walk, another base hit drove in the winning run.

"Tony told me a few years later, early in his career, that there was more talent on that legion team than any team he had ever played on," Cueto said.

La Russa hoped to erase some of the disappointment from that loss with an outstanding senior season, hopefully capped off by winning a state championship. Nearly every major league team had scouts watching him.

"I reach down and pull up my sock, then I look at the stands and think, 'I wonder if they liked that,'" La Russa told the *Tampa Tribune*. "Then I straighten my cap and wonder, 'Was that OK?' Wonder if they thought I did that OK. Then I make a good play, or a bad one, and I wonder what they're thinking. Sure, I know they're there."

Accustomed by now to the attention of the scouts, La Russa thrived on the field, hitting .479 with five homers and 21 RBIs through 20 games.

The rules for signing amateur players were different in 1962 because major league baseball had yet to implement the amateur player draft. Any team was eligible to sign any player once his high school eligibility was completed. The only stipulation was that if the player received a large signing bonus, the major league club was required to keep him on their active major league roster for the next full season.

With the end of the regular season drawing near, along with his high school graduation, La Russa noticed that there was a gap between the final regular-season game and the start of the state tournament. In an effort to keep himself in shape and his skills sharp, he asked his coach if it would be all right for him and catcher Andy Alfonso to play a few games in an amateur municipal league in Tampa.

The coach apparently either misunderstood what La Russa was asking, or didn't know that playing in that league would make the players ineligible for the state tournament. He gave his permission, La Russa and Alfonso joined the Moose Club, and someone noticed them and informed the Florida State High School Athletic Association.

After its investigation, the association said it had no choice but to declare the players ineligible for the state tournament, depriving Jefferson of its two best players. "It definitely hurt our chances of winning," Carrasco said. "We went to the tournament and lost 3–2 to North Miami Senior High School.... I found out several years later that the pitcher who beat us was Steve Carlton." Carrasco was the losing pitcher.

A few days later, La Russa was still very upset over being disqualified from that game and missing the opportunity to play in the state tournament. "This may sound corny," he told the *Tampa Tribune*, "but that was the greatest disappointment of my life." To his family and friends, who knew how important baseball and winning were to La Russa, it did not sound corny at all. They knew that the only thing more important than baseball to La Russa was his family.

La Russa was free to sign a professional contract as soon as he graduated from Jefferson. "A lot of general managers had called and said they were going to come down and watch him in the state tournament," said Cueto. La Russa had asked Cueto to help him meet with the scouts and sort through all the contract offers. The best offers came from La Russa's favorite childhood team, the New York Yankees, and the Cleveland Indians—until the Kansas City Athletics, and a man named Charlie Finley, arrived on the scene.

CHAPTER 2

Bonus Baby

Of all of the teams interested in signing La Russa, the only three that were willing to offer a large enough signing bonus to guarantee him at least one year in the major leagues were the New York Yankees, Cleveland Indians, and the Kansas City Athletics. The A's, through the recommendations of the team's scouts, quickly became the front-runners when the team's owner, Charlie Finley, flew to Tampa to personally meet with La Russa and his family.

La Russa's cousin, Bobby Cueto, was with him at the La Russa home when Finley arrived. "He was pointing out that even though the team was not doing well, they had a lot of good infielders coming along in the system," Cueto said. "I remember asking him, 'If you have all these great young infielders coming along, and Tony is an infielder, why would he sign with Kansas City?' Finley turned to Tony and said, 'Now I know why he's here.'"

The family had told interested clubs they only wanted to receive one offer, eliminating the possibility of back-and-forth negotiations. La Russa and Cueto discussed the situation and wanted to see if Finley and the A's would agree to give La Russa a new car as part of their package. The A's already had pledged $8,000 toward a college education, which made them the family's first choice because the Indians had initially refused to include a scholarship as part of their offer.

"I asked Hoot Evers, an executive with the Indians, about a college scholarship and he said they could offer it but that Tony would never use it," Cueto said, adding that he told Evers, "You don't know Tony."

Finley kept calling, and La Russa worked up enough nerve one night to ask about including a car in the deal. "He said on the phone that Cleveland had offered a car, which wasn't true," Cueto said. "Finley said, 'You want a car? I'll give you a car. I'll give you a new Thunderbird. I'll give you my daughter's Thunderbird, it's brand new.'" Instead, La Russa picked out a white Pontiac Bonneville with black leather interior. He also had the college scholarship and a total signing package that came to $100,000. After La Russa and Finley reached a verbal agreement on the phone, Finley asked to speak to Cueto.

"I had gotten to know Finley a little bit through our meetings," Cueto said. "He thought I had something to do with getting Tony to sign with Kansas City. He said he wanted to give me a choice, he would either buy me a new $200 suit or I could come with Tony when he joined the team and work out for a week or so. I was in my last quarter of college, so what was I going to do with a new suit? I accepted his offer to come with Tony."

On June 7, 1962, immediately after receiving his diploma from Jefferson High School, La Russa signed a contract with the Kansas City A's, touching off a huge celebration at the La Russa home.

The decision was headline news in the next morning's *Tampa Tribune*, with the headline "La Russa to Join Athletics Tonight" leading the sports section. The story was complete with even the time that La Russa's flight would be leaving Tampa and arriving in Los Angeles, where he would be meeting the A's.

Joe Bowman, the A's supervisor of scouts, and Charlie Gassaway, the team's area scout in Florida, were pleased that their work in watching La Russa and their recommendation had come to fruition. The signing bonus was one of the highest the A's had ever given, second only to the $125,000 the team had paid pitcher Lew Krausse the previous year.

Gassaway, who had been scouting La Russa since the American Legion state tournament his junior year, was convinced he was worth the money.

"To me, he's one of the two best prospects at this age I ever saw," Gassaway told the *Tribune*. "The other is Tom Tresh [of the New York Yankees]. At the same age, I would say they were just about equal in ability.

"As a runner, Tony has good, average speed. His arm is good enough he could play any position. He gets a great jump on the ball and that's the secret on defense. I think he's going to be a good hitter. He has improved even over last year."

The headline in the *Kansas City Star* was a little more restrained, announcing "Athletics Sign Top Prospect." The newspaper reported that Pat Friday, the A's general manager, said, "The Athletics had rated La Russa the top prospect in the country at the time organization officials evaluated the youngsters who would become eligible to be signed this year."

La Russa was already in Los Angeles, working out with the visiting A's two days later, when Piniella, after one year at the University of Tampa, signed with the Cleveland Indians.

After working out with the A's before the game, La Russa got dressed and sat in the stands with Cueto to watch the game. From Los Angeles, the team went to Portland for an exhibition game against its Triple A affiliate.

"I remember he faced Gerry Staley, who had been a big-league pitcher, and popped out," Cueto said. He said the A's gave La Russa a choice of joining either of their Class D farm teams, in Iowa or in Daytona Beach, Florida. Cueto tried to talk La Russa into going to Iowa, where he felt he would be under less pressure because less people would know him, but La Russa chose to start his professional career in his home state at Daytona Beach.

His career did not get off to a bad start, considering he still was a few months shy of his 18th birthday. In 64 games, La Russa hit .258, scored 37 runs, and drove in 32. That performance was good enough to earn him an end-of-season promotion to Class A Binghamton in the Eastern League, a jump of three levels. But he struggled there, hitting just .186 in 12 games at the conclusion of the season.

He returned home to Tampa that winter, committed to honoring his pledge to his parents that he would pursue a college education in the off-season by enrolling at the University of South Florida.

La Russa also made a decision that would affect him for the rest of his playing career. Friends had asked him to play on their slow-pitch softball team, just for fun, and he agreed.

"I went to his house and told him he was crazy," Cueto said. "He said he was just going to be playing first base and that everything would be fine. I told him, 'I know what's going to happen. It's cold, you are not going to warm up, and you're going to get hurt.'"

Cueto said his cousin responded, "You talked me out of playing football and you talked me out of playing basketball, but you're not going to talk me out of this."

Cueto's prediction, unfortunately, came to pass. "One day I was late getting to a game," La Russa said in a 1981 interview. "I rushed right over after lunch and ran out to shortstop. I threw a ball to first base without warming up and I tore a tendon in my arm."

The injury would haunt La Russa for the rest of his playing career and also served as a precursor to more injury problems that stayed with La Russa for the next 15 years.

Because of his signing bonus, La Russa knew he would be kept on the major league roster for the entire 1963 season. He also knew that he would likely only receive a limited amount of chances to play, even for a team that was destined to finish eighth in the 10-team American League with a 73–89 record, 31½ games behind the world champion Yankees. What he didn't count on, however, was that his arm injury would cause those playing chances to be even fewer and farther between.

He was invited to a special early instructional camp, prior to spring training, along with 36 other young Kansas City prospects. His fellow "bonus baby," pitcher Lew Krausse, was there, along with a young outfielder who would later play an important role in La Russa's life, Ken Harrelson. Instead of participating in the drills and practice sessions, however, La Russa found himself on the sidelines with his right arm in a sling. When spring training began, he was still unable to play. The same was true when the team left Bradenton, Florida, and moved to Kansas City for the start of the regular season.

La Russa, wearing uniform No. 29, did not make his first appearance in a major league game until May 10, as a pinch-runner for Chuck Essegian in the eighth inning of what turned out to be a 2–0 loss to Minnesota. His performance didn't rate a mention in the Kansas City newspaper's game recap. His next 10 appearances were also pinch-running substitutions. On July 20, he entered a game against Baltimore in the ninth inning as a defensive replacement for shortstop Sammy Esposito.

Almost a month later, on August 15, La Russa got his first major league at-bat. With the A's losing significantly to Detroit, he replaced Jerry Lumpe at second base in the fifth inning. In the next inning he faced the Tigers' Hank Aguirre, flying out to center field.

On August 17, manager Ed Lopat called on La Russa to pinch-hit for pitcher Bill Fischer in the eighth inning against the Orioles, and he came through with the first hit of his career, lining a triple to right-center off Steve Barber.

The A's had a doubleheader at Detroit on August 23, and after replacing an ill Lumpe at second base in the middle of the first game, La Russa made the first start of his major league career in the second game, playing second base and hitting eighth. He went 2-for-4, both singles, in a 6–2 loss.

La Russa made his first career start at shortstop in place of an injured Esposito on August 25, in the second game of another doubleheader at Detroit. At the time he was the only 18-year-old to start a game at shortstop in major league history. Since then two other players have joined him: Robin Yount and Alex Rodriguez.

"They should put an asterisk by my name," La Russa once said about the distinction.

After limited opportunities in the first five months of the season, La Russa received much more playing time in September, appearing in 13 games and starting nine. La Russa went 8-for-33 in the month, with a .242 average, one double, and one RBI.

Three of his hits came in one game, against Cleveland on September 28, and he finished the year with a .250 average, 11-for-44. He played in just 34 of the A's 162 games.

Still, La Russa told a Kansas City reporter in September that he did not think the season had been a waste.

"I know I'll be sent down next season and I'm looking forward to it," he said. "I've learned a lot from our players and also by watching such fine short-stops as [Wayne] Causey, Luis Aparicio, Zoilo Versalles, and others. I've had plenty of help from everyone on the club, especially catcher Charley Lau, who detected a hitch in my swing at the plate. Most of the other regulars were busy when I took batting practice and the coaches have been wonderful to me.

"I'll be given the opportunity to earn a spot on one of the minor league clubs and that's the way it should be. I know I've got a long way to go and know there aren't any shortcuts in pro baseball."

The A's coaches, Jimmie Dykes and Mel McGaha, believed La Russa's hard work would one day make him a starting shortstop in the major leagues.

"Game experience has been invaluable to him," Dykes said that September. "At the rate Tony has improved he should be a major leaguer after a couple of years of experience in the minors. The biggest thing in his favor is that he wants to play. He has the size, a good pair of quick hands, and a fine throwing arm. He moves real good toward the ball and gets his throws away quickly."

But La Russa would find out that it was going to be a lot tougher making it back to the major leagues than he possibly could ever have imagined.

For the next four seasons, La Russa found himself in the baseball outposts of Lewiston, Idaho; Birmingham and Mobile, Alabama; and Modesto, California, working as hard as he could to get back up to the majors. There were good days and bad days. For La Russa, the best parts of those years were some of the people he met—men who would become friends and turn out to play a major role in his life for the next 40-plus years.

After the 1964 season ended, La Russa was one of the young members of the A's organization assigned to the instructional league camp in Bradenton, Florida. Also assigned there, after spending all of 1964 in Kansas City under the same bonus-baby rule that had kept La Russa there the previous year, was a young catcher named Dave Duncan. La Russa and Duncan would go on to spend parts of each of the next seven seasons together, forming the basis of a friendship that would last for the rest of their professional lives. Another young player in the camp who also would go on to become a close associate and coach for La Russa in the years to come was Rene Lachemann.

When the instructional league team had a night off that fall, La Russa invited several of his friends to his parents' house in Tampa for dinner.

"I had never been to a true Italian's house for dinner, and we ended up having a seven-course meal the likes of which I had never seen in my life," Lachemann said. "My dad was the head chef at a hotel for four years when I was growing up. We ate as well as anybody, but we never ate like that.

"After about three courses I was stuffed and she kept bringing out more food. We were sitting on the lawn afterward knowing we were going to have to run about 20 extra sprints to get some of the stuff out of us. I looked at Tony and asked him why he didn't weigh 500 pounds when he ate like that."

In 1966, La Russa and Lachemann were both members of the Mobile team that won the Southern League championship. Two other players on the club would go on to have good major league careers: Rick Monday and Sal Bando.

In fact, La Russa played alongside many of the A's players who would play key roles in winning the three consecutive World Series championships in 1972–74, including Bando, Reggie Jackson, "Blue Moon" Odom, Rollie Fingers, and Joe Rudi.

For the most part, however, La Russa had to watch as those players rose to the major leagues while he languished in the minors, trying to fight off injuries. Much of his anguish was the knowledge that he would never be a hundred percent healthy because of his injured arm. Playing for Class A Modesto in 1966, he once even thought it would be better to fake being sick rather than play at what he knew would be less than a hundred percent of his ability.

"My arm hurt so much some days that all I could do was flip the ball from second," La Russa said. "My biggest fear was that I would go there and throw the ball away."

Despite his reservations, La Russa decided to play. The previous day's result left Modesto in a tie with San Jose for the first-half championship, forcing a one-game playoff. Even though the game was played in Modesto, they were playing as the visiting team because they had lost a coin flip.

The game was tied 1–1 in the top of the ninth, then Modesto went ahead by a run. La Russa followed a teammate's RBI single with a grand slam that carried over the scoreboard—his third hit of the game—sealing the victory and the first-half league title.

"From that day on, whenever I was confronted with a challenge and feared failure, I gutted it out and went for it," he said. "Conquering that fear of embarrassing myself and coming out with those results has been something that I've used the rest of my career."

The overall lack of success as a player in the minors, combined with his internal drive and competitiveness, made him more determined than ever to succeed in the classroom, where he was spending the other half of his life.

Fulfilling a pledge made to his mother when he signed with the A's, La Russa spent seven consecutive off-seasons attending classes at the University of South Florida before eventually earning his bachelor's degree in industrial management. When he attended instructional league or spring training, he spent half of the day playing baseball and the other half going to school.

One of the highlights from those years came in spring training of 1967, when he hit the only home run of his major league career—even though it was only an exhibition game—off Detroit's Mickey Lolich.

La Russa spent much of 1967 on the disabled list with another injury to his shoulder. Among the injuries that forced him out of action in those years were two dislocations of his left shoulder, torn ligaments in his left leg, and injuries to his back and right arm.

In 1968, and for the first time in five years, La Russa made the opening day roster for the major league A's, in their first season in Oakland. But the excitement did not last long. He played in only five games before returning to Triple A Vancouver for the rest of the season—though he did manage to get his name in the A's record book by recording the team's first-ever pinch-hit at the Oakland Coliseum, a single off Baltimore's Dave McNally.

For the next three years he spent time going back and forth between the majors and Triple A, never really getting an extended chance to play in the big leagues. In 1969, he was hitting .300 at Triple A in the middle of the season and was promoted to Oakland. He was with the A's for three months. "Most of the time I just sat," he recalled. He played 52 games for the Athletics in 1970 and 23 in 1971.

"It just broke his heart," said his cousin, Bobby Cueto. "He kept trying so hard. Baseball hammered him for so many years, keeping him from playing in the majors. One time he got to Oakland and was playing great defensively and was hitting well. Dick Green had been the starter, and the manager called Tony in his office and told him he was going to have to send him back down because Charlie Finley had called and said he wasn't paying Green $80,000 a year (a big salary at the time) to sit on the bench."

His friend Lachemann, who also rode the shuttle between the majors and minors in those years, said in all those frustrating years together, he never heard La Russa give any indication that he was thinking about trying to become a manager when his playing career finally came to an end.

"He was very intelligent, of course, but I never really had any thoughts that he was interested in managing," Lachemann said. "I was the kind of guy who always thought I would stay in the game some way because there really wasn't a whole lot else for me to do. I didn't have a lot of things outside of baseball to lean on but it seemed he had other plans."

La Russa thought he might be catching a break in August 1971 when he was sold to Atlanta. He played in nine games for the Braves at the end of that season and thought he might fit into their major league plans the following year. One of the highlights of that time was that he had the opportunity to be a teammate of Hank Aaron, a memory he still cherishes.

He found himself back in Triple A for the start of the 1972 season, and even though he hit .308 and made the International League All-Star team, he was not called up by the Braves when the rosters were expanded in September. It was then, he said, that he decided he better come up with a plan for his life that did not include playing major league baseball.

There were other developments in La Russa's life that year as well. He had been married in 1965, when he was just 20 years old, to Luzette Sarcone, who he met as a teenager in Tampa. The couple had two daughters, but the marriage was in trouble. La Russa had met another woman that summer in Richmond, Elaine Coker. La Russa's first marriage ended in divorce in 1973 and he and Elaine were married later that year. La Russa does not speak publicly about his first marriage and two daughters.

With both the baseball and personal woes weighing on his mind, La Russa knew he was at a major crossroads in his life. "The realization kept creeping in that I couldn't cut it," La Russa said a few years later. "You can rationalize all you want, look at the situation from all kinds of different angles, but after a while, the whole thing becomes crystal clear. I was 28 years old in 1972. I had a better year than I had ever had, finished fourth in the International league in hitting. And nothing happened. Nothing."

In La Russa's mind, the best thing that happened that season was meeting the woman he would marry a year later. Elaine was a former flight attendant for United Airlines, and was working as a waitress at a restaurant when La Russa and a Richmond teammate came in for dinner.

"He caught my eye right away," Elaine La Russa said in a 1980 interview with the *Chicago Tribune*. "The hostess stuck him in someone else's section. Then I came out from the back and he asked if he could move to my section. That was it. I went to quite a few games that summer. I'd been a football fan up till then."

That winter, La Russa began thinking about going to law school,. He was also traded from the Braves to the Chicago Cubs in exchange for pitcher Tom Phoebus.

Once more, he thought it could be the break he needed. He knew by then that he would never become a big star in the major leagues, as once had been predicted, but if he could just stick around for a few years, *something* might happen.

The Cubs, for their part, were happy to land La Russa. The headline in the *Chicago Tribune* on March 12, 1973, declared "Cubs Find Hitter in La Russa."

The spring training report from Palm Springs, California, quoted Cubs batting instructor Lew Fonseca as saying, "La Russa has impressed me more than any of the other newcomers. He has a lot of desire, a quick bat, and he spreads the ball around real well. He is an excellent two-strike hitter. He can be fooled and still have enough strength to poke the ball through the infield."

La Russa made the Cubs' Opening Day roster as a reserve infielder, and got into their Opening Day game against the Expos at Wrigley Field. He came into a tie game in the ninth inning as a pinch-runner for Ron Santo, and later scored the game's winning run on a bases-loaded walk to Rick Monday by Mike Marshall.

That moment turned out to be the final major league highlight of La Russa's career. He did not get into another game, and three weeks later he was sent to Wichita, the Cubs' Triple A team. He would go on to spend five more years in the minors, but never again cracked the majors.

"One of the things I hate is when people talk about him and say he was a bad ballplayer," Cueto said. "I saw him play. He was a hell of a player. He never had a chance because of all the injuries he suffered."

La Russa's major league career totaled 132 games, 176 at-bats, and a .199 average. He recorded 35 hits, no homers, and 7 RBIs. The only full season he spent in the majors was his bonus-baby year, 1963. He spent parts of five more seasons in the majors, but never played more than 52 games in a season.

"I never hit in the big leagues," La Russa acknowledged, "but I was a tough out in the minors. I had a lifetime batting average in the minors of about .270 and had the reputation of never cheating the fans or the guy who signed my paycheck."

One of the best days of his minor league career came on June 3, 1973, playing for Wichita. He had four hits and seven RBIs in a 12–3 win over Tulsa. His fourth hit of the night, a single in the eighth inning, earned him a $100 savings bond from Rusty Eck Ford. Typically, however, La Russa found himself back on the disabled list a week later after suffering a pulled back muscle.

A month later, La Russa was angered when he was knocked down by a pitch thrown by Denver's Ed Mims. In an earlier game, Mims had hit La Russa in the helmet with a pitch. Denver trainer Sam Wilkinson and the umpire urged La Russa to sit on the ground to make certain he was OK, but La Russa insisted that he was not injured as he stood up.

"I tell you I'm all right and if you guys don't get out of the way I'm gonna punch somebody," La Russa said. Added Wilkinson, "First time I ever got threatened when I was trying to help somebody."

La Russa had taken the entrance exam for law school the previous winter and after the 1973 season ended, began classes at Florida State University, resuming his undergraduate schedule of playing baseball in the summer and going to school the rest of the time.

His first midterm grades were grim. "I had not done well," La Russa said. "I had some buddies I played racquetball with and they all beat me for grades."

Five years later, La Russa earned his law degree, graduating with honors. "It had little to do with my aptitude for the law or my love of studying, but everything to do with [not wanting] to get beat for grades," he said.

One of his papers actually dealt with how he thought the decisions in the cases involving Andy Messersmith and Dave McNally, arguing free agent rights for major league players, would affect the majority of players.

"It doesn't seem to me that Messersmith and McNally were really aggrieved parties," La Russa said in a spring training interview in 1976. "They weren't the kind of players who should have pressed a grievance.... I understand Messersmith said he did it for the good of a lot of players, that he especially wanted to help the younger guys, the players who are buried behind the established stars."

The actual arbitration ruling, however, would only affect the stars and the superstars, La Russa said.

"Most guys will say, 'I know Tony La Russa. He's a minor leaguer," La Russa said. "'All he wants is a change that would help him in some way.' They can say whatever they want. Messersmith may really believe he is helping most of the players. But he isn't. He'll get more money and so will the other super-stars. And the guys at the bottom won't be affected."

La Russa, of course, was one of the guys on the bottom, always hoping the next move would be the one that would get him back in the major leagues. It happened again when he was traded from the Cubs to the Pirates organization at the end of spring training in 1974. Instead of getting a shot at the big league club, La Russa found himself in Charleston, West Virginia, all season. He was then on the move again, this time to Denver, signing on with the Chicago White Sox for the 1975 sesaon.

It was in Denver that he met the man who, at that point at least, likely had the greatest impact on his life of anyone other than his own father: Loren Babe.

Babe was the manager of the White Sox's Triple A team. He had started managing in the minor leagues in 1961 after a career similar to La Russa's. He played a total of 120 games in the major leagues for the Yankees and Philadelphia A's in 1952 and 1953, hitting .223. Subsequently, he worked as a coach and scout. In nine years of managing, he had led just two teams to a league championship, the Idaho Falls Yankees in the Pioneer League in 1963 and the Columbus Yankees in the Southern League two years later.

Despite his dubious record, it was quickly obvious to La Russa that Babe knew the game and was willing to share that knowledge with his new student. Though La Russa was only a player and not a player-coach, Babe began to treat him as he would a coach.

"I've learned something from every manager I ever played for, but nobody taught me as much as Loren," La Russa was quoted as saying a few years later. "I'd sit next to him in the dugout and we'd talk about squeeze plays, hit and runs, intentional walks…all the moves that have to be second nature to a manager."

More than establishing that dialogue, however, Babe encouraged La Russa to begin thinking like a manager.

"I'd say, 'Why did you bring this guy in?' or 'Why didn't you hit for this guy?' It really whetted my appetite," La Russa said.

One of La Russa's best days in the minor leagues came that year, on June 25, when he hit for the cycle and drove in three runs in Denver's 18–9 win over Wichita. He hit .280 over 118 games that season, and even made the American Association All-Star team as a reserve, playing left field in the exhibition game against the White Sox.

Babe gave La Russa some experience coaching third base, and when the White Sox moved their Triple A team to Des Moines in 1976, both Babe and La Russa moved too.

Mike Squires was playing on the Iowa team that year, and he said a few of the players suspected there was a special bond between Babe and La Russa. "He and Tony talked all the time," Squires said. "I know Loren was officially the manager, but I'm not so certain he didn't let Tony have a little more of the reins than a lot of the players were aware of."

Babe missed a game in Denver because he was ill and asked La Russa to be in charge that day. Because a left-hander was pitching, La Russa was also in the lineup, playing third base. He tied an American Association record that day by going 6-for-6. Iowa lost in the tenth inning on an Andre Dawson home run.

There was at least one instance when La Russa wished he had been in the safety of the dugout instead of on the field. On August 7, when Iowa was playing Evansville, future major leaguer Steve Kemp hit a hard smash that took a bad hop and struck La Russa, playing shortstop, directly in the face.

"The ball hit Tony under the left eye, broke his glasses, and cut him in three places," Babe said. The public address announcer at Evansville's stadium appealed for the assistance of a doctor, but when no one came forward, La Russa walked off the field with help and was taken by ambulance to a local hospital where he received ten stitches. Kemp, who was celebrating his 22nd birthday, also hit a home run in the game.

When the White Sox decided to change Triple A managers for the 1977 season, La Russa moved on as well, signing with the Cardinals' organization, which had moved its Triple A affiliate from Tulsa to New Orleans.

The manager was Lance Nichols, another veteran minor league manager and a strict disciplinarian. He did not allow radios to be played in the clubhouse, and even worse, banned card games, a baseball staple.

"We just found a spot outside the clubhouse in the hallway and played there," said Ken Oberkfell, one of the players.

Another player on the roster who quickly developed a friendship with La Russa was Jim Riggleman, who would later go on to become a major league manager himself with the Padres, Cubs, and Mariners.

"It was my first year in Triple A and I was 24 and he was 33, and he was kind of looking out for me a little bit," Riggleman said. "He became like a big brother to me. He gave me a lot of advice and you knew there was a lot of respect for him among the players."

The team played its games in the 62,000-seat Superdome, and La Russa gave the fans something to cheer about in their home opener on April 30, hitting the first home run in the building. Despite having the second largest attendance in the league, the team averaged just over 1,600 fans a game, so there were plenty more open seats than fans. The Pelicans' stay in New Orleans lasted only one season. In 1978, the team relocated to Springfield, Illinois.

La Russa was officially named player-coach on the team, and when Nichols had to take a short leave of absence to seek treatment for lymphoma, La Russa was placed in charge of the team.

Nichols missed five games, and with La Russa as the acting manager, the team was 3–2. Considering that the overall record of the team was 57–79, La Russa's record looks much better by comparison.

"He put me up to pinch-hit one time against Pete Broberg of Wichita, and I hit a home run," Riggleman said. "Tony was making a big deal about how great a managerial move it was—how he had put me in the right position to succeed. He never gave me the credit for hitting the home run."

Oberkfell also remembers that the players were unconcerned when La Russa took over the club for the week. "He was totally prepared," Oberkfell said. "He managed those games as if he were the full-time manager and it was his team."

Like Riggleman, Oberkfell felt La Russa helped enhance his baseball knowledge during their season together. Oberkfell remembered when he was playing second base against Oklahoma City and was upended in a hard slide by future major leaguer Lonnie Smith.

"I guess it was kind of a cheap shot, but I didn't really know any better and I didn't think anything about it," Oberkfell said. "I got to the bench after the inning and Tony and another older player, Tommy Sandt, came up to me and said, 'Don't worry, we'll get him for you.' I was like, 'Get who for what?' That was a part of the game I really didn't know much about."

As the season began to wind down, La Russa knew his playing career was coming to an end. He also was nearly finished with law school and would soon begin to prepare for the bar exam. It was time to make some decisions about his future.

The Cardinals were impressed by what they had seen of La Russa's ability to run a club. George Kissell, the organization's field coordinator, sat down with him and said he wanted to discuss his future.

There was going to be an opening for a manager at the Cardinals' rookie league club in Johnson City, Tennessee, in 1978 and if La Russa was interested, the organization would be very interested in him taking the job.

La Russa listened politely, then told Kissell that while he appreciated the offer, he had put so much time into the game and to law school as well, it would not be fair to his wife for him to begin managing at such a low level in the minors. He needed a job that placed him closer to the major leagues.

La Russa was not disrespectful, nor was he hurt by Kissell's offer. It was the only job open in the organization, and he understood that. Once again, however, he had confidence in his own abilities and was determined that he could find a job at a higher level.

Once again, he was right.

CHAPTER

Learning to Manage

The White Sox's Double A farm team in Knoxville, Tennessee, was awful in 1977, finishing in last place in their division in the Southern League, 37 games under .500 and 36 games behind division-winner Montgomery, Alabama. The franchise had drawn an average of just 514 fans to their home games.

Roland Hemond, the team's general manager, and Paul Richards, who ran the farm system, knew they needed to make some changes, and finding a new manager was near the top of the list.

Once again, Loren Babe's influence came to La Russa's aid. During his two years managing the White Sox's Triple A team with La Russa by his side, Babe had told Hemond how La Russa would one day make a good manager. When Hemond received a letter in 1978 from La Russa expressing interest in managing, Hemond went to owner Bill Veeck and recommended they hire this 33-year-old kid, who by the way, was also finishing up his law degree.

"He was one of the non-roster players we brought to spring training in an early camp one year and he made a tremendous impression on Bill Veeck," Hemond said. "He is extremely bright and has all the ingredients necessary to get results in any field he chooses to pursue."

La Russa knew he had the option of walking away from baseball and hanging out his attorney's shingle, but the game had not released its grip. He knew his playing days were over, but he thought maybe managing might be worth a try.

"I sat down with my wife and decided that I would try managing on a short-term basis, to see how it went," La Russa said in a 1980 interview with the *New York Daily News*. "I was in my thirties and I was facing a minor league manager's salary. It meant there were things we couldn't do. We couldn't travel. We couldn't buy a house. I didn't feel I had a lot of time to find out how this would go. Some guys manage in the minor leagues for seven years, or 10. After seven years a lawyer is making serious money."

Because minor league managers did not make much money, and because he was uncertain how that career would work out, La Russa spent time that winter working for a law firm in Sarasota, Florida.

One of his first cases was an attempt to restore the competency of a woman who had been sent to a state institution. Years later, White Sox owner Jerry Reinsdorf would not let him forget what happened. "He prepared all of his arguments and got all of his papers and everything in order and went to the courtroom," Reinsdorf said. "The judge called the case and then said, 'Where's your client?' He had forgotten to bring the client to court."

Another time, as La Russa readied to take his first case to trial, one of the parties died. The case was delayed, and the new date conflicted with spring training, so it was assigned to another lawyer at the firm.

When La Russa decided to go into managing for a short-term basis, he didn't define exactly what "short term" meant. What he did know was that he would do the job the best way he knew how and devote a hundred percent of his time and energy to the job. The results would tell him the rest.

The minor leagues exist for the primary purpose of developing players for the major league level. While teams want to win—and the White Sox certainly wanted to win more games in Knoxville than they had the previous year—it was not the most important aspect for the team. But La Russa's passion for winning was unchallengeable.

A few days before the Knoxville Sox opened the season at Chattanooga, La Russa was interviewed by Tom Siler, the sports editor of the *Knoxville News-Sentinel*. He told Siler his approach to trying to win every game was in line with the philosophy that was being dictated to the minor league teams by Veeck, Hemond, and Richards.

"They told us [minor league managers] they wanted all of their farm teams to win—that is, play to win," La Russa said. "Some figure the big thing is to develop talent and if you don't win in the minors, no sweat. They said they wanted us to use our talent to win games. I was glad to hear that. They want to win the games, use the talent to that end."

Based on spring training, La Russa thought there was a good collection of talent on the team. He had also handpicked a few players himself. It was a combination of young players mixed in with a few veterans.

If La Russa was nervous before the first game, he didn't show it. He sent right-hander Fred Howard to the mound, and Howard limited Chattanooga to three hits over seven shutout innings in an eventual 8–1 Knoxville win. The date was April 13, 1978. History did not record La Russa's first managerial victory as a memorable event.

La Russa was right about the talent on the Knoxville team. The team's strength was in its young starting rotation, led by Howard, 19-year-old Richard Dotson, 18-year-old Rich Barnes, and 20-year-old Steve Trout. Nineteen-year-old and future Silver Slugger Harold Baines was the right fielder. Other regulars who would go on to play in the majors included Marv Foley, Chris Nyman, Rusty Kuntz, and Tom Spencer.

Perhaps because of the relative youth of the team, there was never a question about La Russa's own age. He quickly won the older players over with his level of preparation and his intense desire to be successful.

"I had played Triple A for quite a few years so it was disappointing to me to find out I was going back to Double A," said Tom Spencer. "Tony called me in and said he wanted me to be his cleanup hitter. That sounded good to me. Tony was just so well prepared that he forced everyone around him to prepare as well.

"I don't think I ever played for a manager who was more intense than Tony. He brings out the intensity in the player as well. If you are a laid-back guy, it sort of changes your personality if you are around him for very long. He is looking for the serious type player who puts winning ahead of his individual accomplishments."

With so many young players on the team still learning how to play the game and how to approach the game, La Russa was clear in his message.

"It was my second year in pro ball and he really was the first guy who taught me how to play the game right and to play the game hard," Baines said. "I'm almost positive it got me on a faster track to the major leagues. We grew up together, him as a manager and me as a player. He was learning how to manage a game and I was learning how to play as a professional."

Kuntz said he could tell after being around La Russa for only a short time that there was a special quality to him. "One thing he has always had is his passion for the game," Kuntz said. "You are not going to out-prepare or outwork the guy. That's been his MO ever since he got into managing. One of the things that drove you as a player is you could see how hard he took losses. It wasn't just another game. The message was, 'If I'm going to put the time and energy into this, I want the final outcome to be in my favor.' That's part of his passion."

The Knoxville Sox got off to their best start in franchise history and finished April with a 13–5 record. They continued to do well in May. Still, La Russa was affected by the occasional loss. He would dissect every detail of the game, looking for a move he made or a move he didn't make that might have changed the outcome.

"He didn't go home when we lost. He slept at the ballpark," Baines said.

In the midst of it all, he was spending what free time he had, including on the long bus rides in the middle of the night, studying for his upcoming bar exams. One night he had a very different bus ride.

"We were coming back to Knoxville from Jacksonville and it turned out our bus driver was drunk," Spencer said. "Tony noticed it right away. He made the guy get up and go sit in the back of the bus. Tony sat down and drove the bus. I didn't know he was multitalented. I was standing next to him in the stairwell when a deer jumped out right in front of us. He clipped it; there wasn't anything else he could do."

In Chicago, the White Sox's hierarchy was noticing Knoxville's turnaround. After charging to a 36–16 record, the team finished the first half of the season with a 49–21 record and led its division by 9½ games. The major league club, however, was struggling and on June 10 fired manager Bob Lemon, replacing him with Larry Doby. That move was followed by a shakeup in the team's coaching staff. On July 4, La Russa was given a new assignment as the first-base coach on the major league staff, replacing Minnie Minoso.

La Russa was happy with the promotion. It showed that his bosses had recognized his performance and success. But the return to the major leagues also had an extended benefit. When La Russa had last appeared in a major league uniform, for the crosstown Cubs in 1973, he was 86 days short of qualifying for a major league pension. Spending the second half of the season as a coach for the White Sox would accomplish that goal.

Unfortunately for the big-league club, the change in managers did not produce much change in the team's performance. The team went 37–50 under Doby, and at the end of the year, Veeck named shortstop Don Kessinger as the player-manager.

La Russa had done well enough that Hemond and others in the front office invited him to remain on the major league coaching staff in 1979. La Russa knew that the organization was looking for a manager for its Triple A team in Des Moines. Instead of making the easy decision, and the better decision financially, to stay in the major leagues, La Russa said that he wanted to go to Des Moines. He told Veeck and Hemond that his goal was to become a major league manager, not a coach.

Before reporting to Des Moines in April of 1979, La Russa had another managing assignment to complete. He had agreed to run Estrellas of the Dominican Republic in winter ball, an assignment not for the faint of heart. La Russa knew the challenge he was facing firsthand; he had spent two winters in the Dominican as a player. He took seven Americans with him, most out of the White Sox organization, and the rest of the team were Dominicans. Since La Russa spoke perfect Spanish from his childhood, the language barrier was one problem La Russa did not have to worry about.

There were other problems, however. On an off day, he and Elaine had gone to Santo Domingo when he received a frantic telephone call from the manager of the apartment complex where the Americans on the team were living. "She told me the guys had been playing around and had done a lot of damage, and one had fallen off the roof and busted his head," La Russa later told the *Chicago Tribune*. "When I got there five of the players were in jail, three of them pitchers the Sox felt were going to be aces on their staff the following summer. The guy who had split his head open was our trainer.

"I [pled] with the people at the jail and got them out shortly. I told them the boys had been pent up for weeks and were just feeling their oats."

Another moment that La Russa can now laugh about came when the team was returning home late one night after a road game.

"Our bus driver was old and afraid," La Russa said. "Whenever he'd see upcoming lights, he'd take his foot off the gas and coast for a while, so the trip took forever. At one point, he thought he saw a white light and took his foot off and it turned out it was the moon coming up over the horizon. As far as the players were concerned, that was it. When we finally pulled in, all our American players promptly lined up in front of the bus and mooned the driver."

La Russa did not have the same kinds of worries once he got to Des Moines, but that didn't mean there were no problems. It is a common belief that managing in Triple A is one of the hardest jobs in baseball because basically none of your players want to be there. The youngsters on the team are eager to get called up to the majors, and the veterans all want to be called back. Trying to build team unity in that type of environment is tough for even the most seasoned of managers, but was an especially tough task for a 34-year-old man with less than a year of managing experience.

La Russa now also found himself in the American Association, a league ripe with managerial talent: future major league managers Jim Leyland, Jack McKeon,

Hal Lanier (a former high school and Legion opponent of La Russa from St. Petersburg, Florida), and Lee Elia, to name a few.

Once again La Russa was taking over a team that had finished last the year before, 12 games under .500. Luckily he brought many of the same players who had helped him win at Knoxville with him to the Triple A level. There were more rough times than the year before, starting with losing a double-header to Evansville—Leyland's club—on opening night. La Russa also saw his team come out on the losing end of a perfect game, by Denver's Jamie Easterly, and he became enraged one night against Denver because he thought the opposing pitcher was throwing at his hitters.

Perhaps nothing about the game bothers La Russa more than when he thinks pitchers are intentionally throwing at his hitters. He does instruct his pitchers to pitch inside, but never, *ever* at a batter's head. It was something that upset him as a player and has never changed.

"The genesis of protecting players came when I started managing in Knoxville. Paul Richards told me one of my essential responsibilities was to protect my roster from efforts to intimidate or even hurt somebody," La Russa said. "He used Harold Baines, our best prospect, as the example. He said, 'Don't ever let them abuse or hurt Harold.' I've taken that responsibility personally."

One such incident happened in a game during the winter in the Dominican Republic. La Russa thought pitcher Silvio Martinez had intentionally thrown at one of his hitters. "Tony had his foot on the top step of the dugout when Martinez knocked one of our players down," said catcher Mike Colbern. "He said, 'That's it,' and started straight for the mound. The whole club went with him, but he led the way. It was a pretty good scrap before it was over."

When it happened on May 11 against Denver, La Russa engaged in a lengthy, heated discussion with the umpires, then before leaving the field, picked up third base and threw it into foul territory. In a final salute, he tossed a garbage can onto the field as he headed for the clubhouse.

The small headline in the *Sporting News* after that episode was "La Russa Goes Wacko." But his reaction also exemplified many of his best qualities: his intensity, his belief in playing the game fairly and by a code of conduct, his fierce loyalty to his players, and the fact he would not back down when challenged.

"He objected to pitchers throwing at people's heads," Baines said. "Throwing inside is part of the game, but when you throw at somebody's head you are messing with his livelihood." La Russa himself had been hit in the head when he was playing in the minors, as well as thrown at intentionally. It was a lesson he vowed to never forget, and never to let pass unnoticed.

Another brushback incident in a game against Omaha later that summer sparked a fight between two Iowa players in the team's dugout. Bob Molinaro was upset because he thought that an Omaha pitcher had thrown at him and teammate Harold Baines. When their pitcher, John Sutton, did not retaliate by throwing at an Omaha batter, Molinaro challenged him and the two came to blows. La Russa dismissed it as "an inner-family fuss." He did not think the incident upset the team unity he had worked so hard to create, and felt that he had convinced the players that the name on the front of the jersey was far more important than the name on the back, not an easy opinion to teach minor league players with the singular goal of making it to the major leagues.

"One thing that was a lot of fun that year were our games against Evansville," Kuntz said. "Tony and Leyland would go head to head, and kept going back and forth. We had great games against them all year. Tony had so much respect for Jim that he said, 'If I ever get a big-league job that guy is going to be on my staff.' They learned so much from one another."

One player that La Russa was going to remember in years to come made his Triple A debut for Evansville against La Russa's squad on May 21. Kirk Gibson hit a homer and double and drove in three runs in the Triplets' 8–4 victory.

La Russa told the *Chicago Tribune* in a 1985 interview that as far as he could remember, he and Leyland had only one confrontation that season, when the Iowa shortstop, Harry Chappas, stole second late in a game in which Evansville had a big lead. "Evansville had us down by five or six runs," La Russa said. "The first baseman wasn't holding Chappas on, so I gave him the steal sign. I wanted to do something. Maybe it would start a rally for us. Or at least give us some momentum for the next night's game.

"As soon as Chappas slid into second, Jim began yelling at him. I thought he yelled, 'I hope you break a leg, Chappas.' I came out of our dugout. We had a big argument. The umpires had to separate us."

When the two managers came out to home plate the next night to exchange the lineup cards, La Russa started in again on Leyland, telling him his remarks were out of line. In this calmer environment, Leyland told La Russa what he had actually said: "I hope you lead the league, Chappas."

Even at this early stage of his managerial career, La Russa always was looking for an edge, something that would give his team an advantage for its next victory. He didn't care if an idea was new or not in keeping with baseball tradition. If he thought it would give his team a better chance of winning, he would do it.

La Russa knew that Veeck, Hemond, and the others in the White Sox's front office were constantly evaluating the performance of the players in the minor leagues. What he didn't know as the Iowa team reached the end of July was that his own performance was under the microscope. With no overwhelming change in the success of the major league club, one of Veeck's top assistants had been dispatched to Des Moines to study La Russa without his knowledge. The mission was quite specific: Veeck wanted to know if La Russa was ready to manage at the major league level.

After a few days, Veeck got his answer: "Yes, he's ready."

CHAPTER 4

"Yes, He's Ready."

On Thursday morning, August 2, 1979, La Russa accompanied his wife Elaine to the doctor's office. She was about eight months pregnant with their first child. After the appointment, the couple went out for lunch and stopped to buy some baby supplies.

The White Sox had lost their seventh consecutive game on the night before, a matter that La Russa likely did not discuss over lunch. He had no reason to believe what happened in the major leagues had any impact on his job managing the Triple A club. He had no way of knowing that while he and Elaine were eating, Chicago owner Bill Veeck was having a lunch meeting of his own with his current manager, Don Kessinger.

Veeck had been disappointed with the way his club was performing and he was particularly upset with the latest loss, a 9–1 defeat to the Yankees. He believed that the team was too lethargic and accepted defeat too easily. The White Sox had been outscored 23–6 in the three losses to the Yankees, which concluded a 1–8 homestand.

It was Kessinger who had called the day before and asked to meet with Veeck. "We're just not very sharp," Kessinger told reporters after the game. "I don't know what we can do about it. Obviously a lot of things have been discussed. If there was any way we could get some help, I think we would have done it by now. The plan now is just to sort of go with what we've got."

Veeck had a different plan in mind.

During their meeting, "Don suggested that maybe it would be in the best interests of the ballclub to make some changes," Veeck said later. "Don felt it would be helpful to the club and to Sox fans if we'd try to shake up some of the athletes with different management."

Said Kessinger, "I just felt the club needed more enthusiasm. I wondered if maybe somebody else could supply it. When Bill agreed with what I said, I had no alternative." What Kessinger didn't know was that Veeck was already considering a change of managers. If he expected Veeck to try to talk him out of resigning, he was sorely disappointed.

As soon as the meeting was over, Veeck called the Iowa office looking for La Russa. After his own lunch, La Russa made a routine call to the Iowa office to check in. He was told to call Veeck in Chicago immediately.

La Russa recalls, "He said he wanted to see me in Chicago tonight. I told him we [the Iowa Oaks] had a game tonight. That's when he told me he wanted me to be the manager."

The news came as a tremendous shock to La Russa and also to Elaine, whose first thoughts weren't about her husband being named to manage a club in the major leagues, his goal, but about their unborn baby. "I should have been the most ecstatic person in the world," Elaine La Russa told the *Chicago Tribune* in 1980. "I mean, how many days do you get a call like that? I cried.... My gosh, here I was, pregnant and one month away from my due date, and we had everything planned so perfectly...the doctor, the hospital, natural childbirth and all."

So if La Russa did not have enough on his mind just with the job change, he also had his wife and unborn child to worry about. He accepted the position, and flew to Chicago in time to join the White Sox, who had the day off before beginning a series in Toronto the following night.

Ordinarily, the news that Kessinger had resigned and the White Sox had named La Russa as his replacement would have been the biggest sports headline of the day in Chicago and around the baseball world. The news quickly became a secondary item when a private plane piloted by Yankees' captain and catcher Thurman Munson crashed that afternoon at the Canton-Akron airport in Ohio. Munson, 32, was killed. Munson's final game had been the previous night against the White Sox.

However saddened La Russa was by Munson's death, he had to put aside his sorrow, just as he had to put aside worries for his wife and baby, in order to prepare for the first game of his major league managing career. Fortunately he knew many of the players on the White Sox roster, from managing them himself over the past two years, from his coaching stint in Chicago during the second half of the 1979 season, or from playing and managing against them in the minor leagues.

The club had experienced more than its share of problems that year, starting in spring training with the death of pitching coach Fred Martin from cancer. La Russa was the team's fourth manager in less than two seasons, following Lemon, Doby, and Kessinger, and he knew firsthand that too much change was not good for the players.

Veeck and Roland Hemond had no way of knowing how successful he would be, but they had seen enough of La Russa in action to realize that he would never be complacent. He would expect a hundred percent effort out of his players every day, and if he didn't get it, they knew he would not hesitate to make changes.

"Tony relates well to the athletes," Hemond said. "He's very bright and very creative. He's familiar with the personnel and Bill is very fond of him.... We hope Tony is the White Sox manager for a long time."

At age 34, La Russa became the youngest manager in the major leagues. He knew he was taking over a club that was 46–60 and 14 games behind AL West leader California. Those facts were the basis of his immediate expectations in his new job.

"I'm not scared but I am a little apprehensive," La Russa said. "I don't expect to work any miracles." What he did expect, and what he told his players in a 35-minute meeting before his first game at Toronto's Exhibition Stadium, was that he wanted to see effort and that he wanted his players to perform to the best of their abilities.

"Don't embarrass me, and I won't embarrass you," La Russa told the players. "Play hard all the time…[and] come to me any time you want to talk."

Later, La Russa said that he expected to be successful because it was the way he was raised and the only way he knew how to play the game or manage.

"I'm a hungry manager," he said. "I have the fire that burns inside me and it tells me I want to win any way that I can."

That statement may never have been more true than before that first game against the Blue Jays. He didn't have to wait long for his team to take the lead. Jim Morrison, also a Tampa native and who had played against La Russa's teams in the minors, led off the game with a home run against Toronto starter Balor Moore. The Blue Jays countered with two runs in the bottom of the first. Kevin Bell, who had played for La Russa in Iowa, hit a three-run homer in the second. Morrison also contributed a two-run double and a former La Russa teammate, Lamar Johnson, homered. The White Sox went on to an 8–5 victory. Steve Trout, who had pitched for La Russa in the minors, got the victory with ninth-inning relief help from Ed Farmer.

Trout said the players were motivated by La Russa's pregame speech.

"We played aggressive," Trout said. "Tony told us that if we played the way we had been playing [previously] it would be a long two months."

La Russa did let himself enjoy his first victory as a major league manager, but the knowledge of just how difficult a task he faced was brought home to him again very quickly. Hemond delivered the news of a postgame telephone call from Veeck, "congratulating the major league's only undefeated manager."

"All I had to do was pick up the newspaper the next morning to see how far out of first place we were," La Russa said. "It's my goal to build a champion. I feel the challenge and the responsibility."

La Russa knew the job was not going to be easy, but that didn't concern him. Hard work and challenges had never deterred him. Before he even thought about becoming a manager, La Russa had been unknowingly preparing for the job. His childhood and high school friends and his former teammates in the minor leagues were not surprised. Nor were the players he had managed in the minor leagues. Nor was his mentor, Loren Babe, who La Russa quickly added to his coaching staff.

La Russa and his father had gone to visit Al Lopez, the former White Sox manager and Tampa icon, the previous winter. "My dad and I went by and we talked a couple of hours about managing. I wanted to pick Al's brain," La Russa said.

Lopez later told the *Chicago Tribune*, "He wanted to know what I felt were the most important things for a manager to be a success. He must have talked an hour or two, and I told him I felt he had to have the respect of his players.

"I told him I didn't associate with my players off the field as much as I wanted to because if you get friendly with one or two of them, the others might feel left out. I told him that my thinking was that you find out where a player does best and then leave him at that position. He might make a few mistakes at the beginning, but he'll gradually get better."

Lopez and La Russa also discussed the specific challenges of managing the White Sox and playing at Comiskey Park. "In that park up there, you've got to get a team that lets the other club make the mistakes," Lopez said. "That's what we had in 1959. It's foolish to get a big, slow club, especially in that park."

La Russa would continue to seek advice from those he respected for years to come. He had learned from every manager for whom he had ever played, in the majors and minors, and filed those lessons away for future use. He was impressed by the way Dick Williams handled the flow of the game. He remembered how John McNamara cared for his players.

He also never forgot when he saw managers do something wrong, and remained mindful of repeating those mistakes himself.

"I played for a manager in Oakland who talked to me eight times in two months," La Russa said. "The only thing he said was, 'Get a bat.' I felt like I was scum. Here he was, always kidding around with Reggie and Sal and the others. That's easy to do.

"I think the manager's number one responsibility is getting the most out of his players. If a fan goes to the park and sees that a player isn't hustling, he should boo the manager. If a guy refuses to give his best on the field, then it's [the manager's] responsibility to get him out of there."

The two things La Russa hoped to quickly convey to his players on the White Sox were how much he wanted to win and how much he cared about them and the game.

"I'm not just sitting in the corner of the dugout, idly watching the scoreboard, trying to be a strategical genius in the eighth inning, " La Russa said. "Another manager once told me that the first five or seven innings belong to the teams on the field, and that if the game is still close in the seventh, the last three innings are his; that's when he really gets into it. I don't agree with that. I get into it from the first to the ninth."

La Russa did not have as many rules as some managers, but he knew what he wanted out of his players and he knew that discipline would be an important key to his team's success.

"I don't believe in organizations that build discipline by telling you how to wear your socks," La Russa said in the spring of 1980. "The way you can build discipline is by having everyone play like a pro. I won't say, 'Geez, we're not running it out to first base, so you have to cut your hair shorter.' That doesn't make sense. The public doesn't like to see rubber-stamp players, and part of our job—besides winning games—is to provide entertainment. I like guys to be individuals."

La Russa also knew that he had to overcome an opinion that many fans, reporters, and others had around baseball: that the primary reason he was hired as the White Sox manager was because Bill Veeck was too cheap to hire a real manager.

"I had no credentials," La Russa said, almost agreeing with his critics. "I didn't blame anybody. But I knew I had to earn that benefit of a doubt."

He also had to overcome what he considered another handicap. Always quick to downgrade his own accomplishments as a player, La Russa was managing several players who he had played with or against in the minors.

"I accepted that I wasn't good enough," La Russa said of his playing career. "I was a horsefeathers player and I have to remember that because I'm managing a lot of guys who saw me play."

Fortunately for La Russa, many of those players were not as negative about La Russa the player as he was on himself.

"He was a hardnosed, hustling kind of player," Chet Lemon said. "He was a Pete Rose kind of guy." And if he needed to create a model for the kind of player he wanted to manage with the White Sox, La Russa knew that would be it. Unfortunately, he was stuck managing the players he had inherited, and that wasn't always easy. The White Sox had won 90 games in 1977, finishing third in the AL West but they had enjoyed only one other winning year in their previous 11 seasons.

"To me, you judge a manager on what he gets out of the club that you have provided him," Hemond said. "You know in the front office if your team is not a pennant contender. You have to be very realistic and not make the manager a scapegoat if you have failed to provide him with a talented club. That was not a talented club. He didn't take a choice job."

La Russa did his best to try to light a fire under the players, regardless of what his fate might be at the end of the season. Veeck and Hemond never called him an interim manager, but he was only signed through the 1979 season.

La Russa, who knew that controlling his temper would be one of his challenges in the major leagues, quickly found himself getting into trouble with the umpires. He was ejected in his sixth game in the majors, in Yankee Stadium, and got tossed two more times during his first six weeks on the job. In so doing he followed the first piece of advice he had been given months earlier by Al Lopez; he earned the respect of the players.

"I think I can do the best job just being myself," La Russa told the *Chicago Tribune* in 1980. "If I have to kick a bat once in a while, I'm going to have to do it."

Those players who had been with La Russa in the minor leagues saw that he was not managing any differently just because he was in the major leagues. If anything, he was working harder and longer and trying to educate himself as much as possible, not only about his team but about the opposing club as well.

"He earned the respect of the players because he was smart and everybody could tell he knew what he was doing," Jim Morrison said. "He knew how to take care of guys."

One person who was paying very close attention to the team's performance was Veeck, then 65 years old and with a virtual lifetime invested in baseball. His latest run with the White Sox had begun when he purchased the team in 1975. He still was as motivated to win as he had been when he began working for the Cubs in the 1930s, when his father became president of the team.

"Hardly anyone has noticed how we've played under Mr. La Russa, but it's quite well," Veeck said near the end of the 1979 season. "He and the pitchers are the high spots of the summer. They are the redeeming feature of the season."

The club finished with a 27–27 record under La Russa, not great by his standards but a major improvement in the 14-games-under-.500 performance of the club before he was named manager. He said he never believed the club's record would be the only factor in determining whether he returned as manager in 1980, but he still was glad to finish at .500.

"Realistically, I knew if I did poorly I would not be back," La Russa said. "I started feeling pretty good about my chances in the early part of September when Bill and I would get together and he'd talk about 'next year this' or 'next year that.'"

At the end of the season, Veeck rewarded La Russa with a contract to manage the club in 1980. Armed with the knowledge and experience gained in just two months on the job, La Russa was quick to acknowledge that he was still very much in a learning position. He spent as much time with the owner as possible. When Veeck routinely had visitors come up to his private dining room following home games to talk baseball, La Russa was always there, soaking in every word, even if the sessions ran well into the night.

"It was always fascinating," Hemond said of those sessions in the "Bard's Room." "Tony was not a yes man and he would ask questions and also express his thoughts about the game. Tony never had any fear whatsoever. Some managers would probably have dodged the issue and said they had somewhere else to go, but Tony was always there.

"Bill was very smart and he would often ask questions just to see what kind of answers he would get, not only from Tony but from the other scouts and baseball people there. Bill was great at initiating arguments and he would purposely plant the seeds, even if he knew what he was saying was technically incorrect."

La Russa had things on his mind in addition to what was happening with the White Sox. His wife Elaine gave birth to the couple's first daughter, Bianca, with two weeks left in the season. In his free time, he was also studying to take the final section of the bar exam. Most of his time, however, was spent thinking about baseball and how he could get the White Sox to be a better team in 1980. His first taste of managing in the big leagues had only increased his desire to be successful.

"If I ever lost my enthusiasm and just had to sit in the dugout and not show emotion, I'd get out of managing," he said. "Before every game there's a little fire that burns inside me. When I saw us play Baltimore, the best ballclub in baseball, it gave me goosebumps. When you play with enthusiasm you don't cheat the fans."

Veeck also was looking forward to seeing what La Russa could do given a complete season on the job.

"I think we're going to find that he is one of the really outstanding managers before he's through," Veeck told the *Chicago Tribune* at the start of the 1980 season. "His intelligence was the thing that first attracted me; and his dedication. Anybody who puts himself through law school while playing ball, you know is going to work at whatever he does. When he was managing in the minor leagues, his leadership ability was obvious.

"In baseball, the better managers usually weren't outstanding players. All the star has to do is go up and hit the ball out of the park. What does he care about the finer points of the game? But when you're a scuffler like Tony was—up and down, trying to stick with limited talent—then you have to learn the nuances that give you a little bit of an advantage, things that will keep you afloat.

"The difference in our club the last six weeks of the season was so noticeable. Not only the won-lost record but attitudes, spirit, enthusiasm. Don

Kessinger was too nice a guy, and too many people took advantage of that niceness."

Veeck knew in La Russa he had found a manager for whom competitiveness was paramount, as illustrated by La Russa's comments when asked the reasons why he did so well in law school.

"I enjoy competing," he said. "In law school, I made good grades and people would say, 'You've got a good head for the law.' Nah. It was very simple. I had friends in school, and when the grades came out, I wanted mine to be higher than theirs. They'd quit studying at 11:00, and I'd stay up to 2:00 or 3:00 in the morning."

La Russa applied the same logic when it came to baseball. He was now competing against some of the greatest managers in the history of the game. In the American League in 1980, when La Russa stared across the field into the opposite dugout, he saw the likes of Earl Weaver, Billy Martin, Sparky Anderson, Gene Mauch, or Dick Howser staring back at him.

Some young, inexperienced managers might have been intimated, but not La Russa. He thought back to his law school days, and knew there was only one way he could compete with those managerial giants—he would outwork them by learning as much about the game as possible. In was in that mind-set that he arrived at his office for spring training shortly after the crack of dawn, a tradition that would continue well into the future.

"I was at such a disadvantage experiencewise," La Russa said years later. "I was just trying to narrow the gap. It's a habit that stuck…. When you take a test, don't you do better if you study as opposed to walking in and trying to wing it?"

Anderson, for one, was immediately impressed with La Russa—after their relationship got off to a somewhat rocky beginning.

"I was out at the mound arguing with an umpire, and I saw something out of the side of my eye," Anderson said. "I wasn't sure what it was. I turned and saw it was [La Russa]. I said, 'What the hell?' He wanted to listen to what I was saying.

"The next day I called him on the phone and arranged to meet with him in the dugout. I asked him, 'What the hell were you doing?' He said, 'I just wanted to hear what you were saying.' I said, 'Let me tell you something. It's a very simple rule and if you follow it you are never going to have any trouble. You always take care of your dugout, and let the other manager take care of his dugout. When you do that you will never have any trouble." From that moment on, Anderson had his eye on La Russa—perhaps because he might have seen a little of himself in the young White Sox manager.

Anderson was only 36 years old when he was plucked from relative obscurity and named manager of the Cincinnati Reds in 1970. He had spent one year as a player in the major leagues, hitting .218 as a second baseman for the Phillies in 1959. He managed for five years in the minors and coached first base for the Padres in 1969 before taking over the Reds. After eight years, he joined the Tigers in 1979.

"I never saw anyone catch on as fast as he did," Anderson said. "When you talk to him, you realize he is very intelligent. You're not talking to a bozo. He learned so fast that you were never going to trick him. He knew what was going on. I always played him straight up, but I never let him play any tricks on me either."

Hemond, for one, appreciated the time Anderson and the other veteran managers spent with La Russa, helping with his transition to the major leagues.

"Tony was being tested in his first years in the dugout," Hemond said. "That was where some of those guys learned to respect him. At first I'm sure they thought, 'Who the heck is this guy?' When you start managing against somebody, you have to react to the way he is managing. There's a lot of gamesmanship that goes on. All of a sudden you realize 'that guy is pretty good.'

"Tony was smart enough to pick up the wisdom those guys were willing to pass along. I don't think Sparky would have spent so much time with him if he thought he was talking to a guy who would not be around very long."

As part of his major league education, Hemond had taken La Russa with him to the 1979 World Series between the Pirates and Orioles. It was the first World Series La Russa had attended and he was in heaven, surrounded by some of the greatest and smartest people in the game, sitting for hours talking about baseball.

La Russa could not believe how much these men second-guessed and analyzed the moves of Earl Weaver and Chuck Tanner, two of the most experienced managers in the game. It reminded him all over again how much he had to learn.

La Russa had yet to develop a reputation of being an innovator and a free thinker, but it would not take long. His team prepared to open the 1980 season with an unusual starting rotation of four left-handed pitchers, all 28 years of age or younger. His fifth-best pitcher was also a young left-hander, 20-year-old Britt Burns.

While he especially liked the talent and potential of those pitchers, La Russa already had found another bonus in going with a youth-laden roster.

"I don't have to motivate these kids," he told the *New York Times* that spring. "All they want to do is get out there and play. Some managers have stars with big egos. On the other hand, of course, they've got stars."

The young players also knew they had a manager who believed in them and would back them a hundred percent. Even the older players, such as closer Ed Farmer, quickly saw and appreciated that.

"The managing experience might not have been there, but he was a good manager from day one," Farmer said. "He knew how to manage the game and how to manage the guys. There were three men in my life who were influential to me as far as baseball went. Two were Cal Ripken Sr. and La Russa. [La Russa] didn't want any tricks. He had come there to do a job. He wanted guys on the team who were going to do it, and if you didn't want to jump on board he would send you someplace else."

Another thing his players appreciated was that he made it a point to speak to each of his players at least once every other day.

Joe Goddard, covering the team for the *Chicago Sun-Times*, wondered if that was really true so he made a special point of arriving very early before a game one day just to watch La Russa in action.

"He was down sitting on the tarpaulin talking to some guys, then I saw him behind the batting screen in the middle of the field," Goddard said. "Next he was in the dugout, then behind the batting cage. He really did talk to almost everybody on the team while they were on the field. I was impressed with that."

La Russa's first unconventional move that spring came with the decision to see if first baseman Mike Squires, who was left-handed, could be used as an emergency catcher. That idea actually was born in a conversation between Squires and Roland Hemond, when Squires said he had always wanted to be a catcher like his father, but nobody would let him do it because he was left handed.

"Roland's eyes lit up and he said to me, 'Would you consider trying?'" Squires said. "I still had no idea what he was talking about. He said, 'Bill Veeck would like that.' Most teams carried three catchers back then and they knew if I could do it, even on an emergency basis, it would free up a roster spot.

"They put me behind the plate for batting practice to see if my eyes closed, which they didn't because when I was a kid in the backyard I had always been the catcher."

Squires' one concern was that he had an incentive clause in his contact that kicked in if he played a certain number of games. He was worried that if he got hurt while catching he might not reach that incentive, so he talked the White Sox into guaranteeing him the extra money if he got hurt.

"Tony had enough guts to put me in a couple of games when we were getting blown out just to see if I could do it," Squires said. "The situation never came up where he had to use me."

The White Sox's players could tell with those types of decisions that La Russa was looking for an edge, something extra to give his club an advantage.

"I don't really think Tony cares what other people think," Squires said. "If he thinks there is enough value to something he'll try it."

La Russa was extremely superstitious, which led to some lighthearted moments in the dugout. "If there was a piece of trash on the floor of the dugout, he would always kick it down to the other end of the dugout," Squires said. "At times guys who were not playing threw stuff down on the floor just to mess with him. He would come along and kick it to the other end of the dugout."

The lighthearted moments had to be shared with serious ones, however, and the White Sox had more than their share of those episodes as well. More often than not, La Russa's outbursts would be triggered by what he perceived as pitchers intentionally throwing at his hitters.

The first battle of the year came on April 20, at Baltimore, when Doug DeCinces of the Orioles charged the White Sox's Mike Proly when he thought a pitch had come too close to his head. After order was restored, Harold Baines came to bat and La Russa told him to "dig in." La Russa thought a warning had been issued to both teams that there would be no more dangerous pitches.

The first pitch from Sammy Stewart came in under Baines' chin. La Russa found out no warning had been issued. "Harold said to me, 'Are they really paying you to manage?'" La Russa said. "He said it with his eyes."

That battle, as it turned out, was only a preamble for more fights to come, starting with a full-scale brawl against Milwaukee on May 5. This fight again started with Proly on the mound. Ben Oglivie charged the mound after he was hit by a pitch, and in trying to separate the players, La Russa suffered the worst injury in the fight, dislocating his left shoulder.

Then on June 20, Ed Farmer—who had hit Al Cowens with a pitch in 1979, breaking his jaw—saw Cowens, who had moved from Kansas City to Detroit in the off-season, try to get revenge when he attacked Farmer in the eleventh inning after hitting a ground ball to short. Instead of running to first after hitting the ball, Cowens charged the mound and starting punching Farmer.

Chicago police went into the Detroit clubhouse after the game to try to arrest Cowens on assault charges. He also was suspended for seven games and fined by American League president Lee MacPhail. La Russa said the attack was "about the most gutless move I've seen."

Farmer fought back against Cowens with his postgame comments. "If that's his best shot, he won't scare anybody," Farmer said. "It wasn't even a punch. He scratched me with his fingernail, just like a fight with a woman."

When the White Sox were too busy playing baseball to get into fights, the season was going about as well as La Russa could have hoped. The team remained in contention in the AL West throughout the first half of the year, arriving at the All-Star break in second place, three games under .500 and 8½ games behind division leader Kansas City.

He felt that he had established a good relationship with his players, possibly because his age helped him relate well to many of them. He walked through the clubhouse listening to Bruce Springsteen tapes on his headphones, and he became good friends with Dennis DeYoung, the lead singer for the band Styx, who was from Chicago and was a frequent guest at Comiskey Park.

Ed Farmer was selected for the All-Star Game, and La Russa made it a point to congratulate him and remind him that he was representing the team. He also told him that the Sox had a workout on Wednesday, the day after the All-Star Game, and that it would mean a lot to the team if Farmer could be there.

Farmer pitched in the game, caught the redeye flight back from Los Angeles to Chicago, and was at Comiskey Park for the 11 AM workout.

"I didn't think you would let me down," La Russa told him. "This is huge for the team."

La Russa didn't quite have the same reaction when Farmer called him before the team's kangaroo court. La Russa had been fined $50 when he fell down in a mud puddle going out to argue a call. La Russa wanted to challenge the fine, which meant if Farmer, the judge, ruled against him, the fine and court costs would increase to $150.

"I told him to state his case and he said he was going to go out and argue the call, but when he slipped and fell his uniform looked terrible and he thought he would be better served by going back in the dugout," Farmer said. "I told him that was understandable, but the team was screaming for him to argue the call and that I was going to have to rule against him.

"I said, 'The fine is $150,' and he said, 'I'm not paying.' Lamar Johnson was the bailiff, and I told him, 'Go to Mr. La Russa's office and do whatever you need to do to get the $150.' He came out with the money."

Farmer was on the other end of a fine when he overslept and missed a flight from Chicago to Texas. He caught another flight and actually beat the team to Texas and was waiting when La Russa walked into the clubhouse.

"He fined me $500," Farmer said. "I wrote him a check. He asked if I was mad at him and I said, 'I missed the plane. Those are the rules, and I abide by the rules. But I've done everything you've asked of me and you know that.' He said, 'I have to do it for you because your needs are not bigger than anybody on the team. If I do it to you, everybody else will fall in line.'

"He told me, 'If you don't screw up for the rest of the year I will give you the $500 back.' We were in Oakland the last week of the season and he called me in his office and handed me the check back. He had never cashed it."

Unfortunately for Farmer, La Russa, and the rest of the team, the second half of the season had been a major disappointment. After going just three games under .500 in the first half, the team limped home with a final record 20 games under .500, in fifth place, 26 games behind the division champion Royals. The record would have been even worse had the team not won eight of its final 10 games.

La Russa knew that it had been a tough year, but he didn't believe the White Sox's final record truly reflected how much progress the team had made. He especially liked what he saw from the three rookie pitchers who ended the year in the starting rotation: Burns, Richard Dotson, and LaMarr Hoyt.

"We've learned some things the hard way," La Russa said. "The one thing we haven't lost sight of, the point of going through all this, is that we are going to become a winning club. It is the prevalent feeling on the team that we will. Any player who does not share that feeling will not survive here."

The biggest uncertainty about La Russa returning as manager for another year was the unknown status of the club's ownership. Veeck had decided to sell the team, but other owners had blocked Edward DeBartolo's bid to buy the team. With the sale still up in the air, Veeck went ahead and hired La Russa for the 1981 season so he would be under contract no matter who bought it.

Veeck eventually sold the team to Jerry Reinsdorf, a real estate investor, and Eddie Einhorn, a sports television executive. Though he was upset and disappointed that Veeck's tenure as owner was coming to an end, it would turn out to be good news for La Russa.

Unfortunately, La Russa's two most vocal critics, broadcasters Harry Caray and Jimmy Piersall, remained.

5

CHAPTER

The Critics
Speak Up

Harry Caray had been broadcasting White Sox games on radio or television since 1971, after 25 years in the broadcast booth for St. Louis. Jimmy Piersall, an ex-player who spent most of his career with the Red Sox, joined Caray in 1977.

The two were quite popular with the nucleus of the White Sox fans in the working-class neighborhoods on Chicago's South Side. The team's new owners, Reinsdorf and Einhorn, were well aware of that, but they also believed that the future success of the franchise, from a marketing standpoint, would be in making the team more appealing to the increasing number of people moving to the Chicago suburbs.

Even before the new owners took over and started making changes, however, Caray and Piersall had already made up their minds that they did not like La Russa. They believed, as did many others, that La Russa was hired because he would work for a low salary and that he was a puppet for Veeck.

La Russa acknowledged that there had been moments in his first couple of months on the job when the broadcasters had criticized him, but he had been around the major leagues enough as a player to realize that came with the job.

As long as the attacks were not personal, he would not comment on what either of the announcers said.

When the attacks became personal, La Russa took the criticism hard. He wasn't used to people criticizing him and wasn't sure what to say or do about it.

"They're popular because they say what the fans would like to," La Russa told the *Chicago Tribune* in the spring of 1980. "The only thing that would bother me would be if they said it after the fact. Like if I brought in a pitcher and they said it was a bad move after he got shelled. If they said it while he was walking in from the bullpen, then they'd be running a risk too."

Said Hemond, "They were on him right from the beginning. It was almost like a crusade. Bill was always very supportive of Tony. They could have said anything and he was still going to be in Tony's corner. Some other owners might have succumbed to the pressure early on and changed managers, thinking that the announcers were more popular than the manager so we'll keep them. Bill wouldn't do that."

La Russa did appreciate the fact that Caray and Piersall would ask him later about particular moves, seeking his opinion, even if they still disagreed with the move. Searching for that extra edge, La Russa even asked Piersall, a former outfielder, to work with the club's outfielders at spring training in 1980. Piersall agreed, doing it free of charge, because he wanted to be more involved in the game and believed that he had knowledge to pass on to the current players.

In his autobiography, *The Truth Hurts,* published in 1984, Piersall discussed his relationship with La Russa that spring.

"I told La Russa at the outset that, if he ever felt there was a problem with me up in the press box and coaching at the same time, he should just let me know and I'd step out of the coaching job," he wrote. "Well, there was a lot to say about the way the White Sox were playing that year. The team stunk.... I had a lot to say about the performances and the mistakes I saw on the field."

While the White Sox were on a road trip to California in June, La Russa approached him and said he thought it would be better for the team if he stopped helping out on the field. Piersall agreed, since it was a promise he had made to La Russa in spring training. What later angered Piersall, however, was that he found out from a couple of players that La Russa had conducted a vote about whether Piersall should continue coaching. It was reported in some newspapers that the poll had been Piersall's idea, which he said was not the case.

La Russa acknowledged that he had sought out the players' opinions about Piersall continuing in both jobs, which he thought, given Piersall's constant on-air criticism, had become a conflict of interest.

The issue escalated on July 2, when the White Sox returned to Chicago. Before a game at Comiskey Park, Piersall attacked sportswriter Rob Gallas of the suburban *Arlington Heights Daily Herald* in the White Sox locker room. Gallas had not been on the road trip to California and was asking players about the decision to discontinue Piersall's coaching duties.

Piersall reportedly had both of his hands around Gallas's neck when the two were finally separated. After Veeck—who was still officially the owner of the team—heard about the incident, he sent his son, Mike Veeck, to look for Piersall, whom he found in the broadcast booth. The two of them fought, witnesses said, because of earlier negative comments Piersall had made about the younger Veeck's mother, Bill Veeck's wife.

Piersall ended up in the hospital. He had been under psychiatric care earlier in his life, and was again examined by a psychiatrist. While he was off the air, the *Chicago Sun-Times* polled fans about whether he should be fired or should keep his job. More than 6,000 fans voted for him to come back; less than 800 thought he should be fired. He returned to Caray and the booth about a month later.

It was against this backdrop that the sale of the White Sox was finalized, with Reinsdorf and Einhorn taking over before the 1981 season. The problems that Caray and Piersall had experienced with Veeck would only get worse under the new owners.

Reinsdorf, for one, was appalled by how critical Caray and Piersall were of La Russa during the broadcasts. He knew about Piersall's problems with La Russa from the previous year, but he did not understand why Caray did not get along better with the manager.

"They [Caray and Piersall] tried to destroy him [La Russa]," Reinsdorf said. "I never could figure out what Harry had against him.

"Harry has done a lot to undermine Tony. He has a great following, and he has caused Tony a problem, a problem he'll overcome only by winning."

Reinsdorf's problem was Caray and Piersall's popularity. He knew that if he changed broadcasters he would alienate his fans. He didn't think at that point that he had any choice but to tell La Russa to endure the criticism.

"They [Caray and Piersall] had everything to do with public perception," Reinsdorf said. "I had no problem resisting public perception. We had been 20 games under .500 in 1980 and in 1981 we were two games over .500 so I couldn't figure out what there was to complain about the guy."

The fans were listening to Caray and Piersall, however, and seemingly anytime La Russa came out of the dugout he was getting booed. Reinsdorf and Einhorn met with Caray and Piersall and asked them to tone down their criticism, but their entreaties fell on deaf ears.

Piersall soon added additional targets—the umpires, the players, and even the wives of the players.

In the first game of a doubleheader against the Angels on May 31, Piersall thought a third strike to Mike Squires, called by umpire Joe Brinkman, had been outside. He stood up in the broadcast booth and held his hands about a foot apart from each other, a nonverbal indication of how far outside he thought the pitch had been. Brinkman didn't see Piersall, but first-base umpire Dale Ford did. He called time and ran toward the plate, urging Brinkman to look up at Piersall. The two then exchanged various gestures toward each other, the umpires asserting Piersall had "flipped them off."

Ford was behind the plate for the second game, and he said that if Piersall continued to target the umpires, trying to incite the crowd, he would not hesitate to forfeit the game to the Angels. It didn't happen, but Piersall said he would continue to criticize the umpires if he thought they deserved it, the same way he felt about La Russa and the rest of the team.

"Lots of people would like to see me fired," he said. "Umpires now, too. But I'll tell you one thing…I'm gonna keep plugging. Lazy, gutless fat cats.…

You know why I called Ken Kaiser [another umpire] a whale? Because he is a whale, that's why."

The player's strike prevented Piersall from getting into more trouble until September. When play resumed, the owners had figured out a way to separate Caray and Piersall most of the time. Caray called all but two innings of the game on television, while Piersall was kept on the radio side for the entire game.

Piersall still managed to criticize the White Sox's Greg Luzinski for not running out a ground ball. Luzinski did not hear the comment, but several players who were listening in the clubhouse heard Piersall say, "With the money he's making he's got to run that ball out."

La Russa called the comment a cheap shot, and said Luzinski had been instructed not to run at full speed because of a thigh injury. Piersall said later he had not been told about the injury.

La Russa's comments in defense of his player made Piersall even more upset.

"No matter what, it couldn't be a player's fault," Piersall wrote in his auto-biography. "It was Harry or me who was the problem, he would say. He'd find some cock-and-bull excuse for his player and then rant about how we were maligning his wonderful players.... What bullshit.

"A couple of innings later, when Luzinski doubled to drive in the winning run, he didn't dog it. He ran like hell. And what kind of managing would it be to put an injured player in a game and then tell him to take it easy, don't bother hustling? Pure unadulterated bullshit. But that's the way it was with La Russa, a million excuses and a hurt little boy when somebody said one of his players loafed or goofed up."

Luzinski said the players were united with La Russa in the dislike of Caray and Piersall.

"You really never saw them except at the ballpark," Luzinski said. "They didn't spend much time in the clubhouse, yet they had a lot to say about things. I have no idea why."

On September 6, Piersall appeared as a guest on Mike Royko's television show and made critical remarks about the players' wives. According to a transcript of the show, which appeared in the *Chicago Tribune*, Piersall said, "I think each ballclub should have a clinic once a week for the wives. I don't think they know what baseball is. First of all, they were horny broads who wanted to get married. They want a little money, they want a little security, and a big, strong-looking ballplayer. I traveled, I played. I got a load of them broads, too."

The remarks naturally angered the players, and Reinsdorf and Einhorn hit Piersall with an indefinite suspension that would last through the remainder of the season.

"I don't think players have to be immune from criticism, but their families shouldn't be brought into it," La Russa said at the time. "It came home to one of our players today when his wife was confronted by an acquaintance in a store and the friend said, 'I didn't know you were that horny.' That's just not right."

Reinsdorf and Einhorn didn't like Caray's style of announcing much better than Piersall's, but they knew how popular he was with the fans. They didn't think they had any choice but to try to re-hire him for the 1982 season. Caray had a choice, however, and he jumped over to the crosstown Cubs.

That move allowed the owners to bring in Don Drysdale and Ken Harrelson as the new broadcast team. But Piersall was not entirely out of the picture—or La Russa's hair—just yet. The Sox gave him a job as a pregame and postgame commentator on their pay television channel, Sports Vision, for the 1982 season. They hoped to appease the fans and entice them to purchase the pay-per-view games. Piersall also was hired to do a postgame radio show on WMAQ, the studios of which were in the same building as the Sox's broadcast network.

Those forums still provided Piersall with plenty of opportunities to criticize La Russa, and he did so frequently. Shortly after the All-Star break and with the team playing poorly, media reports began to surface that speculated that La Russa's job status could be growing shaky.

One night, accompanied by coaches Jim Leyland and Charlie Lau, La Russa went to the studio after the game and came face to face with Piersall right after he went off the air. "He said that I was managing so poorly that even my father was ashamed of me and the job that I was doing," La Russa said. "That was unfair and crossed the line."

Piersall wrote in his autobiography that La Russa called him "a liar" and that the two men had a heated verbal exchange but did not get into a fight.

La Russa said the next day that he had reached the point at which he could no longer ignore Piersall's criticism, not only of him, but of his coaches and players.

"You have to look at it two ways—one, as a professional and two, as a person," La Russa was quoted by the *Tribune* as saying. "As a professional, the only answer for Piersall or anybody else is what happens on the field. Nobody else has a say in whether a team wins or loses, only the players and the manager.

"But when I take the uniform off and put street clothes on, I'm a person, like any other individual, with the right to speak up. Piersall has been saying certain things about me and my club and I wanted to talk to him about it, face to face. I did it the way I think it should be done. There was nothing physical."

Piersall kept his television show going into the 1983 season, for one game. He was fired after the opening game of the season for what Reinsdorf and Einhorn said was a failure to keep his promise not to make "personal attacks" on members of the White Sox organization.

He remained on the air for his WMAQ radio show through the 1983 season, and was then dismissed. Years later, he would continue to criticize La Russa whenever a reporter somewhere provided him with an opportunity.

"He just doesn't know the game well enough to lead the team or teach the players," Piersall told the *Sun-Times* in 1986. "He wasn't a good manager when I was broadcasting the games with Harry and he can't be much better now."

One hard lesson La Russa had learned in his first few seasons in charge of a major league team was that he needed to expect criticism. Another was that a manager had a much greater chance of being successful if he was surrounded by great players. Going into the 1981 season, when he looked at the White Sox's clubhouse and saw Carlton Fisk and Greg Luzinski coming through the door, he knew he had a couple of big reasons to smile.

CHAPTER 6

Building a Foundation

The White Sox's new owners, Jerry Reinsdorf and Eddie Einhorn, told La Russa they were committed to putting a more competitive team on the field for the 1981 season. Unlike Veeck, they had the money to support that pledge.

In two bold moves during spring training, the White Sox signed catcher Carlton Fisk and purchased outfielder Greg Luzinski from the Phillies. Fisk was a seven-time All-Star during his 10 years with the Red Sox before becoming a free agent. Luzinski, a Chicago native, had made the NL All-Star team four times in his nine full years with the Phillies.

"It's hard to think of a player in either league who could help our club more," La Russa said about Fisk, who immediately starting producing when he hit a three-run homer on Opening Day to help the White Sox win at Boston. When the team played its home opener, Fisk followed suit with a grand slam.

In addition to signing Fisk and Luzinski, the White Sox had picked up another outfielder with great potential, Ron LeFlore. The moves only cost the club money and allowed them to keep their young pitching staff intact.

"We've tried to assemble a roster of players who care," La Russa said. "Care about giving effort every game, because fans pay to see effort, and care about winning. Whoever doesn't meet my standards of caring won't stay.

"You're enthused because the Sox are improved. We would be more optimistic if the other clubs had stood still or gone backwards, but almost all our opponents have improved too. It will be a dogfight. I want to be in that dogfight so much I can taste it."

La Russa told *Sports Illustrated* early that season, "Last year we had more ways to lose than we had to win. This year it's just the reverse."

The White Sox did indeed get off to a better start, staying near the top of the AL West standings with the Oakland A's, who were managed by Billy Martin, one of the managers who La Russa had been quietly studying for the previous seasons, beginning in 1978 when he first joined the major leagues as a Sox coach.

"I was intrigued by the way he would change his pitchers to draw pinch-hitters off our bench," La Russa told the *Chicago Tribune*. "In the late stages of the game, it would turn out that we were short of pinch-hitters…didn't have a great choice, and Martin would have the pitcher he wanted mopping up the game."

La Russa admitted he had tried to pattern some of his decisions after watching Martin, but not completely copy what Martin did.

"I may copy strategy," he said, "how a certain manager handles pitchers to get the most from them, but I don't believe in emulating another man's style or personality. When it comes to how you deal with players, you have to be yourself. So I'm not Billy Martin or Paul Richards. I'm Tony La Russa."

As the midpoint of the season neared, La Russa really had only one reason to doubt whether the club's winning ways would continue. That reason was the growing tension between baseball's team owners and the player's union, the likelihood increasing by the day that the two sides were headed for a work stoppage. When the strike deadline of June 12 arrived, La Russa still hoped that there would be a last-minute compromise, but no such settlement was forthcoming.

The White Sox had a 31–22 record when the strike came, in third place in the division but just 2½ games behind division-leading Oakland. Both sides were optimistic that the strike would be short-lived. As days turned into weeks, however, the prognosis for a settlement evaporated.

The White Sox assigned their coaches to minor league teams, to help with extra instruction; Hemond and La Russa took off on an extended scouting trip throughout Mexico. As the strike stretched to a month and then six weeks, the biggest question became what to do with the schedule if and when play resumed. La Russa had his own idea.

"If we had only, say, an 80-game season, it wouldn't be fair to have the play-offs and World Series to determine the champion," La Russa said. "What I think we should do is start from scratch, have a playoff system of best-of-five series with the winners playing each other for the championship."

Rumors increased that the major leagues would play a split season, with the winners of the "second half" meeting the winners of the "first half" (the pre-strike games) in the league playoffs. "My gut won't let me even consider the possibility," La Russa said.

When a strike settlement finally was reached and the continuation of the season was scheduled to begin on August 10, La Russa learned that the plan for qualifying teams for the playoffs was indeed the split-season plan. He became livid, not only because he found major flaws in the model, but also because he thought the Sox were going to be at a major disadvantage—they were opening the second half with a 15-game road trip.

The plan, as it was originally announced, created the very real possibility that it would be better for the White Sox to lose a four-game series at Oakland in late September than to win. One stipulation stated that if one team from a division won both half-seasons, they would have a playoff against the team with the next best overall record in the division. La Russa and his players admitted that would be something they would have to consider, which touched off a firestorm throughout major league baseball.

"To play a series where you don't play to win would go against everything in my brain and my body," La Russa said. "It's clear to me that nobody is going to take care of us except ourselves. The league and the commissioner have not proven to me they are concerned with the White Sox franchise to any great extent.

"My feeling now is that even if it would go against everything I've been brought up to believe in, under those circumstances I'd do everything I can to take care of my club and our fans.

"The bottom line is this…if it gives the fans and our club the best chance to win, I'm going to try to put our club into the playoffs, and if the powers in baseball would criticize that statement, I would criticize those powers for putting us in that position."

La Russa later revised his statement to say that if that situation did exist where the team would benefit more by losing, he would rather see his team forfeit those games instead of playing them and deliberately trying to lose. His stance was not appreciated by commissioner Bowie Kuhn, who said he would not discipline La Russa but did listen enough to the comments that the baseball officials devised a new playoff plan which eliminated any incentive for losing games.

Still, the basic concept of the temporary playoff structure remained. The team that won the first half—when teams didn't know they were playing for half a pennant—would play the team that won the second half. It was possible that a team could have the best overall record in its division for the entire season but if they finished second in each half, they would not make the playoffs at all.

It turned out that was exactly what happened in the National League, where the Cardinals and Reds had the best overall records in their respective divisions but neither team made the playoffs.

The White Sox started on a positive note, going 9–6 on their extended trip to Boston, Baltimore, New York, Toronto, and Milwaukee, but then hit the skids, losing 10 of 11 games. By then, any realistic hope of remaining in the race was gone and the team limped home with a 23–30 second-half record, sixth in the AL West.

When the team lost for the 13th time (in 16 games) on September 12 at Minnesota, La Russa held a closed-door team meeting and paid an attendant $100 to remove the traditional postgame meal.

"It was a chicken thing to do," La Russa said. "I've been on teams where you only have a meal when you win. I don't believe in that. This is not a policy but just a way to make my point tonight.... There's no way we can accept losing."

Only 3,129 fans came to Comiskey to see the White Sox officially eliminated from the race with a 6–0 loss to the Angels on September 28. A season that had started with so much promise had ended with a dramatic thud. No one took the defeats harder than La Russa.

The team owners, Reinsdorf and Einhorn, believed the strike had played a major role in the outcome of the season and therefore did not blame La Russa for what had happened on the field. They gave him a new two-year contract and listened when he made another big request: hiring two new coaches for 1982, Jim Leyland and Charlie Lau.

La Russa knew both men well. Leyland had been his managerial opponent in the minor leagues, and he had come to appreciate his skills and desire. Lau was a former playing teammate who, many years earlier, helped him fix a hole in his swing.

During the financially strapped Veeck years he knew that the team could not afford to bring in the coaches he wanted. But he felt that sometimes a different coach could have just as big an impact on a team's success as adding a new player.

Reinsdorf and Einhorn asked La Russa to rate his coaching staff on a scale from 1 to 10. Until all of the coaches received a 10 rating, they would set out to make changes.

"In the end, it's the players who win games, but our coaches make a big enough difference in enough games to justify their expense," La Russa said. "Actually, all they have to do is make a difference in a few games, and that can help you distance yourself from the rest of the league."

La Russa also realized the value of specialization. Teams had always had a pitching coach and a hitting coach, but he wanted his other coaches to also work with players on specific areas of the game—base running, infield defense, outfield defense, and so on. Specialization was a lesson he had learned in the minor leagues as well as when he was in a college classroom.

"Paul Richards told me a good manager looks after all the pieces of the game: hitting, pitching, defense, base running," La Russa said. "There just isn't enough time for me personally to devote the needed time to each of those pieces. So you pick the best men possible to help.

"In my undergraduate management courses, we were always talking about the delegation of responsibility and how you let people feel that they are worthy. If I tell a coach what to teach and how to teach it and he's just parroting me, he's not going to feel good about me or his job. When a coach comes to Chicago, he knows it's going to be a challenge."

One of the reasons La Russa might have taken a liking to Leyland was that the two had a lot in common. Leyland was the son of a factory worker who learned the importance of hard work and personal ethics from his father. Leyland loved baseball and respected the game deeply.

Leyland played seven years as a catcher in the minors but never rose above Double A before he was hired at age 26 to manage the Tigers' club in Bristol, Virginia, in the rookie Appalachian League. By the time La Russa hired him as his third-base coach with the White Sox, Leyland had managed for 11 years in the Detroit farm system. He won three Manager of the Year awards and directed his teams to five first-place finishes, including in 1979, when his Evansville team beat out Iowa for the American Association title. It was the same Iowa Oaks squad that La Russa had managed before coming to the White Sox as manager.

Leyland's path to the Tigers' managing job was blocked by the presence of Sparky Anderson in the Detroit dugout (a spot he would occupy for 16 years). He had developed the same respect for La Russa as La Russa had for him, but when the offer came from Chicago, Leyland declined out of loyalty to the Tigers, where he had spent all 18 years of his professional career.

"He was going to pass up a chance to go to the majors because he felt so much loyalty to the Detroit organization," said La Russa, who ultimately was able to convince Leyland to change his mind.

Lau, La Russa's former teammate, had a tougher decision. He was coaching with the Yankees and also had a job offer to return to Kansas City, where he had worked in the past with George Brett.

"Charlie came here because of his love for Tony," Reinsdorf said. "Tony convinced him that he needed him more than George Brett did."

Lau, who was one of the first hitting coaches to make specific use of videotape, also came because of a six-year contract, four years longer than La Russa's own.

In making the announcement, Reinsdorf said that La Russa "had been Lau's one failure."

Neither Reinsdorf nor La Russa expected Lau to fail with the White Sox, especially with two new hitters, outfielder Steve Kemp and first baseman Tom Paciorek. Those changes produced the best offensive lineup in La Russa's years in Chicago. But going into the 1982 season, he still believed the key to the team's success would be the pitching staff.

The young starters were at a point, La Russa believed, where they could no longer use their age or inexperience as an excuse if they did not perform. He was counting on Britt Burns, Steve Trout, Richard Dotson, and Dennis Lamp to be better than they were in 1981. If they produced, he did not see any reason why the White Sox could not compete for the AL West division title. La Russa began the year expecting LaMarr Hoyt to be in the bullpen, but the pitcher was quickly moved into the rotation once the regular season began.

The year could not have looked more promising in early April, when the White Sox started the year 8–0, a mark that included two doubleheader sweeps. The team then fell into a cycle in which they played well for a while, then slumped.

The team was 14 games over .500 by May 26, but was only 45–37 at the All-Star break. A 13–3 streak in early August improved the record to 64–52, but it was quickly followed by a 2–10 slide.

After every game, win or lose, La Russa questioned himself, replayed the game's key moments in his mind, and wondering if he had made the right moves. He sometimes wondered if there was a way to change his intensity— not to the point where he didn't care if his team won or lost, but maybe enough that he wouldn't worry so much about losing a game.

"I do think I sometimes push too hard," he told the *Chicago Tribune,* "I do think I could learn to relax. Sometimes I wonder about myself. You do this 162 times a year, there are nights when I have left so much out there that I'm sitting here and it's tough to get out of the chair. I've thought about it…. I've tried to be a little composed, but I felt worse when the day was over.

"I'm always looking to accomplish something, and when that day comes, I'm immediately looking for another thing to get me going. My wife kids me that I'm not a good vacationer, but I can't relax. I can't afford to relax. I don't have that ring on my finger."

With the Sox pitching staff struggling in midseason, the heat was building on pitching coach Ron Schueler. As media reports that Schueler was about to be fired, he beat the owners to the punch and resigned on July 10.

A few weeks later, reports began appearing in the Chicago media that La Russa's job also could be in jeopardy. The headline in the *Chicago Tribune* on July 30 read "Sox May Dump La Russa."

Reinsdorf told reporters after a 7–3 loss to Boston, "This is a critical time. If we keep playing like this we'll be dead. Tony didn't make the two errors at shortstop tonight, but at the same time he's the commander of the ship that isn't doing too well."

Still, Reinsdorf sounded as if he supported La Russa's efforts. "If Tony La Russa is fired, we'd be firing a good manager," Reinsdorf said. "A decision like that would be made because the team is going so badly and you can't fire the team, so you fire the leader."

There were many occasions when Reinsdorf was impressed with La Russa's decisions during a game. "We were playing the Orioles once, and we had guys on first and second with nobody out," Reinsdorf recalled. "It was an obvious bunt situation. Earl Weaver put the 'wheel' play on and Tony called for the hit-and-run. The batter hit a ground ball through the hole on the right side and a run scored.

"Another time we were playing the Yankees when Billy [Martin] was the manager. They had a runner on and Tony pitched out. He didn't go and it was ball one. He did it again and the runner still didn't go. Now the count was 2–0. I knew he was not going to pitch out again and so did Billy. Tony pitched out and the runner was thrown out.

"One of the biggest things I learned from him about managing is that a manager has to understand what each of his players is capable of doing, and to be successful he has to put the player in a position where he can do what he is capable of doing. A manager cannot ask a player to do something he is not capable of doing. If a guy can't bunt it doesn't matter what the situation is— you don't ask him to bunt."

Everyone connected with the White Sox knew that La Russa was very superstitious. That night after the loss to the Red Sox, it was chilly at Comiskey Park, and La Russa wore a heavy wool jacket. The team won, and so La Russa continued to wear the jacket, no matter the weather. For a couple of games the temperature was above 90 degrees, but La Russa would not take off the jacket.

"We went 15–3," La Russa said of that stretch.

"We went to Texas and it was like 115 degrees," Squires said. "Tony was in the dugout, wearing the jacket."

At one point during the season La Russa had more to worry about than just winning a game. After receiving a death threat, he wore an armored jacket under his jersey for two days. "Nobody would stand next to me," La Russa said. "I'd go over and sit next to Leyland, and he'd say 'No, no, no, I'm going for a smoke.'"

La Russa was able to laugh off the situation, and his negative press and the fan reaction. He told a story about how his two-year-old daughter Bianca was watching *Sesame Street* and they were talking about rhyming words, with the examples of moo, boo, and so on.

"My daughter asked me what 'boo' means," La Russa said. "I told her I would bring her out to the ballpark. When Dad shows up, she'll know what boo means."

In the midst of all that controversy, the La Russas welcomed the birth of their second daughter, Devon, a pleasant distraction from what was happening at the ballpark. But La Russa could never completely turn his thoughts away from the performance of the White Sox, his own performance as a manager, and creeping doubts about what he should be doing differently. He and Leyland often talked late into the night about every aspect of a game.

On the field, there were continuing problems with beanballs and other cheap shots. The Tigers accused LaMarr Hoyt of throwing at Alan Trammell's head. Detroit first-base coach Dick Tracewski called La Russa a "minor league punk manager" in the *Sporting News*, a charge La Russa responded to by calling Tracewski a "weasel."

In a series against Kansas City, La Russa took exception to Hal McRae of the Royals colliding hard with second baseman Tony Bernazard. "I don't think his teammate [Frank White] will appreciate it when we knock him into center field, which we will do sometime in this series," La Russa said. That threat was not carried out, although it got the umpire's attention enough that Bernazard was called out for interference on a slide that was described by observers as "ordinary." The call cost the White Sox two runs in an eventual 4–3 loss.

"When guys got hit he used to react almost immediately," Luzinski said. "Tony was almost always the first guy out of the dugout. I had to tackle him one time and tell him, 'Now is not the time. We'll get them later, the game is too close.'"

Luzinski recalled one game when Don Baylor, playing for Baltimore at the time, was on second base and La Russa thought he was sending signs to the batter to tell what pitch was coming.

"Tony was screaming at him, and I looked over and thought, 'What is wrong with this guy?'" Luzinksi said. "He said, 'We're going to drill you,' and sure enough, the next time Baylor came to bat, we hit him. It took a while, but Tony finally started to calm down a little and wait for the right situations and opportunities to react."

La Russa also received a lesson about timing one day from veteran umpire Dave Phillips. Phillips was working second base, and after a close play—but not a call anyone could argue—he noticed La Russa trotting out from the dugout. Before La Russa reached him and could begin his argument, Phillips began yelling at him.

"You are always coming out here, you've delayed this game something awful," Phillips said. "You get this guy up, you bring this guy in. We're three hours and 40 minutes into this game and you trot out here on a play that should not be argued about."

Phillips knew he had embarrassed La Russa, and that was not his intent. After the game, which was the final game of the series, the umpires were in their dressing room when there came a knock on the door. It was La Russa, asking for Phillips.

Phillips invited him into the room and listened to what he had to say, then told La Russa, "You screw around more than anybody. You come out and make every kind of move possible. I like you and I respect you. You have every right to argue, but be fair about it. That was not a close play." Another umpire on the crew, Steve Palermo, joined the discussion and La Russa finally left, knowing he had lost that argument.

Many years later, Phillips and La Russa crossed paths and Phillips asked La Russa to autograph a couple of baseballs that he could donate to a charity auction. La Russa also gave him a personal baseball that was inscribed, "To Dave, the guy who taught me to be a professional." Phillips knew La Russa was referring to that day in Chicago.

One of La Russa's biggest issues was with a player on his own team, Ron LeFlore. The White Sox had signed LeFlore as a free agent prior to the 1981 season, hoping he would fill their need for a leadoff hitter. LeFlore, who had learned to play baseball at prison in Michigan, had played six years with the Tigers before one season with the Expos, during which he stole 97 bases. While there was no denying LeFlore's ability, the White Sox worried that LeFlore's bad habits off the field—showing up late for games or practices and missing team flights—and his laid-back attitude would clash with La Russa's personality.

The two didn't have any clashes during 1981, though the White Sox were somewhat disappointed by LeFlore's 36 stolen bases and .247 average. Trouble did develop during the 1982 season, however, when LeFlore missed a post All-Star Game workout and then a Sunday afternoon game. La Russa suspended him for three games, costing LeFlore about $10,000.

LeFlore also missed a flight to Cooperstown, New York, for the Hall of Fame exhibition game and again was suspended, though he was reinstated after convincing general manager Roland Hemond that his wife had been ill.

He finished the1982 season with a .287 average in 91 games, and even though the White Sox did not think he figured in their plans for 1983, they invited him to spring training. When he had a poor offensive camp, the White Sox summarily released him.

Having survived a tumultuous 1982, La Russa was certain that 1983 would be a better season. Hoyt had won 19 games in 1982. Harold Baines had hit 25 homers and driven in 105 runs. Luzinski had 18 homers and 102 RBIs. La Russa had plenty of reasons to think the White Sox had more than enough offense to be a winning team. What the club needed was an improved performance from the pitching staff, and La Russa had just the right man for the job, another former minor league teammate, Dave Duncan.

Duncan's relationship with La Russa went back 20 years, to their days together in the A's farm system. Duncan enjoyed more success as a major league player than La Russa, and after a 13-year career he moved into the coaching ranks with Cleveland in 1978. He was named Seattle's pitching coach in 1982, working for his friend Rene Lachemann.

After that season, La Russa came to Seattle to appear at a roast for Lachemann, who was also a former teammate and minor league roommate. Duncan and La Russa got to talking, and La Russa learned that Duncan was unhappy with his contract situation. The Seattle owner refused to give Duncan a $5,000 raise, even though the Mariners' staff had led the American League in strikeouts and finished second in saves and shutouts in 1982. La Russa got on the phone with his bosses in Chicago, and in no time Duncan was his new pitching coach.

Duncan, La Russa thought, was one more piece of the puzzle that would make the White Sox a winning team. Another piece was former Gold Glove infielder Ed Brinkman, who was brought on board specifically to work with the infielders on defense.

"In spring training he gave his coaches a lot of authority and let them do their work with their group," Brinkman said. "He would assign me a field to do whatever I wanted with the infielders, whatever I thought we needed to work on. I've heard a lot of managers over the years say if they are going to go down they are going down their way, but Tony gave his coaches a lot of authority and a lot of leeway."

Duncan was just as serious about his job as La Russa, preparing and analyzing ways to improve each of the pitchers on the roster. He used a computer to prepare some of his information, and the knowledge he had acquired as a major league catcher added one more advantage.

La Russa was not surprised that Duncan had gone into coaching after his playing career, nor was he surprised about how seriously he took his assignment. "It made sense," La Russa said. "I knew he had a love for the game and was really inquisitive. He wanted to know "why" a lot. If somebody says, 'You have to throw a sinker in with a runner on third base to a right-handed hitter,' he'd say, 'Why?'"

That philosophy was a perfect match for La Russa's own personality, and their relationship appeared headed toward a long, happy marriage—as long as La Russa didn't get fired first.

Even though he had been given a one-year contract extension through 1984, there was pressure on La Russa from the start of the 1983 season. His critics, even without Caray and Piersall to lead them, were howling when the team began the season poorly. When the White Sox lost eight times in a nine-game stretch in mid-May, their record dropped to 13–20. Then they were swept by Baltimore and were shut out in the last two games.

"We had a better club, but some of the players were not hitting up to par, including Carlton Fisk," Hemond said. "The wolves were out for Tony, but also for me too. We both were on the griddle."

Meanwhile, his wife Elaine and two young daughters had stayed behind at their home in Sarasota, Florida, when the season started. They would come to Chicago in late May or June. Elaine called one night to tell La Russa she had come down with pneumonia and needed to go the hospital.

It could not have happened at a worse moment. Thanks to Elaine's support, La Russa did not need to devote any time or attention to family duties during the season. She had done it all, freeing him up to concentrate entirely on baseball. He was torn between his sick wife, who needed him, and his team, which he felt needed him just as much. Instead of flying to Florida to care for his sick wife and two children, La Russa called his sister and asked her to take care of the girls. He stayed with his team. La Russa now calls that one of the biggest mistakes he ever made in his life. Happily, Elaine recovered and the family was soon reunited in Chicago.

La Russa also was shaken by the news that his longtime mentor, Loren Babe, was diagnosed with cancer. Now working as the team's advance scout, Babe needed 57 days of major league service time to qualify for his pension, which also provided medical benefits. The White Sox elected to add him to the coaching staff so he could fulfill that requirement.

Because only four coaches could earn pension credits at one time, Lau, already vested in the plan, ceded his place to Babe. Tragically, just a month later, Lau saw a doctor because he was feeling ill and losing weight. He was told that he also had cancer.

When faced with the news that his two friends were dying, La Russa did what he knew best throwing himself even harder into his work.

Concentrating on how to fix what ailed the White Sox, La Russa targeted his attention on Fisk, mired in a season-long slump. La Russa came to the conclusion that Fisk's struggles offensively were also affecting the way he was calling the game behind the plate. His average dipped to .136 when La Russa took him out of the lineup for a game against Milwaukee.

Fisk did not take the move well. "I've never had a 'going rotten' day off," Fisk told reporters. "I guess you could classify it as being benched for the first time."

Fisk had shown his frustration a day earlier when he grounded into a double play and fired his batting helmet to the ground. "It hit the floor and bounced back up at me and almost hit me in the chest," Fisk said. "I caught it, threw it on the ground, and jumped on it with both feet. That SOB didn't even break. I picked it up and threw it again and it bounced and hit Tony in the leg."

Fisk tried taking extra batting practice. He tried taking no batting practice. Nothing worked. Finally, La Russa took a bold step: he moved Fisk from the middle of the batting order to the number two slot, a spot usually filled by a mediocre hitter.

The move began to produce positive results almost immediately. On May 30, Fisk recorded his first three-hit game of the season. The next day he saw his average climb past the .200 mark for the first time since mid-April. He hit .315 during the month of June, and the White Sox's record began to improve along with him.

All was not well between La Russa and Fisk, however. Before a double-header at Oakland on June 12, Fisk found out the White Sox had recalled catcher Joel Skinner from the minor leagues. Backup Marc Hill was going to catch one game, and Skinner the other.

Fisk confronted La Russa on the field before the game, but neither would say much about their heated discussion. La Russa insisted Fisk was still the team's first-string catcher and he was back behind the plate the following night.

"I was lucky enough to play with a lot of Hall of Famers, and every one of them was different," Luzinski said. "They all had a uniqueness to them. Pudge [Fisk] beats to his own drum."

Hemond downplayed the tension between the two, submitting that both were professional enough to not let their disagreements reach a point where it became a distraction for the team, as it had earlier in the season.

"Sometimes the player doesn't completely understand a situation," Hemond said. "Players are not always going to agree with the manager."

One person La Russa had found that he could confide in and discuss whatever was happening with the team was his third-base coach, Jim Leyland. The two men became close personal friends and shared the utmost respect for each other.

"From day one, Tony was never afraid to try to do things that he thought gave his team the best chance to win," Leyland said. "He had a good feel for it because he knew what he was doing and he studied the game."

After every game, and especially after a loss, La Russa replayed key moments and moves that he could have made or should have made. Nobody was ever a more critical judge of La Russa than La Russa.

"I'll put myself through a tougher test than any fan could put me through," said La Russa, who was still often booed when he went to the mound to make a pitching change. "As long as I pass my test, then I can compete on the field. I haven't changed one decision because of the boos and I'm proud of that."

La Russa had Leyland sit in his office with him after games when the media filed in because he wanted him to see that side of managing as well.

"I think what I learned the most from Tony was the process of the daily chore of managing," Leyland said. "One of the greatest things he taught me was how to manage my time. One of the best pieces of advice about managing I ever got was when he told me that if you are thinking about the questions you are going to have to answer after the game, you are not going to be very successful."

There were still some lingering doubts about just how successful La Russa and the White Sox were going to be in 1983. The headline in the *Chicago Tribune* on June 19 said, "La Russa May Be Next to Go."

"Despite his recent contract extension, La Russa is on the spot," wrote columnist Jerome Holtzman. "If the Sox are 10 to 12 games under .500 and foundering at the All-Streak break, La Russa will be replaced on an interim basis by Bobby Winkles." The team owners asked Winkles, one of their advisers, to watch the team for a week and report back to them. Winkles's report concluded that La Russa was not the problem.

When the All-Star break arrived, the White Sox were three games over .500 and tucked 3½ games behind division-leading Texas. There was no talk about a managerial change.

As the second half of the season began, La Russa, Leyland, and everyone around the White Sox began to realize that predictions for a successful 1983 season were on the verge of becoming reality. Contributions were coming in from a variety of sources, including an unlikely pair of rookies, Ron Kittle and Greg Walker. Kittle had been signed out of a tryout camp after he had been released by the Dodgers because of a neck injury. He had hit 50 homers at Triple A the previous year and quickly showed he could hit homers at the major league level, too.

La Russa had been impressed with Kittle since 1979, when his Des Moines club played the White Sox in an exhibition game. Chicago catcher Wayne Nordhagen split his thumb on a foul tip, and Kittle volunteered to catch.

"I heard Tony say, 'Don't worry, we're not going to run on you,'" Kittle said. "I knew I had better be ready for anything. Sure enough, they tried to steal right away with runners on first and third. I threw out Bobby Molinaro at second base, took the throw home and buried the guy sliding in. Double play. I flipped the ball to Tony and said, 'You can run on me anytime.' He wants to win, no matter what, and he knows I do too."

Walker had been plucked out of the Phillies' minor league system but had missed much of the 1982 season with a broken arm.

"I didn't think I was going to make the club out of spring training," Walker said. "We were leaving Florida and Tony called me in his office. I didn't like my chances of what I was going to be told. But he said, 'We think we are a better club with you playing first base tomorrow night in Texas.' Then I went out and made two errors in the first inning. He stuck with me and made me believe I could play up here. He really became almost a fatherlike figure for me because I was such a young, impressionable player."

After the White Sox were swept in the opening series at Texas, La Russa could have cracked the whip and yelled at his players, but instead he threw a party—a belated bachelor's party for pitcher Kevin Hickey, who had gotten married just before the end of spring training. The party helped ease the pressure in the clubhouse and the White Sox flew to Detroit and won two games against the Tigers.

The team's success as the season continued provided for a few more light moments.

"When we were at home, the guys who weren't in the lineup ordered a pizza every night," Squires said. "We'd order it right when the game started and then take it into the umpire's room, which was right behind home plate. I don't know for sure, but Tony probably knew about it because you could smell the pizza in the dugout. I'd like to think that if he knew he didn't care because we were playing so well.

"We ate the pizza and watched the game on television. One time, Tom Paciorek was running to first and pulled a muscle and I had to hustle down to the dugout and go in and run for him."

La Russa also occasionally had parties when the club was on the road. He felt it was another way to build team unity. Every player was required to attend, even if he only stayed a few minutes.

Squires also remembered a game that season against Baltimore when La Russa got into a heated argument with the umpires. An apparent home run by Fisk was taken away when the umpires ruled a fan had interfered with the ball. Third-base umpire John Shulock had initially called the hit a home run, but it was then changed to a double when umpire Jim Evans said a fan had reached over the wall to catch the ball.

La Russa was livid. His tirade ended as he picked up third base and threw it in front of his dugout, then returned to his dugout and calmly sat down.

"I happened to be sitting next to him, and the umpires wouldn't resume the game and kept looking into the dugout," Squires said. "He looked at me and said, 'What's going on?' I told him, 'Well, Tony, they threw you out of the game and they're waiting for you to leave.'

"He got upset all over again. 'What do you mean they threw me out of the game?' He didn't realize picking up a base and throwing it would get him ejected."

While the players no doubt chuckled behind La Russa's back at moments like that, there was no laughing about how some unconventional coaching methods were beginning to pay dividends for the team. The first was the increased dependence on computer technology as a preparation tool. This was in the '80's, long before the ascendance of the Internet, and before many clubs were taking advantage of the technology. Dan Evans, who was 23 years old at the time and a future general manager, compiled all of the information provided by the computer and met with La Russa before each series, pointing out whatever statistical data he thought might be of the greatest use and interest to the manager.

"My job is to help him as much as I can before the start of a series," Evans said. "Once the game begins he runs everything. The day a computer starts dictating what a manager does, it won't be a very fun game anymore."

The second and perhaps more bizarre method was the use of a hypnotist. Harvey Misel never threw a pitch or swung a bat for the White Sox, but the team definitely benefited from his presence. Misel was a hypnotist hired by the club to work with individual players, including pitcher Richard Dotson.

"People have a stereotype about hypnosis," Dotson said. "I wasn't under a spell when I went out there on the mound. I just sat in a chair in the locker room before the game, 30 minutes at the most, closed my eyes and listened to the man. I figured it couldn't hurt. My concentration was very high in the game."

Misel's basic message was about relaxation, confidence, and concentration. "I can't make a player hit a home run or throw a certain pitch," Misel told the *Chicago Tribune*. "I'm not a miracle worker."

La Russa endorsed the hiring of Misel, which was actually Reinsdorf's idea, he said.

"It's a can't-lose situation," La Russa said. "Harvey met with our players before the game, and he made a good point that if a player has problems, most of them are mental and not physical."

La Russa did stop short of saying he would undergo hypnosis himself. "I'd hate to give my many fans that much ammunition," he said. "If I made a move they didn't like, they'd start yelling that I must be under some kind of hypnotic spell."

Under a spell or not, the White Sox could do little wrong in August. They began the month five games over .500 and with a three-game lead over Kansas City. By the end of the month they were 18 games over .500 and their division lead had ballooned to 10½ games. The superstitious La Russa thought his lucky cap might have had something to do with the team's success.

"I got into an argument with the umpires one night and threw my cap," he said. "It got all dirty and nicked, but I wore it the next night, and we won.

And I kept wearing it for home games and we won 17 straight (at home) and 18 of our last 20."

Grudgingly, La Russa was starting to earn respect around the league.

"He hasn't gotten a lot of that respect yet because he's too young [38] and didn't have much minor league experience," said Paul Richards, one of La Russa's mentors who was working for Texas at the time.

"Frankly, there is considerable jealousy now toward Tony. But to me, Tony is far ahead of the average run of managers. He has things to learn, but one of his strong points is a willingness to learn.

"When Ken Silvestri and I took Tony under our wing in 1978 and 1979, he was prone to question a lot of things on how to manage. We went to dinner and debated back and forth. But he isn't one of those guys who are never willing to listen and change their mind. He has a strong determination to be successful....

"An area he has to improve in is learning to accept things better and not get emotional over things he can't control. He has to learn to use more restraint."

His own players, including veteran pitcher Jerry Koosman, who was two years older than La Russa, believed he had earned the praise that was now coming his way.

"Tony has a knack that is rare in managers," Koosman told the *Chicago Tribune*. "He can be friendly with his players and he can be a disciplinarian. He can talk with a player about a mistake and not make it seem like he's jumping on him.

"It's funny, but he has almost a grandfatherly manner. He's someone who is very versatile in the way he handles a team."

What La Russa really wants out of his players has not wavered over the years. He wants players to give a hundred percent, to do whatever it takes to win.

"He will tolerate guys who don't have ability, but if somebody doesn't give everything he's got, that's when he gets upset," Reinsdorf said. "He knows that in order to win you've got to want it more than anybody else."

La Russa naturally tried to deflect all of the praise toward his players, but he was as happy as anyone when the White Sox officially clinched the division title on September 17 with a 4–3 win over Seattle. The White Sox players were just as happy for their manager. They understood the pressure and difficult conditions he had endured in his still-burgeoning career. What La Russa hoped was that if the division title did not earn him overwhelming respect, he could at least get the benefit of the doubt.

"When I go out to change pitchers, maybe the people will say, 'Well, maybe he knows what he's doing,'" La Russa said. "Do you have to be 16 games up or win your division before you get that? I don't know."

Texas manager Doug Rader, who once almost came to blows with La Russa before a game, coined the White Sox's nickname, "Winning Ugly." "I just said, the way they were winning games was ugly," Rader said. "I said they didn't win games in a classic way. And they don't. I have great respect for their club, but when you get three hits and score three runs, that's not considered a classic game."

Not everyone shared Rader's sour grapes. One especially important congratulatory note La Russa received was a telegram from Al Lopez.

The White Sox's opponent in the American League playoffs was the Baltimore Orioles. Unfortunately for the team, the magic that had helped them climb to 99 wins in the regular season disappeared over four playoff games. The Sox did not hit in the series and their pitching could not overcome the lack of offense. The Orioles outscored the White Sox 19–3, primarily because Chicago had only four extra-base hits and left 35 runners on base, including a whopping 18 from the seventh inning on. After squeaking out a 2–1 win in the opening game, the White Sox lost three straight and the American League pennant flew in Baltimore.

Did La Russa's lucky cap, the one he wore when the team won 17 consecutive home games, have something to do with the loss?

"I thought it was too classy an occasion to wear a scruffy old cap," he said. "So I wore a new one, and we got beat 11–1."

The White Sox, true to their nature, did not go down without a fight. When Richard Dotson brushed back Eddie Murray (after first hitting Cal Ripken Jr.) the benches emptied. La Russa was one of the first to get to Murray, where he launched a verbal assault.

While the series loss to the Orioles left La Russa the most disappointed person in Chicago, a look back told him how far he and the White Sox had come in a year. In June, he had been on the verge of losing his job. Four months later, the team had won a division title and he was named the league's Manager of the Year. La Russa even received additional publicity with an appearance on the *To Tell the Truth* television show, where he stumped the judges. None correctly picked him as the contestant who really was a major league manager.

In a quiet moment, celebrating with owners Reinsdorf and Einhorn, La Russa asked them just how close he had come to losing his job.

"Jerry said it was not that close," La Russa tells it. "My gut says it was. When times were rough this year, Eddie was trying to decide what was good from the marketing side. Not would it help the club, but would the public support me as manager? We had one discussion about the public's perception of me. What can the manager do to make himself popular? He was honestly asking me.

"If somebody tells me I've got to be fired because the public's not coming to the park, I can understand that. If I get fired because they think I'm not doing a good job on the field, I challenge that. I don't think Eddie was unfair to me. If he was, I never would have forgiven him."

Leyland knew how hard La Russa had worked that season. He also knew that despite the team's success, La Russa still wouldn't receive the credit that he was due.

"If the media doesn't like you they will say you won because you had good players," Leyland said. "If the media likes you they will say you won because you were a good manager. There is no magic behind the manager's desk. Nobody in any sport throughout history who has ever coached or managed has won without good players."

La Russa knew that Leyland was right, and he also knew he wasn't going to be satisfied with one successful year and one division title. He wanted to prove his team could win again, and the sooner next season started, the better.

CHAPTER 7

Searching for an Edge

For all the professional successes of 1983, there was also sadness. La Russa watched both Loren Babe and Charlie Lau as cancer weakened and ravaged their bodies. Over the course of the season, both coaches had to leave the team at times to undergo treatment, and often got tired and needed to return to the hotel before the game's end. The hardest part for La Russa was not being able to help the men who had helped him so much in his life.

Babe died on February 14, 1984, at his home in Omaha, Nebraska. Lau died three weeks later, on March 19, at his home in Marathon, Florida. Babe was 56 years old, Lau was 50. That spring La Russa was also saddened by the death of Rose Silvestri, the wife of Ken Silvestri, "They were like second parents to me," La Russa said.

"There couldn't be a more fitting tribute to Charlie in his final year than the fact that we scored 800 runs to lead the majors," Hemond said. "He made everyone around him better than they were because of his knowledge and because he was a compassionate person who took the time to understand people."

La Russa knew that the sadness that surrounded the club from the deaths of Babe and Lau would eventually subside. It was his job to determine why the

White Sox got off to such a slow start in defending their division title. The team had picked up future Hall of Fame pitcher Tom Seaver, who should have improved their pitching. There was no indication that the White Sox's performance should be much different than it had been the year before. As La Russa knew all too well, however, quoting that famous anonymous person, "That's why you play the games."

He also had added a new coach, Joe Nossek, who brought with him a reputation as being one of the best players in the game when it came to stealing an opponent's signs. Nossek and La Russa had once been roommates in the minor leagues.

"Tony leaves nothing unturned," Nossek said. "He goes for every angle and usually finds something that is going to give him a little extra edge."

Even deciphering their opponents' signs, the games did not go the White Sox way in 1984. The season started poorly, continued poorly, and ended poorly. They came out of their slump briefly around the All-Star break, won seven consecutive games and moved into first place, but the troubles soon returned. By early August, La Russa was wearing a sweatshirt with a picture of a mouse caught in a trap. The inscription was "How in the hell do you think my day went?"

One bright spot in the season was a 25-inning victory over the Milwaukee Brewers. The game started on May 8 and was suspended after the seventeenth inning because of the American League curfew. It resumed the following day and ended with a Harold Baines home run.

The game lasted eight hours, six minutes and fell one inning short of tying the record for the longest game in innings in major league history.

Another game, on July 16, was almost as memorable, producing the newest installment of the battle between the Tigers and White Sox. Fisk was hit by a pitch in the sixth inning. Two innings later, Britt Burns hit the Tigers' Lance Parrish with a pitch that umpire Ted Hendry ruled intentional. Burns was kicked out of the game. Parrish walked to first base, yelling at Burns, and La Russa came out of the dugout and started yelling back at Parrish. The two were separated without incident, but the war of words continued after the game.

"I really believe Tony La Russa tells his pitchers to throw at people," Parrish said. "I don't think I've ever liked La Russa. I should have punched him in the mouth. They ought to throw him out of baseball. I told him, 'There's no way we were throwing at Fisk.' He said, 'Oh yes you were.' I lost a lot of respect right there for him. I think he better stay as far away from me as he can."

La Russa didn't back down from the challenge.

"I'm not here to make friends with the other side," he said. "If they want to throw inside, we'll throw inside. I'll be by the batting cage if Parrish wants to find me, but I'm not going to say anything to a guy who's big enough to throw me into the stands.

"I don't care what Parrish believes. He's not my catcher. There are a lot of guys who used to pitch for me. You can talk to anybody. I don't order guys to throw at players. But there's no doubt in my mind that that the pitch which hit Fisk came from the bench, the pitching coach, or the catcher."

The Tigers, of course, were not the only team that got into battles with La Russa's club. After a bench-clearing brawl in Oakland in early September, the perception was increasing throughout baseball that at least some of those incidents were incited by La Russa himself.

"It bothers me a tremendous amount," La Russa told reporters. "It gets to be a joke. Every time an incident happens, you read a lot of things the other club says about us, and not much is said for our side. If I could go on national television and say it, I would. There are a lot of pitchers who are no longer in the league who played for me. Ask them if I ever told them they had to go hit a batter because he was doing a good job against our club. Exactly the opposite is true.

"People believe I order them to throw, that we're head hunters, and the opposite is true. A pitch that goes at a batter's head scares me. I always have a meeting to tell them I won't allow head hunting. Anybody who does is gone.

"I believe like the other 13 clubs that if someone messes with our ballclub that we have to send a message back. But it is sent from the shoulders down, and it doesn't have to hit a guy. Where a guy is hitting .500 against us and he's nailed the first time? Never. Throwing at his head? Absolutely never. This whole thing is getting tiring. I'm not sure how it's cured, but we've got a chance if our side gets out."

The perception that the White Sox were head hunters was just one of many problems in 1984. The team suffered the worst one-season drop of any division winner in the AL since 1969, falling from 99 wins to just 74. The decline went somewhat unnoticed throughout the city as, across town, the Cubs rose to a division championship.

La Russa signed a one-year contract to return as manager in 1985, knowing his job security depended on a bounce-back season from his club. He thought it would be better for the team if his players had the same attitude—that they were playing for their jobs.

"Generally, multi-year contracts are not good for the game," he said. "I've told players the same thing. Almost every player is better off to have a survival instinct. No matter how motivated, this survival instinct makes you play better in many cases."

If La Russa was hoping life would be calmer for his club in 1985, he learned even before the year began that that would not be the case. The team traded pitcher LaMarr Hoyt to San Diego for three players, including 20-year-old rookie shortstop Ozzie Guillen. Fisk publicly criticized the move, saying, "We traded a sure thing for three question marks."

La Russa was upset by his latest disagreement with Fisk. "Carlton's points are zeros," he said. "If he cared to discuss his disagreement with us, Roland Hemond or myself may have been able to explain things to him, things he has no access to and wouldn't know. This makes me angry. I respect his opinion, but instead of these negative statements in the media, he should have called us first and listened to what we have to say. We are loyal to our players and expect a certain amount of loyalty from them."

Fisk stood his ground, pointing out that Hoyt had tied Detroit's Jack Morris for the most wins in the AL the previous three seasons (56). "If I had to pick one guy on the team who would come back from last year's fiasco and avenge himself, LaMarr would be the guy. It isn't something I can say about a lot of guys."

La Russa's response: "If he is minding his own business, the first guy he ought to pick to come back from the fiasco is Carlton Fisk. We all should point those fingers at ourselves."

When Fisk concluded by saying it was a trade he would not have made, La Russa got in a final shot. "He's a player, not the general manager," he said.

La Russa had realized already during his few years with the White Sox that the duties and responsibilities of being a major league manager had changed since his days as a player. Even the fact that he was closer in age to the players than many of his fellow managers did not change that relationship, he said.

"A manager today knows the players expect explanations," he told the *Sporting News* in 1985. "And while they are not entitled to them it's often more effective to explain, when asked, because players do a better job if they know their roles. Most outsiders misunderstand this. They think if you explain something to a player, you are giving him a role in the decision making. That simply isn't so.

"The crap a manager has to deal with today, before and after the game, takes away a lot of the enjoyment of the job…. It's more of a challenge because you have to deal with a lot of personnel problems besides just evaluating the playing talent on the field. You have to learn to simplify in order to succeed. You must try to control only that which is necessary to the playing of the game."

La Russa went to spring training counting on his players' pride to inspire them to work harder and avoid a repeat of the dismal previous season. "This club understands how it worked for three years to gain credibility and respect, and it lost it all so quickly," he said, knowing he could just have easily been speaking about his personal status. He could have signed a two-year contract, but he wanted the personal challenge of proving he could get the club back into a pennant race, and counted on his own survival instincts to deliver it.

"Every manager always has a one-year deal, no matter how the contract's written," he said. "You're never guaranteed a spot in the dugout, only money. What gets you going is winning and losing, the fear of how bad things could be, the thrill of how good things might be. I am as romantic as the next guy about baseball, but I only care about the final score."

In April, the White Sox won only one game more than they lost, going 9–8. Speculation about La Russa's status was already brewing. *Sports Illustrated* declared La Russa the winner of the "Manager Most Likely to be Fired" sweepstakes, putting the odds at 8–5. Reinsdorf responded with a telegram to the magazine, declaring, "I'll put up whatever money you're willing to cover at 8–5. Will not be the next manager fired."

Before the end of May, Davey Johnson was fired by the Mets and replaced by Bud Harrelson.

The White Sox continued to struggle at the .500 level for much of the season, barely climbing over the mark, then falling back under. That level of baseball was not good enough to please La Russa. But he got even more upset in early August when the Major League Baseball Players Association went on strike for two days.

"I was mad, darned mad," La Russa said. "People who know very little about baseball came into our clubhouse saying they represent the game and the players and that the players have worked hard for what they get, that they have their rights to get more. These people, who pass themselves off as lawyers and agents and whatever, think they are bigger than the game. They aren't. No one is. It's our national pastime. It's not an industry, it's a game, and we should have kept playing it.

"The people who told us to stop playing, and I'm including the owners, equate themselves with the game but they don't realize that the game transcends them. It doesn't occur to them that you could bring in a whole new set of players, a whole new set of owners, and a whole new set of writers and the game would still be the same. There would be singles and home runs and strikeouts, and there would be writers to write about it."

Unfortunately for the White Sox, the team played only marginally better when the season resumed. An 18–11 month of September allowed them to finish the year at 85–77, in third place, six games behind the division champion Royals. Guillen played well enough to be named the AL Rookie of the Year.

Reinsdorf and Einhorn, as would be expected, were not happy that the team was never really in the race. In early September, media reports circulated that general manager Roland Hemond's job might be in jeopardy but Einhorn said that "isn't in our current thinking."

A couple of weeks later, the thinking changed. Hemond was removed as general manager and given a job as a special assistant to Reinsdorf and Einhorn.

Placed in charge of the team's operations was Ken Harrelson, La Russa's former minor league teammate, who had been working as a broadcaster for the White Sox.

"We're going to butt heads on things, no doubt about it," La Russa said.

While La Russa had never had the problems with Harrelson as he had had with Jimmy Piersall, he was not thrilled with the idea of Harrelson as his boss. Even though he still had the full support of the White Sox's ownership—Jerry Reinsdorf said he should have been the Manager of the Year—it took La Russa nearly three weeks to decide to return as the team's manager for 1986.

Part of the reason was that Harrelson wanted to make some changes to La Russa's coaching staff, including his original idea that the team should have two pitching coaches, one for the starters and one for relievers. Harrelson finally relented to La Russa's demand that Dave Duncan remain the pitching coach, but got his way, adding former reliever Moe Drabowsky as a second pitching coach, working out of the bullpen. He also hired former pitcher Don Drysdale as a consultant and broadcaster and, against La Russa's wishes, had a special phone line installed connecting the booth and dugout.

La Russa also endured the loss of one of the confidants from his staff when Jim Leyland was named manager of the Pittsburgh Pirates.

It was obvious from the get-go that Harrelson and La Russa had opposing ideas on many issues. The unanswered question was just how well or how long the relationship would last once the season began. In spring training, La Russa pleaded with the press to avoid creating unnecessary controversy and to focus on what was happening on the field, not off it.

"All winter I heard about the arguments people expect Hawk and I to have," La Russa said. "I don't expect big arguments and I'd be surprised if Hawk did. A few disagreements perhaps, but that's healthy.

"Everyone also thinks that with all these people here"—referring to the special assistants and coaches hired by Harrelson—"we're going to make decisions by committee. Not true. There will be discussions by committee, not decisions. The final decisions will be mine and mine alone."

La Russa and Harrelson did agree that moving Carlton Fisk to left field was a good idea, but Fisk disagreed and said so publicly. "They say this is good for prolonging my career, but I've worked so hard on my conditioning that I never get tired catching," Fisk said. "How come I hit 37 homers? It's not like I lost the catching job. I just got up one morning and read that I was the left fielder."

The two did not agree on the status of another future Hall of Famer, pitcher Tom Seaver. Harrelson was doing his best to trade Seaver, particularly to either the Mets or Yankees, while La Russa wanted to keep him with the White Sox. It did not take long for Reinsdorf and Einhorn to realize that the pairing of La Russa and Harrelson in jobs where they needed to work so closely together probably had been a mistake. It certainly didn't help matters when the team won only two of its first 12 games.

The two owners made a quick trip to Milwaukee to meet with La Russa, reassuring him that his job was not in danger despite whatever was being reported in the media. They hoped the team would be able to string together some victories and curb some of the talk that La Russa was about to be fired. The team did perform marginally better, reaching the end of April with a 7–12 record, but a six-game losing streak followed, and speculation became rampant that the team was about to make a change.

La Russa was grieving the May 4 death of Paul Richards, another of his career mentors, when he woke up to the headlines in the Chicago newspapers on May 6. The *Sun-Times* said, "Sox Lose Game, Maybe La Russa." The *Tribune* was a little more direct, "La Russa on Rocky Road; White Sox Manager's Status 'Isn't Good' Harrelson Says."

Reinsdorf admitted that he had another meeting with La Russa before the White Sox lost 4–1 to the Yankees. "Sometimes a manager can be doing a good job but you have to make a change because the public demands it," Reinsdorf was quoted as saying in the *Sun-Times*.

When reporters asked La Russa after the game about his "possible demise," the manager said, "Demise? Demise to me means going to bed. If that's what you mean, I haven't had much sleep lately."

La Russa tried to convince the reporters that he was unconcerned about his job status. "Believe it or not, I don't care if I survive managing this club," La Russa said. "If you tell me that you'll guarantee me a job, but that we wouldn't have a chance to win September 1, I'd say no. The thrill of this game is finishing first.

"I'm concerned now about being below .500. I want to get this club well, so we can go about the business of contending. If that happens, all the other stuff will take care of itself. We're 7–16. I have to do a better job as a manager. As a manager you're judged on your win-loss record. Right now I'm not doing too good."

Reinsdorf was not as worried about the win-loss record, except for the negative impact it was having on the team's attendance. He was trying to find a workable peace for Harrelson and La Russa's relationship. He knew it was not easy for La Russa to hear all of the speculation about his status, and to keep reading in the newspaper who Harrelson liked and didn't like as his candidates for the team's new manager. The most popular name thrown around was Billy Martin, who had been replaced by Lou Piniella as the manager of the Yankees before the season.

As it happened, the Yankees were in Chicago for a three-game series. Under normal circumstances, the media might have been focusing on the first-ever game between former child teammates Piniella and La Russa in their roles as major league managers. But Piniella was serving a two-game suspension for bumping an umpire, so the first game between the two was not played until May 7. In step with the way things were going for La Russa, the Yankees won that outing 5–1.

Writing in the *Sun-Times* on May 8, columnist Ray Sons said, "Tony La Russa broke the American League record last night for nights spent twisting in the wind with a smile on your face after the trapdoor has been sprung beneath you."

La Russa was even to the point where he had developed kind of a "gallows humor" about the situation. He noted that instead of booing him when he stepped onto the field at Comiskey Park, he overheard fathers telling their sons, "Hey, son, get your last look at him."

The question all around Chicago and the baseball world was, "Has La Russa been fired yet?" By May 9, it seemed that if the White Sox were not going to take any action, he would. The team was 7–18 and he came to an off-day workout at Comiskey Park ready to resign. He called Reinsdorf and told the owner what was on his mind.

"I told them I couldn't make it work," La Russa said. "They [Reinsdorf and Einhorn] told me that I might not have to worry about it. I didn't give them an ultimatum. They've known how I felt about this for a long time."

Before the team left for Cleveland, Harrelson called a news conference at O'Hare Airport. He announced that La Russa was staying, but that two of the coaches he had hired, Drabowsky and hitting coach Willie Horton, were being reassigned to other positions in the organization.

"The players have not responded," said Harrelson, who admitted he also had thought about resigning. "Tony now is going to have a situation that he's been familiar with for the last seven years. It was unfair to impose the Hawk's will on him the way I did.

"I'm not backing off the concepts one bit. But when you're talking about a man who has been around as long as Tony, and then ask him to change his style, it's like asking Nolan Ryan to start throwing sinkers."

La Russa might have won a temporary victory, but he knew he had not won the war. The players were glad that at least the public speculation about La Russa's status was over and hoped it would allow them to concentrate as a team on how to turn the season around. One move La Russa agreed to make was to gradually return Fisk to working behind the plate.

"[The speculation] was wearing Tony down," Seaver said. "You could see it. He was good at hiding it, but it's not healthy to hide behind cosmetics. I don't know how he did it."

La Russa did admit that he was angry about how he and his family had been treated.

"I don't like the fact 22 people called my wife and told her I'm gone," La Russa told the *Sun-Times'* Ron Rapoport. "And now there's an implication I'm only here because the thing with Billy [Martin] didn't work out. I'm offended by that. It bothers me because everybody has feelings about their reputation, about their ego. I have personal feelings about that.

"But I don't underestimate the toughness a person has to have to be successful in this league. You have to put up with some tough things. You can't cower before that. I knew I could deal with it but that doesn't mean I liked it. But I can't afford to make much of it. I can't do my job if I walk around being mad about that stuff. I can't walk around saying people feel sorry. You acknowledge it and put it aside."

In his five years of owning the White Sox, Reinsdorf had become very fond of La Russa from a personal standpoint, and he also had developed an appreciation for his skills as a manager. He was enough of a businessman to be able to separate his personal feelings when a decision had to be made, but it wasn't an easy one.

"As a manager he was always three innings ahead," Reinsdorf said. "A lot of times he would make a move in a game that I didn't understand and which I thought was pretty dumb. Later, I would ask him about it, and after our discussion I thought *I* was the idiot. His decision always had to do with the move that was coming next. He had a reason he did something. It didn't always work out, but I don't think I ever came away from one of our discussions thinking I was right and he was wrong.

"I realized what a terrific manager he was and over the years I found out what a great human being he is. There are only a few people that I put in his class."

Reinsdorf was hoping that the decision to change the coaching staff and putting La Russa back into a familiar situation would produce positive results, or at least buy the team some time before the owners needed to make another move.

"Tony and Hawk just were not getting along and I did everything I could to try to get them to work together," Reinsdorf said. "I just told Tony, 'Get me to the end of the year,' and we would work something out."

A seven-game winning streak brought some temporary relief, but that was quickly followed by a seven-game losing streak. It was during that stretch that La Russa's frustrations got the best of him. He was ejected in two consecutive games on May 27 and 28 because he forgot a lesson taught to him by umpire Rich Garcia in 1979, letting an argument from one day carry over to the next. Garcia was the one to remind him of that after ejecting him in the second straight game.

When the White Sox were swept in consecutive series at Texas and at Toronto, they found themselves with an 18–28 record at the beginning of June, sixth in their seven-team division. Unable to make a managerial change, Harrelson decided to fire Dave Dombrowski from his job as vice president of baseball operations. Only 29, Dombrowski had worked for the White Sox for nine years, steadily rising through the organization's front office under Roland Hemond's guidance.

"It's just a simple fact that I felt a change was in order and I made it," Harrelson said.

The decision removed one more person from the front office with whom La Russa had a good relationship. Tension in the ballclub was slowly mounting.

As media reports again began to flurry, La Russa decided to go on the offensive. "If these people want to say these things to my face, they might find me standing on their chests," La Russa said. "You get in a certain mood sometimes and you want somebody to insult you. It would be a mistake to say something to my face."

La Russa was particularly upset by a headline in the *Minneapolis Star-Tribune* when the White Sox came to town to play the Twins. The headline referred to the ongoing battles within the team's organization as a "soap opera."

"Those are pretty close to fighting words," La Russa said. "If push comes to shove, this is our organization and I'll stand up for it. These 24 guys on this team deserve better than that kind of treatment. You'd better be careful saying those kinds of things to my face."

Harrelson was in Indianapolis, watching the Sox's Triple A team play and listening to the Sox's 10–9 loss to the Twins on the radio while driving back to Chicago. A 9–8 victory the next night concluded a 2–5 trip and the White Sox came home to start a series against Seattle 12 games under .500 and 26–38.

When the team plane landed in Chicago, Harrelson told La Russa he had made his decision: La Russa and pitching coach Dave Duncan were out.

"Tony couldn't get to the end of the year because Hawk kept attacking Duncan," Reinsdorf said. "Tony can take all kind of shit himself, but don't say anything bad about his friends, especially Duncan. He and Harrelson were bickering over Duncan all the time.

"I've always believed that you can't make a general manager have a manager that he doesn't want. You can't make the head of the accounting department have a bookkeeper he doesn't want. I reluctantly let him fire Tony. I should have fired Harrelson instead, that's what I should have done."

Before he gave Harrelson his permission to make a change, Reinsdorf called his friend Roy Eisenhardt, the president of the Oakland A's, who he knew had long been an admirer of La Russa.

"I told him things weren't going well here and I asked him, 'If we make a change and let Tony go will you hire him?' He said, 'In a heartbeat.' So I knew even before we fired Tony he was going to get another job right away."

Someone else who felt that way and told La Russa how to handle his departure was his fellow manager, Sparky Anderson.

"I told him, 'You don't say one single thing bad about anything,'" Anderson said. "You thank Mr. Veeck for bringing you here. You thank Mr. Harrelson for having you here. You thank everybody in the White Sox organization for the time you worked with them. I'm going to tell you something. You are going to go home, keep your mouth shut, and end up with a better job than you ever dreamed you would have.'"

La Russa told the media his two daughters, now six and three, had actually been rooting for Harrelson to fire him so he could come home and spend time with them.

"When I called and said I had been fired I could hear the girls singing and laughing," he said. They said, "'Daddy's coming home.'"

La Russa accepted the decision with a positive attitude.

"It bothers me when someone says you have failed," La Russa said. "It bothers me that there will be people in uniform out there who I will not be working with. But I understand. You live and die with wins and losses. [At] no time this year were the wins and losses acceptable. I could have been fired at any time. I was vulnerable."

Dotson, who had played for La Russa since 1978 in Knoxville, disagreed with the decision to change managers.

"I kidded him all the time that he was the best manager I had ever played for, because he of course was the only manager I had played for," Dotson said. "Thirty years later, however, I can honestly say he was the best manager I ever played for. Players would run through a brick wall for him."

La Russa acknowledged that he and Harrelson had their differences, but said he thought it was the overall performance of the team that prompted the decision, and not personal feelings. "There were differences of opinion," he said. "I understand that you are supposed to work together and this has been a problem. You can't have a situation where you don't have teamwork and trust, and that has been a problem here.

"I had my chance to not come back so I obviously thought we could make it work. Hawk called me the most stubborn person he's been around and I took it as a compliment. I knew I was resisting him. I knew it wasn't a healthy situation."

Reinsdorf blamed himself for putting both La Russa and Harrelson into a situation that was doomed to fail from the beginning.

"I was incredibly naïve," Reinsdorf said. "Eddie [Einhorn] and I spent a lot of time with Hawk and he was diagnosing the team's problems and he was right on. We thought he was the guy to fix the problems. He wasn't. That was the mistake we made. We brought the wrong guy in to try to fix the problems. Hawk's heart was in the right place.

"I never should have allowed Tony to be fired. I've often said that was the biggest mistake I've ever made. I knew it was wrong. I knew it was a mistake. And I let it happen anyway."

CHAPTER 8

A New Beginning

La Russa was already planning his immediate future as he packed up the photos and other items from his office at Comiskey Park and then flew to Florida to join his wife and daughters at home in Sarasota—and the plans had nothing to do with baseball.

For the first time, the family was going to spend the rest of the summer traveling around the United States. La Russa's list of anticipated stops included historic venues—Washington, D.C., Williamsburg, Virginia, and Mount Rushmore—places he had never been during his nomadic baseball life.

La Russa knew another managing job likely was in his future too, but it seemed to make more sense to wait until the 1986 season was over and see what jobs opened up. Then he could make a decision about which spot seemed to offer the best fit instead of taking over a club in the middle of the season. He knew well that the only reason a club changes managers in the middle of the year was if the team was losing. The opportunity to spend quality time with his family was preferable to inserting himself into another bad situation.

La Russa, of course, had no knowledge of the conversation that had taken place between Jerry Reinsdorf and Athletics President Roy Eisenhardt. Nor was he paying enough attention to the baseball transactions on June 26, five days after he was fired from the Sox, to notice that Jackie Moore had been dismissed as Oakland's manager.

La Russa quickly learned about both, however, when he received a phone call from Sandy Alderson, the A's vice president and general manager. It was the first of many conversations the two would have over several days.

Despite the fact Alderson and the A's were offering him some security in the form of a three-year contract, La Russa had reservations about saying yes. He really did want to spend time with his family and away from baseball, having been mentally and emotionally drained in his final weeks in Chicago. He felt that he needed that break from the day-to-day pressures of the game.

"I told the A's I didn't think I was ready," La Russa recalled in a 1989 interview with Bob Verdi of the *Chicago Tribune*. "I was carrying a lot of excess baggage from the White Sox thing. I wanted to put it off until September, or spring training. These people wanted me right now.

"When you get in trouble, like I was in Chicago a couple of times, you hear other teams say that you'll hear from them if you ever get let go. But until you get let go, you never know for sure. You never really know whether you'll get that call."

So, despite his reluctance to say yes to another team so quickly, La Russa accepted the A's offer and canceled his family's summer vacation plans. He was hired as the A's manager on July 2, just 11 days after he had been fired by the White Sox.

"The fact remains there's only 26 of these jobs around," he said at a news conference the following day. "Of the 26, there are only a few that can be termed as good situations."

With the A's struggling and in last place in the American League West, it was not immediately apparent why La Russa thought Oakland fit the description of a good situation. He explained that he thought the club was better than its record reflected at that point in the season, that he felt more comfortable since they were in the same division as the White Sox, and that he liked the challenge of seeing if he could help turn the club around.

"I thought there was a legitimate talent base to be competitive," La Russa said in the book *Champions*, a history of the A's. "They had traded for Carney Lansford and had made a couple of other moves that made sense. I think there were expectations that the club would be at least a winning team—that was the buzz around the league over the winter.

"But if the team gets off to a bad start, guys get discouraged, and they end up playing below their ability. My impression was that the A's were better than they were playing."

It would have been hard for them to have been playing any worse. When La Russa and new pitching coach Dave Duncan joined the A's on July 7 in Boston—coincidentally for a nationally televised game against the Red Sox—the A's were 31–52 and had lost 25 of their previous 31 games. They had the worst record in the major leagues and not only were they playing Boston, the team with the best record in the American League, the Red Sox were starting Roger Clemens, who was coming into the game with a 14–1 record.

A couple of days earlier, La Russa had called Duncan at his home in Arizona to discuss the Oakland pitching rotation. They basically had three choices about who to start in the first game against the Red Sox: veteran Rick Langford, rookie Bill Mooneyham, or a journeyman named Dave Stewart, who had signed with Oakland as a free agent on May 23, two weeks after being released by the Phillies. La Russa and Duncan were familiar with Stewart because they had discussed bringing him to the White Sox after he was released in Philadelphia. They had gotten a look at him when he had pitched a couple of games against the White Sox for Texas.

"We thought we'd take a shot with him," La Russa said. "We didn't have much to lose."

Stewart did not have a record for the A's and had a 4.85 ERA in 10 appearances, including one start. With the A's in Milwaukee for the weekend, La Russa picked up the telephone and called Stewart to see how he felt about starting the game on Monday night, on national television, against Clemens and the Red Sox.

"Give me the ball," Stewart said.

Not only were La Russa and Duncan getting a fresh start, so was Stewart, then 29 years old. He knew it was an opportunity he might not get again. He took the ball, and thanks to back-to-back home runs from Dave Kingman and rookie Jose Canseco in the sixth inning, along with some bullpen help from Dave Von Ohlen and Doug Bair, Stewart and the A's posted a 6–4 victory. Stewart allowed eight hits and all four runs in six-plus innings of work.

The following day, Stewart, who had gone to high school only a couple of miles from the Oakland Coliseum, sat down to discuss his performance with Duncan.

"Stew was known for a strong arm and live fastball," Duncan told *USA Today* in a 1989 interview. "But I noticed he threw an off-speed pitch a couple of times and asked him what it was.

"He told me, 'It's just a little split-finger I play around with some. Texas and Philadelphia told me to forget it.' I told him we'd work on it on the side the next day."

That pitch, of course, became the key to Stewart's future success, which coincided with the team's overall success. He finished 1986 with a 9–5 record and a 3.35 ERA as a starter.

"Tony told me he wanted to have somebody he could count on to go out there every five days and give the team a good chance to win," Stewart was quoted as saying in *Champions*. "I wanted to be that guy. I wanted to carry the team on my shoulders."

Stewart's confidence was bolstered by his happiness being home in Oakland and pitching in front of his family and friends, and the belief that both La Russa and Duncan were counting on him and showed they believed in him.

"I never had the confidence to throw my other pitches in critical situations," said Stewart, a catcher in high school who turned down 26 college football scholarships to sign with the Dodgers. "Now I want to throw them. I use the forkball to get the big out. If you can't be comfortable in a situation where everything is positive, you can't be successful."

La Russa had enough experience already in his career to realize how important the mental aspects were to a team's and an individual's success, and that was one area he really emphasized in his first few days in the Oakland dugout. He knew the team's confidence had been destroyed by all of their recent losses and that the team would continue to struggle until they recaptured the feeling that they were good enough to win.

"I'd like to challenge the club a little bit," La Russa said. "I know what some of these players are capable of doing when they're on their game. I want to get them to play to that ability."

While La Russa had to get to know his new players, the players also needed time to get to know their new manager. One player who wasn't sure what to expect was third baseman Carney Lansford, who had played against La Russa's White Sox for eight years while with California, Boston, and Oakland.

"He gave me a hard time and never said hi to me when he was with the White Sox." Lansford said. "He also had a couple of pitchers who used to drill myself and Dave Kingman on a regular basis. When he got the job I asked him why. Of course in a typical Tony La Russa response he said, 'I always pick the best hitter of every team.' He was trying to make me feel good, but that didn't work."

Lansford quickly saw a different side of La Russa from the vantage point of his own dugout.

"He was a perfect manager for me," he said. "He made sure guys were ready to play every day, and he had a nice way of making sure you were prepared and doing your job. He wanted you to be ready to give a hundred percent of whatever you had every day. He expected everybody to take their best shot everyday, whatever that was.

"He demands that from his players. To play for Tony you have to be a player who likes to be pushed to play to your capabilities. If you are a soft player it won't work. He will run you out of there."

La Russa always said he never wanted to be "too comfortable," which was the explanation he gave A's traveling secretary Mickey Morabito when asked why he always sat in the first row of the coach seats on the team's charter flights instead of sitting in first class.

"He said it was something he had always done," Morabito said. "I asked him who sat in first class with the White Sox, and he said, 'All the important people.'"

Morabito worked closely with La Russa, and came to appreciate his intensity and focus on his job, even in the hours after a game when he could have been relaxing and unwinding from the pressures of the previous few hours.

"He was an incredible guy to watch," Morabito said. "We used to go out after games and I can't tell you how many nights he sat there and would take out a cocktail napkin and start thinking about the lineup for the next game. His mind was always working."

Being able to manage the team for the second half of the 1986 season turned out to be a big advantage for La Russa, because it gave him a chance to evaluate the players already on the roster, make decisions about who he thought could help the team the most in the future, and identify the areas where the team needed more talent.

He didn't have to look very far to see the talent of Canseco, the 22-year-old rookie outfielder who led the majors in home runs and RBIs at the All-Star break. Even an 0-for-40 slump in August did not dim La Russa's opinion of his abilities.

Another youngster who had a chance to make his major league debut for La Russa was Mark McGwire, a star of the 1984 Olympic team who was called up from the minor leagues on August 20 when Tony Phillips was injured.

The discovery of those two young sluggers, plus the emergence of Stewart as the leader of the pitching staff, helped La Russa realize the A's had a chance to become a much better club in the not-too-distant future. The team finished the season with a 45–34 record after La Russa arrived, moving up from last to third in the AL West.

Included in that tally was his first-ever win against the White Sox, when Oakland came to Chicago for a series in September that La Russa insisted carried no extra meaning for him. He did, however, elaborate on some lingering feelings about how the end of his tenure with the White Sox was handled.

"I have a good idea of who said what or who did what before and after I left," La Russa told reporters. "One thing that surprised me is that most times when a guy gets fired, it's over, you turn the page. I had enough people tell me it was different in Chicago. There were shots taken at me, and some of the stuff was plain untrue. It got back to me. There's no excuse for it.

"There are two things that aggravate me. I've heard too many times that we'd all have been better off if I hadn't come back last October. That bugs me. That makes it sound like we were doomed to fail from the beginning. It could have worked. I have no doubt that if certain things happened, we would have had some success."

La Russa was also bothered by the claims that it worked out for the best. He knew he had moved into a good situation with Oakland, but he cared for some of the people who lost their jobs in the team's shakeup, including Dave Dombrowski and coach Joe Nossek.

"When you invest eight years with one team, it hurts to leave it," La Russa said. "A lot of people also got hurt. I'm lucky that I got into a good situation. Some people weren't as lucky."

His experience in the last three months of the 1986 season convinced La Russa that while many of the pieces were in place for success, the A's were missing one key element: a reliable pitcher in the bullpen who could protect a lead in the late innings. Jay Howell led the team with only 16 saves, 30 less than league-leader Dave Righetti of the Yankees.

That changed, even if almost by accident, two days before the end of spring training in 1987 when the A's traded three minor leaguers to the Cubs for pitcher Dennis Eckersley and outfielder Dan Rohn. None of the three players the A's gave up—outfielder Dave Wilder, infielder Brian Guinn, or pitcher Mark Leonette—ever played a game in the majors.

It seemed like an odd marriage at the time; La Russa once called him "gutless" after Eckersley, then on the Red Sox, hit the White Sox's Jerry Dybzinski with a pitch. Eckersley recalled the incident, but he also admitted that he liked the fire and competitiveness he saw in La Russa from the opposing dugout.

"Those guys who make you mad are the ones you want to play for," Eckersley said.

The relationship got off to a somewhat strained beginning, however. La Russa had determined that Eckersley could best help the club by pitching late-innings relief, but Eckersley felt a strong desire to remain a starting pitcher. They tried to work it out, but came to an impasse.

"I've had guys before who have been in roles they didn't like," La Russa said at the time. "As long as they go about their business, fine. It's not their job to decide."

Eckersley, who had started 305 games in the previous 10 years while making only one relief appearance, might not have been happy, but he stopped complaining. By the middle of May, it was obvious he was staying in the bullpen. And the Athletics were well on their way to relying on Eckersley to pitch the ninth inning in close games.

It was a strategy that originated with Dave Duncan and was new to baseball, but the more La Russa thought about it, the more sense it made to him to have one pitcher who almost exclusively pitched when the team was in position to win a game in the ninth inning. The era of the one-inning closer was beginning.

"You can't win a game in the ninth if you give up the winning run in the eighth, so many managers would bring in their closer in the eighth," La Russa said in the book *Champions*. "We felt we had such a jewel in Eckersley that the fewer outs he had to get an outing, the more available he would be for more outings.

"If you have a good team that's going to be ahead in a lot of games in a week, that's very important. If you have an average team, you might only have the lead in the eighth a couple of games a week, so you probably should use your closer to win those games because you might not have another chance for three games.

"But we had a real good team, so we had four, five, six games a week we could win. Common sense told us we should be able to use Eck as much as possible."

After beginning the year with the worst record since the team moved to Oakland in 1968, the A's finally began to learn how to win during the 1987 season, although it didn't look as if that would be the case when the team opened with a five-game losing streak.

La Russa was in his office the next day when owner Walter Haas, Sandy Alderson, and other team executives came to pay him a visit.

"I thought, 'Here it comes,'" La Russa said. "'They've got the finger out, and they're going to start pointing at people they can blame.' But they sat down and said, 'Are you doing all right?' That just blew me away."

Some more tough losses prompted La Russa to lose his temper. In April, he launched into a profanity-laden tirade after a game in which the A's strikeout total rose to 72 in only nine games. A 4–3 loss to the Orioles in May prompted La Russa to charge out of the dugout and up the tunnel to the clubhouse with a chair in his hands. Several people were watching as he flung the chair 30 feet down the tunnel. Then he called for a clubhouse meeting.

When the A's lost again the following night, a brave reporter asked La Russa if he felt like throwing another chair. "People might think I'm nuts," he said. "I'll wait until you leave. Then I'll do something."

La Russa even blew up at his childhood pal, Lou Piniella, in a game against the Yankees on August 31. Piniella complained to umpire Dave Phillips that Oakland pitcher Curt Young was starting his windup with his front foot in front of the rubber, technically a violation of the rules.

Phillips ruled against Piniella, but after the Yankees' Ron Kittle—a former La Russa player in Chicago—homered, La Russa asked Phillips to confiscate the bat to see if it was illegal. La Russa said the Yankees switched bats before turning it over to Phillips.

"They didn't give us the one he hit the home run with," La Russa told reporters. "But I didn't care. I was just out there to play bush league baseball too, just like them."

It was at a series in Minnesota, however, when the A's really got to see how upset La Russa could get. At the start of the four-game series on August 6, the A's and Twins were tied for the division lead. While neither team expected that series to decide the pennant, each knew the games could well play a factor in determining its outcome. It was not a good series for the A's, who lost all four games, dropping from a first-place tie to four games out in 96 hours.

After the final out in the last game, La Russa could not contain his anger.

"Tony grabbed a bat and ran all the way up the stairs to the clubhouse," Carney Lansford said. "He went in and just destroyed the spread [the postgame buffet]. It went everywhere. I was wearing a suit and I had three or four different kinds of salad dressing on it. It was all over everybody's clothes. He just went berserk."

Added Steinbach, "We had played like crap and he stood there swinging the fungo and knocking food everywhere yelling, 'You don't deserve to eat.'"

Lansford, Steinbach, and their teammates, however, knew why La Russa had reacted in such a manner. "I totally understood," Lansford said. "It was a big series, and we had worked hard to get to that point. It told me exactly how intense he was and how much he wanted to win."

The A's finished the year in third place in the AL West with a .500 record, 81–81, four games behind the Twins. More important to La Russa, however, the team's performance had let him know what he thought he could expect the following year.

In Dave Stewart, he knew he had a top-flight starting pitcher. In Eckersley, he had a closer. In Jose Canseco and Mark McGwire, he had two of the best young sluggers in the game. McGwire lost a chance to become the first rookie in history to hit 50 home runs when he skipped the team's final game to return home for the birth of his first son.

"Given the way the cards were dealt, we did all right," La Russa concluded at the end of the season, still disappointed the team lost six of its final seven games.

La Russa knew, however, that the combination of talent and the knowledge the A's had gained during the year about how to win and the effort that it took to win, created a great deal of optimism about the team's chances to be successful in 1988.

More so than usual, he could not wait for the next season to begin.

CHAPTER 9

Success...Almost

The off-season produced even more reasons for La Russa to smile as he thought about spring training and the start of the 1988 season. A trade with Cincinnati had brought left-handed slugger Dave Parker to the A's, balancing the righthanded power of Canseco and McGwire. Starting pitcher Bob Welch was added in a trade from the Dodgers, and outfielder Dave Henderson was signed as a free agent. La Russa was also convinced that rookie Walt Weiss was ready to be an everyday shortstop in the majors, allowing the A's to move Alfredo Griffin in the trade for Welch, and he liked what he saw from catcher Terry Steinbach in his first two years as a regular.

"It was a classic example of what the front office, with backing of ownership, can do utilizing all of the resources of scouts, coaches, and everyone in the organization," La Russa said. "The guy who orchestrated all of that was Sandy Alderson. We had eight needs, and he identified three candidates for each of those needs. I believe he got one of the top three guys to fill six or seven of those categories. It was unbelievable."

It seemed to the manager that almost all of the pieces were in place for the A's to compete for the division title, his goal at the beginning of every season. On the first day of spring training he told his players he thought they could win the World Series. His answering machine at home had a recording predicting the A's would win 100 games.

Alderson did not try to put too much extra pressure on La Russa when he said at the start of the spring that he too thought the A's were capable of winning 100 games. "I try not to be overly optimistic," Alderson said, "but I'm as excited about this team as I have been about any in the five years I've been here. I think we're legitimate contenders."

About the only distraction was the late arrival to spring training by Canseco, who stayed home in Miami for a few extra days to sign autographs at a baseball card show.

When Canseco finally arrived in Scottsdale, Arizona, La Russa was ready. He had a table set up near where the team ran through its exercise drills, covered by a sheet. When the workout was over, the sheet was removed and on the table were several of Canseco's bats, buttons bearing Canseco's picture, and a large picture. A hand-printed sign read, "Welcome to Jose Canseco Autograph Day. Appearing for the first time, Jose Canseco. 10:00 AM to 2:00 PM. Evening Lecture: Concepts of Team Play. Special guest speaker, Jose (Card Show) Canseco."

Everybody, including Canseco, was able to laugh about the prank. For the serious La Russa, however, his private discussion with Canseco about his responsibility to the team was far more important. La Russa just hoped the distractions would be kept to a minimum once the season began.

Nothing in baseball solves problems more than winning. It has always been that way and will never change, and when the A's began to win a couple of weeks into the season, it seemed nothing could get in their way. After opening the year by splitting their first 12 games, the A's won 18 of their next 19 games, including 14 in a row, the longest streak in the majors in 11 years. On May 9 they were 24–7 and already had an eight-game lead over the second place White Sox.

The wins continued and the lead increased, even though the rival Twins refused to go away. The A's even found themselves playing 50 innings over three days in Toronto and Cleveland in July—two 16-inning wins in a row followed by a doubleheader against the Indians—and came away ready for more action, after a good night's rest.

At the All-Star break, the A's were 20 games over .500, 54–34, and had a 5½ game lead on the Twins. By the end of August they were 84–50 and had a nine-game lead. Still the wins didn't stop, and at the end of the year La Russa's A's had collected 104 wins, tying the 1984 Tigers for the second-most wins by an American League club. The team was in first place for all but five days in April.

The players who had been on the team the previous year were not surprised by their success. La Russa had spent much of his first season and a half as the Oakland manager shaping the team in his image, acquiring players who shared or could buy into his philosophy about how the game should be played.

"There probably are only some select players who can play for Tony," Steinbach said. "He has a definite mind-set of what he wants his players to be like. The number one thing I learned from Tony is that he has one very simple rule: you've got to play the game hard, and you've got to play the game right. He virtually said, 'If you don't want to do that, please let me know and I'll get you the hell out of here.' We are not going to go out there and half-step it, we're not going to go out there and not play hard and not play the game right. It doesn't mean we're going to execute every play, it doesn't mean we aren't going to make errors, but it means we are going to try.

"There have been good successful players who have been on World Series championship teams who could not handle his type of managing. I still don't know if his intensity is a good trait or a bad trait. My observation was that he had a hard time letting the game go, especially if it did not turn out well. If something went wrong, he struggled with that for a long time and really dwelled on it. I don't necessarily consider that a fault. I think his passion for the game and his will to succeed is one of the reasons he has been as successful as he has been."

It didn't take long for the A's players to accept La Russa's intensity and tunnel vision.

"Tony was so into the details of planning out everything that he never left a stone unturned," Steinbach said. "He would have all of spring training planned out and if we had one day that got rained out it would almost send him into a tizzy. It was like he was saying, 'Now everything's going to get screwed up. Mickey [Morabito, the traveling secretary], we've got to get into a gym,' or 'Come on, guys, we've got a 20-minute window, let's run outside and do something.'

"As players we talked to Tony about it that a lot. 'Come on, Skip, what's up?' we said. His answer was, 'I can't play anymore. My only job as manager is to make sure that I have done everything to get you guys ready to play. Once the game starts I can't pinch-hit or pinch-run. Yeah, I can put a bunt on or call for a hit-and-run but if you guys don't do it and don't execute it doesn't matter.' He always was very intense about that."

Weiss quickly came to appreciate what La Russa's presence meant to him and the rest of the team.

"I really learned how to play the game from him, watching him manage," Weiss said. "I learned all of the finer points of the game, the games within the game. He expected you to play at a certain level and to play with a tremendous focus. A lot of guys who played for him probably had a run-in or bumped heads with him at some time or another, myself included. When you have somebody who is as competitive as he is—and competitive players—sometimes they are going to clash, but even if you had differences, there was a mutual respect there."

One player new to the team in 1988 who wondered how he would do under La Russa's leadership was Dave Henderson, who had played against La Russa's teams while with Seattle from 1981 to 1986 and with the Red Sox in 1986 and 1987.

"I think he hated me because I seemed to beat him so often when he was in Chicago," Henderson said. "He didn't care for me because he didn't like my demeanor. I was always smiling and having a good time, and that didn't sit too well with Tony. I never thought of a baseball game being life or death, and because of that I think I had to grow on Tony.

"Rene Lachemann (who had been the Seattle manager) was in my corner and vouched for me and said I could play. I think Tony had his doubts. I could always have fun and be on my toes and play baseball, and that is a tough thing to do, but I could always get it done."

Henderson convinced La Russa that he was more than a platoon player by hitting .304 with 24 homers and 94 RBIs. He also tried to help La Russa forget about the tough losses and show him that people could have fun while playing and still be just as intense and focused on winning.

Several years later, Henderson admitted he had learned more from La Russa than any other manager he played for in his career, comparing La Russa to a schoolteacher.

"You hated that class, but 10 years later you figured out it all was all for your own good," Henderson told USA Today Baseball Weekly. "As a player, you think you're working as hard as you can, but that teacher takes you to a higher level. Sometimes you rebel. After my first year with him I realized pretty quick he was making me into a better ballplayer."

One player who rebelled, and did it often, was Jose Canseco. La Russa already knew about Canseco's talent before he took the Oakland job, but it wasn't until a couple of years later that Canseco began to act like a star and expected to be treated like one. That not only rubbed his manager the wrong way, it affected the players and those on the periphery of the team. It was a nuisance they could all tolerate, however, as long as the team was winning.

"Canseco had a problem with preparation, and Tony hated that," Henderson said. "He wanted his players prepared, and that meant taking batting practice and infield practice. It was a strained relationship, but I tried to be the buffer to make sure Tony didn't kill him. It angered Tony when Jose did crazy things like showing up late or missing batting practice. I cooled tempers and we got it done."

Steinbach and the other players could tolerate Canseco's distractions as long as he played well. And play well he did. In 1988, he became the first player in history to hit 40 or more home runs and steal 40 or more bases en route to winning the AL MVP award.

"There has been a lot of crap written about Jose and probably 99.9 percent of it is deserved," Steinbach said. "But none of that can take away from what his ability was. When he wanted to play, his talent was phenomenal. He was a major force on our ballclub. We had a few of those unique personalities, and

Tony did a good job of balancing them. He had what I call blue-collar workers, who were guys who were going to go out there no matter what and guys who didn't need to be in the limelight. They were guys who wanted to play, who wanted to win, who wanted to make money and didn't care about anything else.

"Tony used to walk around during batting practice and visit with all the different groups. We said, 'Tony, what are you doing?' He said, 'I'm smelling.' We said, 'Smelling for what?' and he would say that he was just trying to measure the mood of the team. He wanted to know if some guys were tired, if his stars were bitching, if his blue-collar workers were happy. He always tried to keep his finger on the pulse of the team at all times and adapt accordingly. Maybe his horses needed a rest or maybe his horses needed an ass-chewing."

La Russa was keenly interested in how other leading coaches motivated their players—even in other sports besides baseball. La Russa had a chance during a road stretch to Texas, to watch the Dallas Cowboys practice and meet with coach Tom Landry. He was always looking for whatever competitive advantage he could gain to improve his team and add fire to his players.

Thanks to their success during the 1988 season, La Russa had time to rest his horses before the playoffs. In addition to Canseco and Henderson's contributions, McGwire hit 32 homers and drove in 99 runs and Weiss was named the league's Rookie of the Year, the third consecutive Oakland player to win that award.

Stewart won 21 games—his second consecutive 20-win season. Welch won 17, Storm Davis 16, and Eckersley, the reluctant reliever, led the AL with 45 saves.

La Russa had accomplished one of his initial goals when he had become the team manager, earning the respect of his players. It might have come grudgingly from some, like Henderson and Eckersley, but it came.

"The thing with Tony," Eckersley once said, "is that when you're on the other side of the field, you think he makes too many moves. But when you're on his team, you understand that the moves help the bullpen, which makes all the pitchers better. He knows what he's doing."

There were more than enough stars on the team to point to for their success, but a major part of the attention, and scrutiny, was on Canseco.

It was on September 28, with only a few days left in the regular season, that the first public accusation was leveled that Canseco had used steroids. Appearing as a guest on a CBS television program, Thomas Boswell, a columnist for the *Washington Post*, said Canseco was "the most conspicuous example of a player who has made himself great with steroids."

Boswell said that he was basing his accusations on conversations he had earlier in the season with La Russa, who said Canseco had made "some mistakes" earlier in his career. Boswell implied that La Russa was talking about Canseco using steroids, which La Russa denied.

"That's a very irritating inference that he took," La Russa told reporters at the time. "It wasn't anywhere near what I meant... It bothers me that he put me in there as a source. It's bull."

Boswell later told the *Miami Herald* that he had asked La Russa if he was worried about Canseco's long-term future because of his use of steroids, to which La Russa made the remark about Canseco having made "some mistakes" in the past. La Russa said Boswell never asked a specific question linking Canseco to steroids and said, "Whatever my response was, it wasn't to that question. Somebody made a mistake, and it's not me."

Canseco denied the charges and Major League Baseball officials said they had no plans to investigate the allegation. But fans in opposing cities, especially Boston, were ready to let Canseco have it when he took to the field at the start of the American League playoff series between the A's and Red Sox.

With chants of "steroids, steroids" coming from the crowd at Fenway Park as Canseco came to bat, he reacted by stepping out of the batter's box, smiling, and flexing his muscles. He also responded by putting the A's in front in the opening game of the series and went on to hit .313 in the series with three homers, a double, and four RBIs.

"They were having fun and so was I," Canseco told reporters. "This is too big a show to get uptight. Anyway, it's a compliment."

The A's won the first two games in Boston, beating Bruce Hurst and Clemens, and returned home needing just two more wins to advance to the World Series, armed with the knowledge that the Red Sox had lost 14 of their previous 15 games at the Oakland Coliseum.

La Russa remembered what had happened to his White Sox in 1983, who had lost the AL Championship Series to Baltimore, and was not about to take anything for granted. The nerves tightened even more when the A's quickly fell behind 5–0 in Game 3.

The offense rallied, however, and pulled out a 10–6 win, leaving La Russa only one win away from his first pennant and a trip to the World Series. There was no drama in the fourth game, as the A's closed out the series sweep with a 4–1 victory behind a Canseco homer and the pitching of Stewart and Eckersley.

Eckersley saved all four games of the series and was almost universally heralded as the best closer in the game—one of the first pitchers to be known by that title.

But even the best closers can have a bad day, and it often only takes one poor pitch to turn a would-be victory into a loss. Such was the case in the opening game of the 1988 World Series, when Eckersley came in to pitch the ninth inning with a 4–3 Oakland lead. Starting pitcher Stewart had lobbied La Russa to stay in the game. He had pitched 14 complete games that season and felt good about going the distance, but La Russa already had made up his mind.

Eckersley quickly retired the first two Dodger batters, but then walked Mike Davis, a rarity. Eckersley had walked only 11 batters in 72 innings in the regular season. The Dodgers lineup for the game did not include the player who would be named the NL MVP, outfielder Kirk Gibson, who was suffering from a pulled hamstring and a wrenched knee and could barely walk, much less run. After receiving treatment in the trainers' room for the game's first eight innings, he came out to the bench for the ninth and told manager Tommy Lasorda that he could pinch-hit if he needed him.

After the walk to Davis, Lasorda sent Gibson into the game. Watching from the Oakland dugout, La Russa might been excused for having a flashback to the first time he ever saw Gibson on a baseball field, playing for Triple A Evansville against his Iowa team. Gibson had hit a home run. Eckersley quickly got ahead in the count 0–2, but Gibson fought back, fouling off more fastballs and working the count to 3–2. Instead of throwing another fastball, Eckersley tried to surprise Gibson with a slider.

Broadcasting the game nationally on CBS Radio, Jack Buck saw Gibson swing and launch the ball into the right-field stands, sending Dodger Stadium into a frenzy, celebrating the 5–4 victory, one of the most dramatic endings in World Series history. Buck told his listeners, "I don't believe what I just saw."

Neither did La Russa, Eckersley, or the rest of the stunned A's. It was only the sixth time in Series history a game had ended on a walk-off homer, the first since Carlton Fisk's famous blast in the sixth game of the 1975 Series for Boston against the Reds. It might have been the first by a hitter who could only limp around the bases.

La Russa tried to speak boldly the next day. "We've had our hearts broken before, and we've come back," La Russa told reporters. "We'll come back and play hard tonight."

He might have honestly believed that would be the case, even if the A's were facing baseball's best pitcher in 1988, Orel Hershiser, in Game 2, but the result was a disappointing 6–0 loss. The heavily favored A's were now returning home, down 0–2.

La Russa had also gotten involved in an off-field controversy with Texas manager Bobby Valentine, who was at the game wearing a Dodgers cap and cheering for Los Angeles. La Russa criticized Valentine for not supporting his fellow American League team. Valentine explained that he was cheering for Los Angeles out of his longtime friendship with Lasorda. He said he was not disrespecting La Russa or the A's in any way, despite La Russa's contention.

"I couldn't allow a 20-year relationship to be affected by what job I was in at that time," Valentine said a few years later. "It would be hypocritical of me if I did anything but root for a friend of all those years."

La Russa admitted later he had been wrong to criticize Valentine. "That was a huge mistake on my part," he said.

Back home for Game 3, the A's rallied for a 2–1 win, but it would turn out to be their last gasp. La Russa was even more intense than normal, uncharacteristically yelling at his players in the dugout. The added emotion didn't help. Los Angeles closed out the Series victory in five games, giving La Russa the most bitter defeat of his managing career.

Recalling the Sox's 1983 playoff loss, La Russa said, "When I was walking up the tunnel, I remembered going over to congratulate [Orioles manager] Joe Altobelli after the 1983 playoffs. I remember thinking, 'I hope I never have to do this after a World Series.' Well, here I am."

Later in the evening, he told a smaller group of reporters, "My heart is broken. We let a lot of people down. It's a very bad feeling."

A couple of weeks after the Series loss, La Russa was signing autographs at a department store. He signed one for a man whose car had been stolen from the Oakland Coliseum parking lot during the last game. "To Doug," La Russa wrote. "You lost your car. I lost the world."

Never one to accept a loss easily, La Russa admitted he didn't know how long it would take him to recover from losing the World Series. One of the virtues of baseball is that, even after a tough loss, there usually is another game to play the next day. This time, however, the next game was five months away.

10

Erasing the Pain

The heartache of losing the World Series might not have gone away, but as La Russa and the A's arrived in Scottsdale for the opening of spring training in 1989, he had found a way to turn that negative into a positive. He had decided to use the disappointing loss as motivation for the team for the new season.

Voted by his peers as the AL Manager of the Year for the second time in his career, La Russa quickly stopped answering questions about "last year" and sidestepped requests to replay Eckersley's fateful pitch to Gibson.

"We missed the biggest piece we were chasing," La Russa said. "We did not choke. We got beat because the Dodgers did more than we did. I'm very proud of this club and I have a great feeling about the A's in 1988. I'm as proud of this club as any I've been around."

The loss, in a strange way, had another benefit for the team. La Russa is fond of saying that he "never wants to be too comfortable," and the World Series loss prevented his team from coming to spring training with a superior, "nobody can beat us" attitude.

"After success, you get a little bit soft," La Russa said. "That's something we're going to have to pay a big price to prevent in the spring. Last year a lot of people picked us and we won. This year the challenge is to repeat."

La Russa was well aware that no AL team had won back-to-back pennants in a decade, since the 1976–78 Yankees won three in a row. He had been down that road, trying to repeat as a division champion when his 1983 White Sox won, then fell apart the following year.

"I learned the lesson well in '84, that you never take anything for granted," La Russa said. "We assumed there was a carryover of how we executed plays. We touched them, but we didn't discuss them. So this year we're not doing that."

La Russa spent the winter reading books by and about people who had experienced long periods of success at their jobs, even if it had nothing to do with baseball or even other sports. He and wife Elaine also took their daughters Bianca and Devon out of school and spent time traveling to Washington, D.C., New York, and Revolutionary and Civil War battlegrounds—the trip they had planned to take when La Russa got the unexpected call from Oakland.

It was a different kind of education for his daughters, 10 and 7, and it led the La Russas to homeschool the girls instead of having them attend traditional schools.

"From mid-February through October, there is a certain sacrifice we have elected to make as a family," La Russa told the *San Francisco Chronicle* that winter. "I think I do as much as other guys in terms of getting to the park early and staying late. But the idea has always been that winters would be for family."

By the start of spring drills, La Russa was refreshed and ready for the next challenge. Always looking for that edge, La Russa had writer George Will speak to the team about excellence. He also invited former Yankee and Oakland great Reggie Jackson to spring training to speak to the players about what it took to repeat as champions.

Another morning, the guest speaker was Doug Williams, the quarterback of the Super Bowl champion Washington Redskins, who talked about the importance of mental preparedness.

"If he could not bring the coach in, he had them videotape a message for us and we would watch it," Weiss said. "He always focused on guys who had enjoyed a ton of success. He was relentless. He never stopped trying to learn or gain an edge."

Mostly, however, La Russa was counting on the leadership and determination of players such as Eckersley, Stewart, and the other veterans to set the tone for how the team would play in 1989.

"I have more drive this year than last," Eckersley said. "I want to prove it was not a fluke."

Added Stewart, "You feel you're the better team, that you're going to win, but you've got to do it."

That was the attitude La Russa hoped to see in his ballclub, which was predicted by many to repeat in the AL West, even though the division was loaded with quality teams like the Twins, who were the 1987 World Series champion and quickly becoming Oakland's biggest rival.

"The most important thing we have to do is make sure our attitude is right so that we can take our best shot," La Russa said. "We're going to give it our shot. We're going to contend. Last year this team set a certain standard about how hard they played everyday. That's what I want to see again, that consistent effort. The rest will take care of itself."

One of the challenges La Russa had not counted on was serious injuries that kept Canseco and Eckersley out of the lineup for much of the season. La Russa already had been worried about Canseco from the beginning of the season. He felt that Canseco's success in 1988 would affect his attitude about how hard he needed to work to prepare for the season, particularly since he was not the hardest worker on the team to begin with.

"After his 40–40 year, he got an awful lot of attention and started to make some serious money," La Russa said in *Champions*. "As happens to so many young guys when they get attention, their values go sideways. You could see it. I had conversations with Jose, telling him he was losing track of what it's all about."

Canseco was now surrounded more by his "friends" and he started listening to them more than to his manager. Canseco bought a red Jaguar with a personalized license plate: "MR 40 40." He was arrested for speeding both before and during spring training, then was stopped by a police officer for having a concealed weapon in his car, a charge that was eventually reduced to a misdemeanor.

Even more upsetting for La Russa was the fact that Canseco had begun the year on the disabled list after undergoing wrist surgery. He did not return to the lineup until after the All-Star break.

"The day I learned that Canseco would need surgery, I remembered something I'd read in a book about Lou Holtz. When he was coaching Arkansas, he had an Orange Bowl game in which the Razorbacks were big underdogs, and he said he told his team to concentrate on what it could do well.

"So I talked to my team about what we still had. I said, 'Do you think with a lineup of Carney Lansford, Mark McGwire, Dave Parker, Dave Henderson, and either Terry Steinbach or Ron Hassey we're not going to score runs?' Then later, when we continued to have injuries, I challenged the players. I told them everybody expected us to have trouble repeating anyway, and now they'd say we'd just fold because of our injuries."

Before Canseco and some of the other injured players could get back in the lineup, Sandy Alderson had stepped in and provided La Russa with another outfielder with Hall of Fame talent who was also known to be the cause of many managerial headaches, Rickey Henderson.

On June 21, the A's brought Henderson—like Stewart, an Oakland native—back to his hometown from the Yankees in exchange for pitchers Greg Cadaret and Eric Plunk and outfielder Luis Polonia.

"We needed something to pick us up," Alderson said about the trade in *Champions*. "I had picked up vibes that that Rickey had worn out his welcome in New York…. It worked out perfectly for us. Rickey was just what we needed that year."

La Russa had managed against Henderson for years and was well aware of his new outfielder's talents—and his reputation.

"Rickey is blessed with an almost unbelievable body, with those strong legs," La Russa once said. "He's taken a beating over the years, because he's been a marked man for his entire career. But teams couldn't stop him. He's a very intelligent guy and very competitive. If you ever see Rickey playing a game, be careful about getting in it, because he's only going to play a game he can win."

That was the attitude La Russa wanted in his players, but Henderson also brought with him his own personal agenda.

"What Rickey needed wasn't always what the club needed," La Russa said. "That really only happened a few times, but every time it did, it seemed to become public and it seemed bigger than it was. Rickey was always very much influenced by those around him, but there was a lot of goodness in him. He was generally well liked in the clubhouse. He didn't carry himself like a big star."

Weiss and the other players welcomed Henderson to the club because they knew his presence gave the team a better chance to win.

"Tony was really good at creating an atmosphere that if you didn't play the game right you stuck out like a sore thumb and kind of became an outcast," Weiss said. "He's the best I've ever been around at creating an 'us against the world' kind of mentality. He thrived on that. He felt like if everybody outside was against us, we would pull together to get it done."

The team concept, of course, was very important to La Russa. He was constantly arranging team get-togethers on the road, where every player was required to show up, if even for a few minutes.

"I think he really understood players more than most managers," said Mickey Morabito, the A's traveling secretary since 1980, who had previously worked for the Yankees. "Tony wanted to be with his players. He had the team parties, which Eckersley called 'forced camaraderie.' It worked. He didn't like players hanging in cliques. He knew enough to respect players. I know the players respected him because they saw his work ethic. They knew he was going to give them their best chance to win."

The A's had a two-game lead in the division at the time of the trade, and Henderson's play through the rest of the season, plus the performance of the team's starting pitchers, helped the team hold off challenges from both Kansas City and California. The A's finished with 99 wins while Kansas City won 92 games and California 91.

Still, it wasn't all good times for the club—such as the game in which the A's lost an eleven-inning game at Kansas City on June 12. La Russa was so upset he threw a chair into a wall, leaving a 10-inch-wide, one-inch deep hole. Those moments were the exception, however, and it was no surprise when the team announced over the All-Star break that La Russa had signed a three-year extension to continue as the team's manager through the 1992 season.

Despite the security of the new contract, La Russa still felt he and his players had to perform well and continue to win if he was going to keep his job. It was one more instance in which he felt that he never wanted to be too comfortable.

He actually seemed to believe that having a fear of losing served as another motivator for his team.

"Fear can be a great motivator," he said near the end of the season. "I used to doubt that, because it seemed like a negative thing, but I finally divided it. If you're paralyzed by fear, if you're afraid to do anything for fear that you'll lose the game, then it's bad. But if it motivates you to play hard because you don't want to blow a lead or look bad, then it can be a positive. It's like Eck—the reason he's so great is that every time he goes out there, he's scared he'll look bad or not pick up the pitcher he's replaced, so he really bears down. He never goes out there casually."

Eckersley, who missed 40 games because of a strained muscle in his rotator cuff, came back to finish with 33 saves for a starting staff that didn't need much help. Four pitchers collected 17 or more wins: Stewart was 21–9, his third consecutive 20-win season; Storm Davis was 19–7; free agent–acquisition Mike Moore was 19–11; and Bob Welch was 17–8.

Henderson hit .294 after joining Oakland and netted 52 stolen bases and 72 runs scored in 85 games. McGwire led the offense with 33 homers and 95 RBIs, Dave Parker hit 22 homers and drove in 97 runs. Canseco, playing just 65 games, hit 17 homers and drove in 57 runs. His strikeout total was alarming, however—69 in 227 at-bats—and led to one angry confrontation between him and his manager.

With Canseco at bat and the potential winning run on third, he took three big swings and struck out instead of shortening his swing and trying for the single, which would have won the game. Canseco reportedly told La Russa afterward, "I'm an entertainer. People would rather see me take three big swings, maybe hit one out of the park, maybe strike out, than just hit a single."

That, of course, was not the kind of attitude La Russa wanted in his players, but Canseco was indeed a star. La Russa knew he had to overlook many of Canseco's faults because of his sheer raw talent.

"We can point to some immaturity and some irresponsibility when we start talking about some of Jose's so-called problems," La Russa told *Sports Illustrated* that summer. "But we're not talking about serious problems, not like so many in sports or society. When we talk about Jose Canseco, we're talking about a person who is completely clean. He doesn't drink, he doesn't smoke, he doesn't do drugs. You never have to worry about his being out of shape. And he's intelligent, which is why he will learn from all of this."

Controversy brewed when Canseco decided to establish a 900-number telephone service, on which he recorded a new message every day and fans could call and listen to him talk about a variety of subjects, including baseball and his personal life. Depending on how long the message was, fans spent as much as $10 per call.

"People weren't getting the story from the horse's mouth," Canseco was quoted as saying in the *Sporting News*. "I just wanted to tell my side of the story."

La Russa learned about Canseco's latest adventure when he saw an advertisement for the number when the A's were in Boston. "I thought, 'This is ridiculous,'" La Russa said. "I once heard him say he was going to be very careful about the types of commercials and endorsements he does. In my opinion, I wouldn't have done this."

With the playoffs approaching, La Russa just hoped that the distractions would not prevent any of his stars from performing well as they tried to earn another spot on the big stage of the World Series. The playoff opponent this year was the Toronto Blue Jays. Henderson turned out to be the star, stealing a record eight bases, hitting two home runs, and generally disrupting the Blue Jays and making their life miserable. The A's won the series in five games.

"When I was traded from the Yankees, my one regret was that I never brought a World Series to New York," Henderson said. "That's the show I've always wanted to be in, ever since I was a kid sitting in the Oakland Coliseum watching the A's. I was a fan. That's why I don't get upset when fans yell at me. I used to yell at players. I just loved a performance. So every time I get out there, I try to give them a performance."

La Russa was thrilled with Henderson's performance, but he had a completely different reaction to Toronto manager Cito Gaston's accusation that Eckersley was using an illegal substance in Game 5. Gaston asked plate umpire Rick Reed to search Eckersley's glove and uniform, which did not reveal anything illegal. Eckersley got upset, as did La Russa—and so did Gaston.

La Russa accused the Toronto manager of gamesmanship and said the only reason there was no retaliatory act was that Eckersley was able to save the game and close out the series.

"We would have done something to show up the Toronto pitchers," La Russa said after the game. "There's a lot of gamesmanship you can play. What bothers me is we won it, and for them to try to taint it is bull. I'm not going to ignore it. This is a charade, a joke. That's why these people should be ashamed of themselves."

One of the worst aspects of the episode, as far as La Russa was concerned, was that it took away from the satisfaction of the A's repeating as the AL champions.

Watching his team work out for a couple of days prior to the start of the Series, this time a Bay Area battle against the San Francisco Giants, La Russa was pleased with the team's intensity. He even saw Eckersley hit Canseco in the back with a pitch when the pitcher thought Canseco was digging in a little too much at the plate during batting practice.

To some of the Oakland players—people such as Stewart and Henderson, both Oakland natives—this matchup was more than just a battle between the AL and NL champions. It was a matter of pride, both trying to wipe away the disappointment of the previous year's loss and best their crosstown rivals.

"There was a lot of stuff in the papers at the time about the San Francisco mayor [Art Agnos] talking about San Francisco being a glamorous city and Oakland being like the ugly stepsister," Stewart said in *Champions*. "We were really fired up going into that Series.... We played the whole Series with a chip on our shoulders."

The Series opened in Oakland, with Stewart on the mound. He backed up his words with a five-hit, 5–0 shutout. When the A's won again in Game 2, 5–1, they were ready to move across the bay to Candlestick Park with a commanding 2–0 lead and Bob Welch, the former Dodger, scheduled to be on the mound. Welch was 19–4 against the Giants, including a perfect 6–0 record at Candlestick.

About 30 minutes before the game's first pitch, an earthquake struck the Bay Area, shaking the stadium's foundation. There was significant damage on both sides of the bay, and baseball officials quickly made the decision to postpone the Series indefinitely. The quake was measured at 7.0 on the Richter scale, a significant magnitude; its epicenter was Santa Cruz, just 70 miles south of San Francisco.

La Russa and his players were naturally more concerned with making certain their families were OK than they were with baseball. La Russa's father and other relatives from Tampa were in town, and had just crossed the Bay Bridge maybe 30 minutes before the earthquake struck. It was late evening before he was able to reach them. Watching on television at home in Florida, La Russa's other family members were just as concerned.

"It was chaos," said Eva Fojaco, La Russa's sister. "We were at home getting ready to watch the game and everything went black. We thought our TV had gone out. Our mom was with us at the house. Vic [Eva's husband] put the radio on and we found out there had been an earthquake. It was hours and hours before we heard anything. Dad finally called and said he was OK."

Once he knew everybody in his family was safe, as well as his players' families, La Russa had something else to worry about. A fanatical control freak, he now was at the mercy of baseball and city executives deciding when to resume the World Series. Two wins away from winning the Series at a time when he felt he most needed to be in control of the situation, he could do nothing but sit and wait. He called a team meeting specifically to talk about the earthquake and its aftermath.

"Talking it out is important," he said then. "You don't want to try to hide from it. You've got to talk about it and talk about our job and what it all means."

As a few days passed and no decisions were made, La Russa became even more restless. There was even talk that the Series would be canceled and not resumed—an opinion that upset La Russa tremendously. As the days passed on, La Russa was as worried about his player's mental state when the games resumed, in addition to their physical readiness.

"I have a lot of problems with people who say the World Series should have been canceled," La Russa said. "As far as a sporting event, this is the most significant thing going on right now. It's our crown jewel.... I'm not being insensitive, but look at the area golf courses the last couple of days. If I'm not mistaken, there have been record crowds out there. What does that tell you? People want some escape."

Both the A's and Giants had workouts at their stadiums while baseball officials waited, then finally decided the Series would resume on October 27, after a 10-day delay.

"We take pride in playing the game right when we take the field," La Russa said. "This is not going to be a perfect way to go, but a lot of what happens will depend on what you do between the ears. I saw Bob Welch pitch here the day after his mother died. I never underestimate what a person can do."

La Russa was even more perturbed with people who said that if the A's won the Series, the victory would be tainted because of the earthquake and the delay. His thoughts went in the completely opposite direction.

"I think the club that wins it may have a claim on being more deserving than any club that's ever played," he said. "Who's ever had to go through this? Do you know how tough it is for these guys to practice? I'm very sensitive to what these players have been through since the first day of spring training.... Whoever can endure all that and win four games, in my opinion, may deserve more credit than any other club has.

"The point is, I don't really give a f—— whether you give the credit or not. I know it my own mind, it would be a tremendous achievement for this team.... It still has a lot of meaning to us."

La Russa tried to ensure that his team had the mental edge by taking his players to their spring training facility in Phoenix for two days of simulated games before the Series resumed. The delays seemed to keep on coming. The team bus was stuck in traffic for two hours en route to Candlestick for Game 3 and missed half of batting practice.

La Russa was anxious to win the next two games as soon as possible. Because of the delay, he was able to make a change in his pitching rotation, going back to Stewart and Mike Moore to pitch the third and fourth games instead of Welch and Storm Davis, as originally scheduled.

His pitching choices did not disappoint; Stewart won Game 3 13–7, a four-run rally by the Giants in the ninth making the outcome seem closer than the rest of the game. The following night, the A's built an 8–2 lead for Moore and held on for a 9–6 win and the championship. The A's never trailed at any point in the four-game sweep.

The celebration was low key. The team was not even treated to a parade, just a small rally in downtown Oakland. Stewart and other players spoke there.

"Last year when the Series was over, the one thing we all said in the clubhouse was that there were two teams that played in the World Series," he said. "One won, but there was only one ballclub that could expect to come back again next year. And we were that club."

The victory produced the usual World Series–winning perks for La Russa and his players, such as a trip to visit President George Bush at the White House. There were also some unexpected invitations for the manager, including one to a formal State Dinner at the White House and an appearance on the David Letterman television show.

While La Russa welcomed those requests, the A's victory also produced at least one unwanted development. The team had won just one World Series, and already the d-word, *dynasty*, was being thrown around. It was another challenge La Russa would have to figure out how to handle.

11

Three in a Row

Going into his third season with the A's, and after a spectacular two-year run of success, La Russa felt confident that his team was now, more than ever, a reflection of its manager. The adjectives that were most often used to describe La Russa—intense, competitive, prepared, focused—were now the adjectives being used to describe his team. It was one of the best compliments the manager could receive.

One player who certainly personified the attitude La Russa wanted in his players was third baseman Carney Lansford. While on vacation in Hawaii, Lansford watched the San Francisco 49ers win another Super Bowl.

"I was trying to figure out how the 49ers kept going, how they kept their intensity level up," Lansford told the *New York Times*. "I wanted to pay close attention to what the players said, and the thing that kept coming up was that they didn't want to be content with the last year. They wanted to stay focused with what they were trying to achieve."

Lansford decided to spend about $1,000 of his own money to have T-shirts made up for the A's players. The shirts contained two messages: "Contentment stinks" and "Stay focused." He gave the shirts to each of his teammates.

"I never felt there would be a problem, not with the guys on this club," Lansford said. "There's too strong a desire to win. It was just to give us some-thing to think about from the beginning. We won the World Series and that was great, but we knew it would be too easy this season to just go through the motions."

Perhaps the only player that La Russa was worried about was also one of the team's brightest stars, Jose Canseco. When he was sidelined in 1989 with his wrist injury, the A's learned that they could win without him. But they also knew that if he was in the lineup and playing well, they were a better team. The problem was that Canseco's personal focus had changed; he was no longer filled with the desire to be a complete player. As he had said a year earlier when confronted by La Russa after a strikeout, he was now an entertainer, putting on a show. He wanted to hit long home runs. Whether the A's won or lost was not as important to him as it used to be.

That attitude bothered La Russa immensely, as it did to the most focused of the team's players, like Stewart. As he said in the book *Champions,* the A's team was tainted by Canseco's attitude.

"We had bad chemistry all that year," Stewart said. "It all centered on Jose. It was always about Jose."

Dave Henderson said that Canseco's individuality was something the other players, and La Russa, had to work around to retain their focus.

Canseco was out of the lineup with a sore back when the A's arrived in Chicago in mid-June, leading the White Sox by only two games. After losing the opening game, 3–2, La Russa spent two hours replaying the game with his 80-year-old father, who was visiting from Tampa for the Father's Day weekend.

La Russa Sr. suggested moving Dave Henderson to the second spot in the A's lineup, and he responded with a 3-for-3 and three-RBI day in the A's win the next day. Oakland went on to win the next two games as well and left town with a four-game lead.

The White Sox came to Oakland the next weekend and swept the A's to cut their lead to one game. Bad blood began to brew between the two teams, particularly when Chicago pitcher Jack McDowell hit Canseco and McGwire with pitches in the middle game of the series.

"I don't think it's good baseball when the guy on the mound doesn't have good command and is trying to bury the ball inside time after time," La Russa told reporters. "If all he is trying to do is hit people, the season would be very short. He lacks command. So when he pitches inside, he hits people. I have an objection to that."

After McGwire was hit, La Russa came out of the dugout and had some heated words for Chicago catcher Ron Karkovice.

"He tried to intimidate me," Karkovice said. "It didn't work. I said a few words to hm, and he kept walking off. I said, 'Just go back to the dugout.'"

McDowell said it was just like college (he pitched at Stanford) where "something happened in every game."

Responded La Russa, "Tell him he [can] save his heroics for Stanford. This isn't college. It's the major leagues."

It was no real surprise when Gene Nelson relieved in the ninth inning and hit Karkovice with a pitch.

When the A's were back in Chicago in August, La Russa asked a friend to set up a visit for him with Notre Dame football coach Lou Holtz in nearby South Bend, Indiana. La Russa, who had been reading Holtz's book, *Fighting Spirit*, even gave a brief motivational talk to the Irish players.

Maybe it was the fighting spirit that also made La Russa mad when McGwire was again the target of a high and inside pitch, this time by Seattle's Eric Hanson, in mid-September. La Russa took out his frustration by whacking a bat against the concrete wall in the Kingdome dugout.

"I thought Hanson was being careless," La Russa said. "Mainly I was mad because McGwire had four homers in a week, and now a pitch like this was going to make him look inside. I want him protecting the outside part of the plate. I don't want anything to get in the way of us winning."

There was no questioning that La Russa's commitment to baseball, but he was also becoming more involved in animal rights issues, a cause he and Elaine strongly supported. Two years earlier, when La Russa learned the A's planned to have a parade of elephants, the team's longtime symbol, march around the stadium before a game, he protested enough to get the promotion scrapped, objecting to the way elephants were treated by circus owners.

La Russa also objected to fur coats being used in a fashion show staged by the player wives. In the off-season, he joined other advocates in a protest march at the state capital in Sacramento.

On one of the A's days off, on August 6, La Russa and his family went to Las Vegas to attend the trial of a man accused of abusing animals in his nightclub show. A sign on the refrigerator in his office said, "Protect Your Right to Arm Bears."

It had been during a home game in May against the Yankees that a cat got loose on the field and ran around for several minutes before La Russa was finally able to control it in the dugout. He turned it over to animal control authorities after the game, but when he and Elaine learned it was going to be euthanized, they claimed the cat, named it Evie after the wife of A's owner Walter Haas, and kept it until they found it a new home.

The La Russas later opened the nonprofit Animal Rescue Foundation, a no-kill facility that more than 17 years later, remains La Russa's biggest interest outside of baseball and his family.

"Tony Phillips [a former infielder] once said, 'Managers treat us all like dogs,'" La Russa said. "I told him, 'I don't treat any player as well as I treat my dogs.'"

La Russa, who had become a vegetarian soon after he and Elaine were married, was sincere about his affection for animals. The family's collection of pets eventually grew to include three dogs, nine cats, and two rats.

"I'm a baseball manager," he was quoted as saying that year in the *Sporting News*. "I'm not going to cross the line and get into something I don't know about. I'm not going to take a stand on animal experimentation. If they're killing animals for perfume, that's wrong. But if they can use it to cure AIDS, then I'm for it. Man is at the top of the hierarchy, but that doesn't mean he can abuse everything below him."

La Russa, of course, saw nothing wrong with his baseball team abusing opponents en route to its third consecutive division title. Even the distractions caused by Canseco did not derail the team from its mission of playing deep into October.

Canseco hit 37 homers and drove in 101 runs, but his average fell off to .274 and his strikeout total climbed to 157 in 481 at-bats, almost one every three times at bat. But when he was not hitting home runs, he was usually getting himself into La Russa's doghouse—which is what happened when he showed up at Yankee Stadium at 6:38 PM for a 7:30 game on September 7, two minutes before his group was scheduled to begin batting practice. Canseco had taken a cab to the stadium from the team's Manhattan hotel, and the driver got lost.

"It will be an expensive cab ride," said La Russa, who did not announce the amount he planned to fine Canseco.

"I got to see a lot of New York I've never seen before and never want to see again," Canseco said. "Worst driving I've ever seen, and my back is killing me from the cab."

La Russa wondered at times if he was losing the battle with Canseco, but he never stopped trying to work with him as a friend and a manager, treating Canseco as both an individual and as one of his players.

"I don't regard Jose just as a professional player who is here just to use his awesome talent," La Russa said. "I've always been struck with Jose as a person, so I deal in a respectful way with his person, and his traits, not just his professional traits.

"We talk. I don't get involved. I'm not his adviser. When he has problems he doesn't come to me, but I always think of him as a person first and a baseball player second. I've said before, I like Jose Canseco. The position he's in, and what he has to deal with, he's remarkable how he handles it."

Rickey Henderson was almost a model citizen by comparison to Canseco, and his numbers were awesome. He hit .325 with 28 homers and 119 runs scored en route to being named the league MVP. The A's were out of first place only nine days all season and all in the first half of the year. They rode the pitching of Stewart and Bob Welch to a 103-win season, making La Russa only the fifth manager in history to win three consecutive division titles.

Stewart won 22 games, his fourth consecutive 20-win year, but was topped by Welch's 27–6 performance. Eckersley was once again the consummate closer, earning 48 saves while allowing just 41 hits and four walks in 73⅓ innings, and giving up only five earned runs to net an almost unbelievable ERA of 0.61.

Eckersley seemed to benefit the most from La Russa's influence. "It took some getting used to for me, because I also was changing from starting to relieving," he said. "There was a lot of transition going on. I came to know him and appreciate him. I never played for anybody who was as wired from pitch to pitch.

"I think I was just as intense when I was pitching, and I was as intense as anybody, almost over the top at times. When I first got to Oakland, I know he was checking me out to see if I still had the fire in the belly. I took it as an insult, but I understood. I don't think anybody would question that about me if they knew me."

La Russa and Eckersley created the mold for the modern-day era of the ninth-inning closer who only came into a game when his team was ahead with a slim lead. Eckersley almost never came into a game before the ninth inning, or with runners already on base. It made him a better and more successful pitcher, he said.

"Why bring in a guy in a situation where if he makes one bad pitch the game is tied?" Eckersley said. "You need to give him some leeway. You should try to bring in a guy when he had the greatest chance of being successful. Some managers wait too long and want the reliever to come in and bail him out of a jam. Tony was the one who figured it out. I was getting accolades for 'changing the game' but it just made sense."

The players who had been with the A's the longest did not think La Russa was receiving enough credit for the team's success. "What he does," Lansford said at the time, "is very underrated."

The presence of Eckersley, of course, gave the A's a big advantage as they moved into the playoffs, once again facing the Red Sox for the American League pennant.

All the A's knew at least one fact going into that series: their manager would be prepared for every game, and he expected the same out of each of his players.

"Other people have pitchers' meetings and hitters' meetings, but here they actually have a plan of attack, how they're going at somebody," pitcher Rick Honeycutt said on the eve of the playoffs. "He gets an edge where other people don't get an edge, and that's what winning is about.

"He's created a workmanlike, professional attitude. Players go about their business. It's common knowledge that a team is going to take on the character of its manager. Tony doesn't let Jose slide or McGwire slide or Rickey slide. If there's something he doesn't like, and it's noticeable by everybody, he brings it up."

What was noticeable to everybody, of course, was La Russa's intensity in the dugout, which always rose to an even higher level during critical games, especially the playoffs and World Series.

"It makes me glad I'm out on the field instead of in the dugout," McGwire said. "People may think this is the easiest ballclub in the world to manage, but I think it may be the most difficult. You have great talent here, but you can have the best talent in the world and if it doesn't jell, you're not going to win. You've got a lot of different personalities here, but he takes that talent and those personalities and puts them together."

La Russa and Duncan had their starting pitchers lined up the way they wanted for the Red Sox, with Stewart again facing Roger Clemens in the opener. They dueled for six innings, with Clemens up 1–0 thanks to a Wade Boggs homer, before a tired Clemens left the game. The A's quickly tied the game up against the Red Sox bullpen, added a single run in the eighth to go ahead, and made the game a laugher with a seven-run ninth.

Welch got the ball for Game 2 and he and Eckersley combined for a 4–1 win. Once again the A's were heading back to Oakland with a 2–0 Series lead.

Mike Moore and the bullpen delivered another 4–1 win in Game 3, and once more the A's were one win away from their third consecutive pennant. Clemens stood in their way in Game 4—although not for long. He was ejected in the second inning after a heated argument with home plate umpire Terry Cooney and the A's went on to complete the sweep with a 3–1 win.

Most observers picked the A's to beat the Cincinnati Reds (and La Russa's childhood pal Lou Piniella) in the World Series, but La Russa admitted later that he wasn't as confident going into the Series as he had been a year earlier.

"We had won 103 games, but I thought we won some of those games on reputation," he said in *Champions*. "There were some slippages. When we got to our third postseason, we had lost our edge. It wasn't new anymore, and we were strutting around. Cincinnati just beat us to the punch in every way.... When we had a meeting before the Series, I could tell they weren't listening. I probably should have yelled and screamed, but I didn't. When we went out there, we were totally flat."

Eric Davis' two-run homer in the first inning of the opener, off Stewart, put the A's behind—and they stayed there as the Reds rolled to the four-game sweep. The loss in Game 2, 4–3 in ten innings, hurt the most. The A's thought they had a chance to win it until Canseco misplayed a fly ball, turning a would-be out into a triple and allowing the Reds to tie the game in the eighth inning en route to the victory.

After the A's returned home and lost Game 3, La Russa made a controversial move, benching Canseco for the fourth game. Canseco's wife, Esther, responded by calling the manager "a punk."

La Russa and Canseco met in the manager's office for an hour before the game, and Canseco publicly said he understood the manager's decision and admitted he was hurt and was playing at less than a hundred percent. That didn't prevent some of his teammates, particularly Stewart, from publicly criticizing Canseco's performance.

"I think too many other things are becoming an interference for him to concentrate a whole nine innings," Stewart told the *San Francisco Examiner*. "Mainly, battling with umpires and questioning balls and strikes. You can't concentrate on what you have to do up there. His concentration level is just shot."

The fact that Canseco was just 1-for-11 in the first three games—the hit was a home run in Game 2—after going 2-for-12 in the ALCS had plenty to do with the manager's decision to leave him out of the lineup, but he also was concerned about Canseco's defense.

Willie McGee started in right, and Canseco came up as a pinch-hitter in the ninth inning and made the next-to-last out of the Series.

The disappointment in the A's locker room was obvious. It didn't help that the star of the Series had been Jose Rijo, a former Oakland pitcher traded away by La Russa and Duncan.

"La Russa put a lot of pressure on me," Rijo said of his experiences in Oakland. "I felt he expected a lot. One day I was just smiling. He told me, 'Why are you smiling? Didn't you see the paper? You got your name by the 'L' [in the box score].'"

Now Rijo was smiling again. La Russa and the A's could do nothing but try to figure out how their team, by many accounts the best in baseball for three straight years, had only one world championship to show for all their efforts.

"He blamed himself," said coach Rene Lachemann of La Russa. "I told him he could not blame himself. Tony's philosophy isn't that the best team will win, it's that the team that is playing the best will win. That was exactly what happened against the Dodgers and Reds. They both played better than we did, even though we had the better team. Tony took both of those defeats very hard."

La Russa soon would have other problems to worry about as well.

CHAPTER 12

End of an Era

On New Year's Eve, third baseman Carney Lansford was riding a snowmobile on his Oregon property when he crashed into a barbed wire fence. Lansford suffered serious injuries to his left knee in the accident.

La Russa didn't know it at the time, but that turned out to be an early indication of what kind of year 1991 would be for the A's. Lansford, one of the steady leaders of the club, underwent surgery and was able to play in only five games all season. He had plenty of company in the trainer's room. On Opening Night in Minnesota, a line drive hit into the dugout broke the little finger of reliever Gene Nelson. By the first week of June, the A's had used the disabled list 13 times.

Part of the team's problems were mental. The biggest bruised ego belonged to Rickey Henderson, who had been upset ever since Canseco signed a new five-year, $23.5 million contract in the middle of the 1990 season, dwarfing the four-year $12 million contract Henderson had signed just months earlier. At the time he signed his deal, Henderson had become the highest paid player in the major leagues. Other contracts quickly exceeded his deal, but it was his teammate's deal that upset him. It said to him that the A's valued Canseco, despite all of his baggage, more than Henderson—quantifiably more.

"Rickey was unhappy with his contract a week after he signed it," Alderson was quoted as saying in *Champions*. "At the time we had the attitude that we wanted to keep all our stars. It was almost like a family feeling. So we went ahead and signed Jose to his contract. That probably contributed to the bad feeling with Rickey, but I think that would have happened anyway."

Henderson broke Lou Brock's career stolen-base record on May 1, but that was about his only highlight of the season. His batting average fell from .325 to .268. His dropoff was matched by several other players. Dave Stewart's four-year run of 20-plus victories ended as he suffered a pulled muscle in his side and won only 11 games. McGwire hit just .201 with 22 homers and did not play the final day of the season to ensure that his average would not fall below .200. Canseco, in fact, was the only star who compiled big offensive numbers, leading the AL with 44 home runs and driving in 122 runs. His average dropped again, however, from .274 to .266.

The A's stayed competitive for the first half of the season but by the All-Star break they found themselves in fifth place, even though they were only 2½ games behind Texas and Minnesota, who were tied for first.

Tom Kelly had arrived in Minneapolis as the manager of the Twins at the end of the 1986 season, and since then the A's and Twins had developed a nice rivalry. They were two small-market teams, led by aggressive managers who had a great deal in common.

Kelly, like La Russa, was a marginal player. He appeared in 49 games in the majors, all for the Twins in 1975, and hit .181. He turned to managing and quickly worked his way through the Minnesota farm system, taking control of the major league club with 23 games left in the 1986 season, just a month after his 36th birthday. Kelly led the Twins to the 1987 World Championship, and he immediately won the respect and admiration of La Russa, perhaps because he had come from a similar background and shared much of the same philosophy about the game.

"You had to be prepared when you played against Oakland, and if you weren't you were going to get run over," Kelly said. "You had to be on the top of your game and be prepared for things to happen. The best thing was to get him before he got you. If you didn't do that you were usually in for a long afternoon."

Kelly and La Russa talked often about their respective teams, and strategy; La Russa wanted to pick his opponent's brain just as he had always done with managers that he respected.

"I think we both had the opinion that you could never collect enough information," Kelly said. "You put all the information in your head and maybe some day you can apply it. The best teacher was always the experience you gained on the field.

"Tony would do different things at times. When they had runners on first and second he would call for a bunt, then he would take it off and try a hit-and-run instead. You had to be ready for that or you were going to get screwed."

One of Kelly's most vivid memories was a conversation with La Russa that concerned Stewart. "He was always interested in trying to figure out what you knew about his team," Kelly said. "For whatever reason, we had pretty good success against Stewart even though he was a great pitcher who every manager would have loved to have had on his team. Tony swore to me that we had his pitches, that somehow he was tipping them. We didn't."

What La Russa did not know, and Kelly never told him, was that the Twins did have the pitches from another Oakland starter figured out.

"The problem was, even though we knew that, we didn't do all that well against that guy," Kelly said. "I just remember laughing under my breath a little bit because it was one of those quirky things. He had the wrong guy."

What frustrated many of Kelly's players about playing against La Russa's team, however, was his strategy of trying to slow down the game in the late innings if he was behind. Part of that was through his constant changing of pitchers, trying to get an edge, but part of it also was no doubt hoping that the opponents would mentally wear down during the delays.

"If the game was maybe not going the way he wanted it to he could slow down the game," Kelly said. "It would really get your people on edge if you were not prepared for it. We constantly talked to our players about keeping their composure. You had to understand that was going to happen, and not get too anxious to get the game over with in the next four minutes because that was not going to happen."

Steinbach had the privilege in his career of playing for both La Russa and Kelly and seeing the A's-Twins rivalry from both perspectives.

"They were both very unique," Steinbach said "They each won, but they had different styles of managing. On plane flights we would sit and talk about what some of those games were like. I think it really is underwritten and not talked about enough about how good the AL West was in those years."

Before the A's hold on the division began to slip away, La Russa experienced a major meltdown in Chicago on June 1, when Steinbach was hit in the head by a pitch from the White Sox's Bobby Thigpen. It was a serious moment. Thigpen's fastball tailed toward Steinbach's head and struck him in the left temple. Luckily he was wearing a helmet with a flap protecting his ear or he possibly could have been killed. Observers said the sound of the baseball hitting the helmet echoed throughout the ballpark, a sickening sound.

Steinbach had suffered many facial injuries during his career, including a broken cheekbone, a hairline skull fracture, and a broken nose. The belief in the Oakland dugout was that, for whatever reason, Thigpen had thrown at Steinbach intentionally, a move that always brings out the violent side of La Russa.

This night, the violence was both physical and verbal. As Steinbach lay motionless near home plate, La Russa came out of the dugout, picked up Steinbach's bat and flung it toward the stands behind home plate. Luckily it hit the protective screen, in place to keep foul balls from injuring fans, but on this night keeping fans safe from a thrown bat.

Steinbach was taken from the field on a stretcher. The game resumed, but it was not long before a brawl broke out. Order was restored, and the A's ultimately won the game. Then came an ugly scene in the visiting manager's office, as reported by the *San Francisco Chronicle*.

None of the reporters in the room knew what to say to La Russa, because they knew he was ready to explode. Finally someone spoke up, "How is he?" La Russa said, "I don't know." Reporter Bob Glass, a 64-year-old man, was in the group of reporters, covering the game for the Associated Press. He spoke up, saying, "That had to be a very scary moment."

La Russa, who had been shaving, turned around and screamed at Glass. "I don't want to talk about that bullshit," he yelled.

"OK, but don't yell at me," Glass said.

"I'll yell if I f—ing want to," La Russa said.

Glass just happened to be the innocent victim of La Russa's rage, but then he compounded the situation. As La Russa was trying to get out of his office and away from reporters, Glass yelled back, "Be a man."

La Russa yelled back, but Glass was not intimidated. "Try to act like a human being," he said.

La Russa had to be restrained from physically attacking Glass. By this point, the players knew something was happening and a group led by Stewart and Rickey Henderson got Glass out of the locker room.

Glass explained later that it was not the first time he and La Russa had been at odds after a game. The first exchange had been years earlier when La Russa was managing the White Sox.

"He's a psycho," Glass told the *Chronicle*. "There was one game in the mid-'80s when Tim Laudner beat him with a three-run homer off Rich Dotson. Later he asked me what the Twins were saying in their clubhouse. I told him they were talking about Greg Luzinski and the cheap hits he got. Tony started screaming and yelling, throwing things around the room. Right then and there I knew what kind of personality he was. The man is a psycho."

The entire exchange between La Russa and Glass was repeatedly shown on Chicago television stations.

Steinbach was hospitalized overnight but luckily he was not seriously injured. He had a concussion and reported some dizziness, a headache, and that his hearing was a "little muffled," but he was allowed to fly back to Oakland with the team.

A day after the incident La Russa had not calmed down, and said he had no regrets about his actions.

"What would I do differently?" he asked reporters. "To me, throwing the bat was immaterial to what happened in the game. What does that have to do with anything?"

That comment inspired the San Francisco media to go on the offensive against La Russa. Writing in the *Chronicle*, columnist Lowell Cohn said, "The A's manager was enraged about everything that had happened, and he needed a victim. He couldn't vent his anger on the umpires, his players, or the White Sox, so he went after the best available target and the one he thought would offer the least resistance. He's used to writers cowering before his anger, but Glass refused, and for that we should respect the AP reporter."

Kit Stier, a veteran reporter and the A's beat writer for the *Oakland Tribune*, witnessed the entire incident and wrote a column for his newspaper entitled "Out of Control" and described everything that happened.

"Any person who throws a bat in the direction of a stadium seating area is guilty of irresponsible and dangerous behavior," Stier wrote in the column. "For the manager of a major league team to do so...is even worse."

When La Russa read the column, he became angry and later confronted Stier when the two were on the field before a game.

"Tony was really pissed," Stier said. "He didn't like the column at all. We were standing along the third-base line at the Coliseum and he said, 'You know, I don't always tell you guys the truth.'

"I said, 'I know that, no manager does. It's kind of an unwritten understanding between writers and the manager and players. But when you are telling me that to my face you lose all credibility to me.' He didn't like that either."

Several months later, La Russa was in a much calmer mood when he talked about the incident with Art Spander of the *San Francisco Examiner*. "The incident seems to represent one of the problems with sports in this era," La Russa said. "The first thing is a hitter was lying on the ground, and when I ran out there I thought he might be dead. That wouldn't excuse me from doing something stupid, like hitting the catcher with the bat or throwing it into the stands. But I threw it into the screen. I'm not proud I did it, but I did it.

"But what's so typical of the '80s and '90s is afterward, by a ratio of 19:1, maybe 99:1, the issue is what happened in the clubhouse, not about the condition of Terry Steinbach. It should have been 99:1 the other way. I had known Bob Glass, and he's not a troublemaker, but I was real hot. And I didn't want to start a verbal war with the White Sox. If I was as cold and calculating as everybody says, I wouldn't have done that, would I?...

"One of the troubles now is that baseball writers don't write baseball. I still believe the fans want to read about how Walt Weiss makes the double play or Dave Stewart worked a hitter. Instead, the dominant attitude is, 'What's the story? What's the controversy? Why worry about why Jose was 10 minutes late to practice?'"

While the public had a good view of that episode, a much more private example of how much La Russa cares about his players occurred several weeks later. On July 25, the A's were playing the Indians in Cleveland and carried a 7–4 lead into the bottom of the eighth inning. With two outs and runners on second and third, La Russa went to his bullpen and called for Eckersley, despite the fact that it was not a typical situation in which the pitcher was brought into games.

Eckersley coughed up a two-run single to Mike Aldrete to cut Oakland's lead to 7–6. Jerry Browne came off the bench and hit a two-run homer, the only home run he hit all season, to put the Indians ahead 8–7. The Cleveland bullpen preserved the lead in the ninth for the victory.

"It was getaway day and we were going to Baltimore after the game," Eckersley said. "I was bumming. We got to the hotel about 4:00 in the morning, and all of the hotel keys were in envelopes laying on a table in the lobby. I got mine, and when I opened the envelope in the elevator to take out the key, there was a note stuck inside. It said, 'Eck, you're the best. Tony.'

"That may not seem like a lot, but it let me go to sleep. I had tears in my eyes, that's how much it meant to me. It said it all about him. What do you say to somebody? How do you keep people on the top of their game and make it where it is meaningful. Somebody can say 'You're all right' and pat you on the back, but that's not enough, it doesn't cut it."

Eckersley went out and earned saves in his next nine appearances. He did not allow another home run in his next 17 outings.

Unfortunately for the A's, Eckersley's good performance comprised most of the positive news in the second half of the season. La Russa spent much of his time puzzling over the increasing problems with Canseco and the effect they were starting to have on the rest of the club.

CHAPTER 13

The Canseco Problem

Canseco was always the focus of fans when the A's were on the road, and when unruly fans crossed the line, Canseco did not hesitate to stir it up. Incidents happened in New York—after his well-publicized trip to Madonna's apartment—and Baltimore. But La Russa was more concerned with Canseco's performance, or lack thereof, on the field. The manager also got upset when Canseco told reporters he did not think La Russa had properly come to his defense in two arguments he had with umpire Joe Brinkman on ball-strike calls. The reporters naturally relayed those comments to La Russa, who, after accusing the reporters of "trying to stir up shit to write," went into the clubhouse screaming at Canseco.

As the team dropped in the standings in September, Canseco complained about the lack of fan support at the Coliseum and hinted that he might ask for a trade, remarks that irritated Stewart and the team's other veterans. Canseco and the team's other controversial star, Henderson, were on Stewart's mind at the end of the season, with the pitcher wondering whether the A's could win without them or not.

"We wouldn't know that unless they were both gone and [we] see how we play without them," Stewart said in an article in the *Sporting News*. "In both cases, if something could be done—a trade, if that's what you're talking about—you're going to get talented players for them.

"And really, as you've seen this year, pitching is the key to winning anyway. It's a matter of how much you can take. It's as if you have a mole on your face. You may not like it and it might be painful to relieve yourself of the mole. Your other solution is to just live with it."

Trade rumors came from Toronto and the Yankees, but in the end, the team decided not to deal Canseco.

"We did some soul searching," La Russa said. "It was real clear, as far as the manager and coaches, that we wanted to keep the club together and try to win it again in '92."

There was no question that team ownership and management had confidence in La Russa. He was given a two-year extension at the start of spring training, running through 1994, and only days later began to earn his money when a moping Henderson touched off a mini-controversy. Lansford was quoted as saying that if Henderson's mood did not improve, he could become "a cancer on the team."

La Russa reacted by chastising the media, then closing the A's clubhouse to reporters, and finally cautioning his players to be very guarded in their comments to reporters. On a radio show he accused the press of "sensationalizing" Lansford's comment.

Only a week or so later, after the tension had calmed a bit, the A's found themselves in another frenzy. Canseco was hit by a pitch in an exhibition game against the Giants, which led to a bench-clearing brawl. Later in the game, with the Giants ahead by a run, Will Clark came to the plate in the sixth inning to face Eckersley. La Russa ordered an intentional walk, a very rare move for the manager even in regular-season play.

When reporters questioned the move, La Russa naturally had an answer waiting.

"The best practice is trying to win," he said. "That's why I like these games with the Giants. It's not your normal, sleepy spring training game. It's intense out there. Why did I walk Clark? That's just what I'd do in that situation. You talk about Eck needing work, well, the thing he needs more than anything else is to come out of that inning with a zero."

Clark was dumbfounded by the move, because it was a game in which the result did not matter to anyone—except, apparently, La Russa.

"That's Tony," Clark said. "Jim Lefebvre once said that 'when the ballgame begins, Tony La Russa has no friends.'"

Columnist Bruce Jenkins of the *San Francisco Chronicle* wrote, "That's Tony. That's an insight into the A's dynasty, a reason they played in three straight World Series and why they've got a shot at returning. La Russa's style might not be appealing to everybody. It might seem downright inappropriate at times. But this is what a competitive, winning manager looks like, and he's not going to change for anybody, any time."

As has been the case throughout most of his tenure in Oakland, La Russa's team was able to put all of the distractions aside and play well when the regular season began. A 14–8 April put the A's at first in the division, where they remained into the summer. Along the way, La Russa got involved in a verbal spat with Stewart and almost came to blows with rookie Yankee manager Buck Showalter, who thought La Russa was yelling at and trying to intimidate his players in a game on May 17. La Russa thought the Yankee pitchers were intentionally throwing at his hitters. When Showalter stood at the top of his dugout steps and seemed to challenge La Russa to a fight, the Oakland manager charged toward the Yankee dugout. Umpire Al Clark had to restrain him. Players on both sides got involved, and the melee lasted for several minutes.

Yankee catcher Matt Nokes was one of the players yelling at La Russa.

"Last year he screamed at me, 'We'll show you what a knockdown pitch is,'" Nokes said. "In the next at-bat they hit me in the head."

La Russa disputed Nokes' account of that incident.

"Trying to throw strikes inside is one thing," La Russa said. "I had no problem with that. Anytime the ball goes above the shoulder, though, that's different. If we do it, I stop it. I don't know if you can document this, but I don't think we have ever hit a guy in the head on a club I've managed since 1979."

That episode proved there still was some fight left in the A's. When the team arrived in Minnesota to open a three-game series on July 27, the A's were three games behind the division-leading Twins. Oakland won 9–1 and 12–10 in the first two games, but trailed 4–2 going into the ninth inning of the third game. A Minnesota win would increase the division lead to two games.

With Twins' closer Rick Aguilera on the mound, the A's Eric Fox delivered a three-run homer that wiped out Minnesota's lead. After Eckersley retired the dazed Twins in the bottom of the ninth, the two teams found themselves tied for first.

The success had come despite the fact the A's projected starting outfield of Rickey Henderson, Dave Henderson, and Canseco had not played one game together that season, due to injuries.

Canseco, in fact, had a terrible July, limited to just 34 at-bats. His average for the season had fallen to .244. In a game on August 10, Canseco struck out in the fifth inning, then asked to be removed from the game, complaining of a sore back. By the time the A's finished a 5–3 win over the White Sox, Canseco had left the stadium.

"Nobody was happy about that," Lansford told reporters. "To me, staying around is a sign of caring. The team is out there busting their butts, and if you leave, it shows you don't care…. I understand his back is sore, but my legs are killing me, and I was here."

La Russa held a closed-door meeting with Canseco, which lasted nearly an hour. Canseco told reporters he had left the stadium because of a personal matter, but would not elaborate. La Russa said Canseco would be disciplined, but "that stays within the family."

Of the multitude of injuries that the Athletics suffered over their season, there was one that left the team amused. La Russa strained a groin muscle while pursuing a foul ball in the dugout.

"I was trying to make a play on the ball and my left foot slipped," La Russa explained. "I went down like a shot. There wasn't one guy in the dugout who wasn't laughing. Nobody asked, 'Are you all right?' They were just laughing. I wanted the ball to ricochet and hit every one of those guys."

Nobody on the A's, however, was laughing at Canseco, who now was publicly feuding with umpires in addition to angering his own teammates. He was ejected from consecutive games for arguing ball-strike calls.

"We try to calm him down because we need him on the field," Lansford said. "But you can only hold him back for so long."

That was a fact La Russa knew as well. "He has to realize that he's not going to get the same strike zone as a Wade Boggs because a batter only gets the close calls after he has developed some consistency over the years," La Russa said. "It takes six or seven years to get a good reputation. I can't get mad at Jose for complaining about really bad calls. But when he doesn't get the benefit of a borderline call, then he has to turn the other cheek and just keep playing."

By now La Russa was used to Canseco's ranting and raving. He had not been so calm in 1987, his second year in Oakland, when the manager watched as Canseco failed to hustle on a play. When the 6'4", 240-pound Canseco returned to the dugout, the 6'1", 190-pound manager said, "Do that again, and I'll knock you on your ass."

Over next five years, the two had battled back and forth. On August 31, with the A's 7½ games ahead of the Twins with 32 games remaining in the season, a headline in the *Chronicle* said, "Feuding A's—A Lock for the Pennant." That night, there would be one less member of the A's to feud with either his manager, the fans, the media, or his teammates.

Canseco was on deck, preparing to bat in the first inning of Oakland's game against Baltimore, when La Russa summoned him back to the dugout. He pulled him from the game and informed him the A's had just traded him to the Texas Rangers.

"I thought it was a joke," Canseco said.

Ths A's had been trying to bolster their pitching staff for September and postseason play, and to be eligible for the postseason roster, a player had to be acquired before midnight on the 31st. The A's wanted pitchers Jeff Russell and Bobby Witt from Texas, and had to include Canseco in the deal. The Rangers also traded outfielder Ruben Sierra to Oakland.

A few days after he joined the Rangers, Canseco told reporters that maybe the trade would work out for the best.

"Maybe I wore out my welcome in Oakland," he said. "I fell into a trap. The shoes people put out there for me are very difficult to fill. And if I fill them, the shoes just get bigger. It's sad, but I don't think I'll ever be able to fulfill the expectations that people have for me."

The A's players applauded the move. "I was one of the guys that had a say and I said to get him out of here," said Dave Henderson. "It got to the point where he thought he was bigger than the team and he started to act like it. One thing we preached was that we were a team, one of 25."

Canseco wondered if his use of steroids had anything to do with the trade but the topic was never brought up by Oakland officials, players, or the media. The players, of course, were aware of Canseco's steroids use but did not believe their use was as widespread on the team as Canseco would claim in future years.

"I showered and used the restroom and hung out in the locker room and I didn't see any syringes or vials or anything of the sort," Steinbach said. "I was the first player there and generally the last one to leave the majority of my career. I'm not saying it wasn't there, but it was not like he depicted it—that right next to the toothbrushes were syringes and a daily dose of steroids."

Added Dave Henderson, "I knew something was going on with Jose, but I thought it was unfair to guys like me who weren't on it. We looked at him and said 'it works.' But the simple answer was that if you were against drugs you wouldn't take steroids. It was that simple. As a teammate, though, we were not going to blow the whistle on him."

Ever since he began managing, La Russa's goal for every season was to get to September with a chance to win, then take the best shot. That was a lesson he repeatedly taught to his players.

Trading Canseco, in almost everyone's mind, gave Oakland its best chance to win.

"Guys started to resent the fact that he was not respecting the game by doing things like not showing up on time," Lansford said. "We wanted to give it our best shot to win." Whether the A's could win without Canseco remained to be seen.

For the first five games after the Canseco trade, that answer to the question was no. Still, they had a 4½ game division lead over the Twins and there were three weeks left in the season. Panic was far from setting in at the Coliseum.

Just two days later, the A's came alive and went on a 10-game winning streak, including a three-game sweep of the Twins. Twelve wins in 13 games boosted the lead to nine games with just 12 games to play, effectively ending the race.

In a fitting end to the regular season, the A's clinched the division while having a team party at Mac's, an Oakland sports bar, watching the Twins lose to the White Sox.

"It almost had to be this way," La Russa said. "Nothing fell into place, and yet we won."

La Russa admirers ranked the 1992 regular season as perhaps the best managing job of his career. It was quite a feat, the way he juggled the injuries, subpar performances, bruised egos, and the Canseco trade and still came away with the team's fourth division title in six years.

He arrived at the party about 30 minutes after the division victory became official, and was immediately doused with champagne by Steinbach and Lansford.

"This one is special," La Russa said. "There is a real talent base on the club, and you can't lose sight of that. Key people would go down at critical times and this team absolutely refused to get discouraged. They refused to get beat."

The A's used the disabled list 22 times, had 44 players appear in at least one game, and used 56 different outfield combinations. They employed 11 different left fielders, seven center fielders, and 12 right fielders. The team had only one .300 hitter and no 20-game winners.

What they had, other than La Russa, was Eckersley in the bullpen. In addition to his 51 saves, the A's were 73–4 when they led going into the eighth inning and 82–1 when they led entering the ninth. In 80 innings, Eckersley issued only five unintentional walks. He had a 7–1 record and 1.91 ERA and was named both the league MVP and the Cy Young Award winner.

Before the playoffs could open in Toronto, the A's had one piece of unfinished business to complete: Canseco's return to Oakland as a member of the Texas Rangers. It was the night after the victory party that the Rangers came to town. Even though Canseco was not in the lineup, he made plenty of headlines by leveling major charges at his former team and manager. Unaware that his former teammates earlier that day had voted him a full playoff share, Canseco said he was never accepted or appreciated by his teammates or manager and that La Russa was not a "player's manager."

Those charges provoked the expected rebuttals.

"This organization supported him, protected him, and literally lied for him," La Russa told reporters. "We humiliated ourselves doing it.

"What really bothers me is the shots he took at the organization…. I would tell half-truths in order to keep things private. We publicly supported him to the point of lying, which was humiliating…. He was offered help for every one of his problems.

"I believe his priorities switched. His emphasis on winning slipped on his priority list."

And to La Russa, of course, there is no greater sin a player can commit than to not be a hundred percent focused and committed to trying to win every game.

"He believes that whatever he does is right," La Russa said. "He can do no wrong. Baseball history is full of big talents who were also big pains. Talent is something to be revered, but what you hope is that you have talent with a good attitude. You tolerate a big ego if the player will at least go out there with a desire to win."

After he had a couple of days to absorb the criticism, La Russa became more analytical with his reaction.

"I was more sad than upset," he told the *Boston Globe*. "I feel betrayed for the entire organization, from the Haases to the clubhouse kids. He doesn't care about winning anymore. He's lost the focus on why he was given that contract, not to be a star personality but to be a star performer…. Not accepted? We have a lot of team parties and he was invited to all of them. It's not anyone else's fault that he didn't show up. He complains that we blamed the 1990 World Series on him. Yes, a lot of us were upset when he made a halfhearted effort at a fly ball that should have been caught, but we blamed him only for that play.

"Maybe he's conned people so well over the years that he starts believing his own con. It's partly our fault, and the fault of the game. Organizations build up young players as franchise cornerstones. They create idols and icons, and they start to believe everything, that they are stars, not baseball players like a Robin Yount or a George Brett or a Kirby Puckett. They believe that they are bigger than their teams. They forget why they have mansions and fancy cars and millions of dollars before they are 25. I see things that make me sick, especially for the game itself."

What made La Russa smile, however, were high notes like seeing shortstop Mike Bordick finish the year with a .300 average. La Russa sat Bordick down on the final day of the season, just to make certain he would maintain that average. After making that mistake once before, he was glad to have the opportunity to preserve his guy's .300.

"It would be a shame if we wound up hitting .299 or .298," Lansford said. "That's the class guy that Tony is. It's what makes Tony Tony. I don't care what any dumb fool says, Tony is a player's manager."

La Russa did not need players coming to his defense, but they did—not only in his home clubhouse, but from across the country. In Baltimore, pitcher Storm Davis, who had played for Oakland in 1988–89 (and would return later in his career), gushed about La Russa to the *Washington Post*.

"He doesn't want the credit, but he deserves it," Davis said. "He knows how to manage people. He knows how to handle them. He knows how to get the most out of them. And then they just go out and do it."

Davis remembered how during his first season with the A's, La Russa initiated what turned into a nearly hour-long conversation about Davis' Christian beliefs.

"He's the only manager I ever had who sat down with me and asked me to go into detail about my religious beliefs," Davis told the *Post*. "He wanted to see what kind of person I was, what kind of competitor I was.... It almost takes you back to high school, and the relationship you had with your coach then."

Eckersley also spoke lavishly about his feelings for La Russa. "I had a personal connection to him." he said. "He was an older brother to me. I felt he cared about me as a person, and that adds to the relationship. Every player wants to feel that their manager has confidence in them. For me, in my job, I needed that more than anybody. I felt he had all the confidence in the world in me."

That was certainly true, and never was it more in evidence than during the playoffs against the Blue Jays. Some observers questioned La Russa's decision in the opening game to bring in Jeff Russell with two outs in the eighth, with a man on second and Oakland ahead 3–2, a spot where he traditionally would have called on Eckersley. Russell gave up a game-tying single to John Olerud, but La Russa's old friend Harold Baines homered in the ninth and Eckersley preserved that lead in the bottom of the inning.

When asked about his reasoning, La Russa had the numbers ready— Olerud was 0-for-4 in his career against Russell while he was 3-for-7 off Eckersley, although all four of the outs were strikeouts.

"If there's nobody on, yeah, I bring in Eckersley," La Russa said. "With a man on second, against a guy who hits him well, I want Russell there. Another thing is that the last couple of times out, Eck wasn't quite as sharp as usual. I just didn't think it was a good shot.

"If I bring him in there, I'm just covering my ass. As soon as you start covering your ass, the players find out."

After David Cone beat the A's in Game 2, the series moved to Oakland. How focused was La Russa on the series? When the team's charter flight arrived back in Oakland at about 3:00 AM, a bus took the team and others in the traveling party back to the Coliseum. La Russa got off, and forgot that his two daughters, Bianca, 13, and Devon, 10, were sleeping in the back of the bus. The bus was headed back to the highway when a frantic phone call alerted the driver that the girls were still on the bus.

A 7–5 win in Game 3 put Toronto up by a game. The A's appeared headed for an easy victory in Game 4, which would have tied up the series, but this time Eckersley failed to come through. Roberto Alomar hit a two-run homer off Eckersley in the ninth to tie the game, then Toronto won in the eleventh and now had a commanding 3–1 advantage. He considered that moment as bad, if not worse, as the Kirk Gibson homer.

Worse than the loss, however, were the outbursts from several Toronto players who were angered by Eckersley's animated reaction when he struck out Ed Sprague in the eighth inning. One of the most vocal critics was outfielder Devon White, which prompted a retort from La Russa. "I'd like to see Devon White make a living trying to hit off Eckersley," he said. "He'd be carrying a lunch pail."

Once again, La Russa was concentrating so much on the game that he left the stadium afterward and didn't realize for a few minutes that his daughters had been at the game and were still at the stadium.

Stewart briefly gave the A's a life with a 6–2 victory in Game 5, sending the series back to Toronto. La Russa was obviously happy about the win, but had another special reason.

He had made the decision before the game to bench Lansford and play Jerry Browne at third base. La Russa was well aware of Lansford's intention to retire at the end of the 1992 season and he knew that if the A's lost that game, the season would have been over.

"Tony told me, 'If we're going to win later on, we need to rest you right now,'" Lansford said. "Hey, I was bone tired yesterday. Tony saw that. He's very good at reading his players and we've been together a long time. I thought it was a great move, getting another left-handed hitter in the lineup. That's why Tony is as good as he is."

There is a sentimental side to La Russa, even though it is not displayed in public very often, and he knew the risk he was taking by benching Lansford. He said after the game, however, that if the A's had been behind in the late innings he would have brought Lansford into the game.

"I think sentiment is a part of managing," La Russa told reporters. "You don't make moves and just forget about somebody's feelings…. At the same time, you can't let that interfere with winning. Yes, you care deeply, but you can't be too emotional. You have to be aware of what the costs are, and what's really going to help the club."

La Russa sent Mike Moore to the mound for Game 6, trying to force the first seventh game of his career, but the outcome was never in doubt. Toronto cruised to a 9–2 win and its first American League pennant.

La Russa spoke to his players before opening the clubhouse to the media.

"That was the most emotional I have ever seen him," McGwire said afterward. "He told us how satisfying this year was, how gutty we were to make it so far. He thanked us for giving such an effort in the playoffs."

La Russa's performance was rewarded by his selection by the Baseball Writers Association of America as the AL Manager of the Year, the third time he had received the award.

La Russa did not want to hear it, but the A's run of dominance in the AL West was over. Free agency and retirements were gutting the club, and when virtually nobody picked the A's to finish higher than third in the division in 1993, La Russa was upset.

"I was amazed at how many people have us fifth or sixth," La Russa said. "Naturally I think we have as good a chance as anybody in the division. We've got a bunch of pluses and some question marks. But show me one club in our division that hasn't got the same thing."

It turned out the critics were right, for once, and La Russa was wrong. He admitted a year later that the season's problems began in spring training when he "misread" the team.

"I blame myself more than anybody," La Russa said. "The manager sets the course in spring training. I believe in the value of a good spring training. It was obvious to me the club wasn't properly prepared. The blame goes to the guy who sets up the camp and that was me.

"You can try to work on it all, but you wind up with a club that has an idea about everything but is prepared in nothing. You have to pick your priorities and touch on the other things. If you pick the wrong priorities, you set your club back…. If you choose wrong, it can hurt you."

The A's fell from first to worst, finishing with 94 losses, the worst dropoff by a major league team since the 1915 Philadelphia A's lost 109 games after a 99-win season.

"[Orioles manager] Earl Weaver told me that he had his biggest problems in the years after he won," La Russa said. "He'd expect players to do the same thing the next year, and he'd be looking at what he expected, not what he was getting. It would be halfway through the season before he realized that he wasn't getting the production he expected, and by that time it was too late."

La Russa knew much earlier that 1993 was going to be a difficult year for the A's. He wanted to make certain his players understood that too, and did not become complacent or lazy, or expect to win the division title without working for it.

"Each year is a challenge," he said. "What you've done before makes no difference once the season begins. Every year we have to prove again that we can do it."

La Russa tried to capture the players' attention when he ordered a mandatory, full-scale workout on what had been a scheduled off day, an unusual decision in the major leagues. "There's nothing unique happening out there, no mysterious force out there against us," he told reporters. "All we have to do is reverse things."

When the team's starting pitching continued to struggle, La Russa and Duncan came up with an idea to have three pitchers each pitch three innings a game, almost like in spring training.

"What have we got to lose?" La Russa said. Added Duncan, "It's something Tony and I have talked about, but primarily applying it to an expansion team. When you have a lot of young talent, this would be one way to develop it."

The idea, however unique, did not work any better than the traditional pitching rotation. The A's went 1–4 in games using the "pitching committees" and then went back to a regular rotation. Using the system could unfortunately only give a starting pitcher a defeat; there was no way for him to collect a victory.

With the team struggling for the first time since La Russa arrived in Oakland, there was a question of how the manager would react—would he decimate the postgame buffet or throw some other kind of tantrum?

"I was always taught there's a professional way to win and a professional way to lose," La Russa said. "I think it's important for our team to be professional. When you're losing you're being tested to see if you're going to be phony. There are managers who will stand by the clubhouse door and yell at their players so the media will hear them and think they're getting something done. That's what I mean by phony.

"I argue with umpires privately. I'm careful not to give into theatrics when times are tough. I don't like it when somebody gives in to outside pressure and puts on a show for others."

No one could accuse him of putting on a show for the media's sake, but La Russa did have plenty of moments during the season when he got upset. After dropping 9 of 11 games on a road trip in July, he refused to let his players eat.

"I'm not trying to make statements," he explained. "I'm just trying to remind people that it's not acceptable to lose when you're not competitive. From our part, today was not acceptable."

The A's had at least *some* fight left in them. In a game against Milwaukee on August 24. La Russa and Eckersley got into a heated argument with umpire Dale Scott about ball and strike calls, and La Russa also got into it with Milwaukee manager Phil Garner. That turned into a full-scale brawl featured nine ejections and a serious injury to the Brewers' B.J. Surhoff.

Perhaps La Russa's most vocal outburst came in response to a commissioner's study about the length of games, in which the A's were cited as the biggest culprits, averaging three hours, three minutes in 1992, but by a negligible margin over other clubs like Toronto and Detroit.

"Later I heard [Bud Selig] said it in a joking manner, but every time this issue comes up, we're the team responsible," La Russa said. "I think it runs a little deeper than that. They say we make too many pitching changes. You'll see us use two, even three pitchers in the late innings of a game. But that's how we operate here. Why should we change?"

The plan to add two expansion teams and split the NL and AL into three divisions, adding a wild-card team to the playoffs in each league, also came under fire from La Russa. "I am not a big fan of not finishing first and still getting into the playoffs," he said. "I have no problem with the extra level of playoffs. I think that might add something. But if they want eight teams in the playoffs, then they should make eight divisions.... My opinion is that if you don't finish first, you should go home. The wild card works for me in football, but I don't think it belongs in baseball."

The players who had been with La Russa the longest, such as Eckersley, knew how hard the 1993 season was for La Russa. "You never enjoy losing," Eckersley said. "But with all the success we've had, it's that much worse. There's a lot of pride in this organization, starting with Tony. It made it tough on Tony. He said, 'Your stats are your stats but last place stays with me forever.'"

The World Series home run that Eckersley allowed to Kirk Gibson had sat with him for five years before he finally got another chance to face Gibson.

"Before he came up, I smiled at him and he smiled back," Eckersley said. "I've been waiting five years to get him out—and he got another hit."

It was that kind of season for La Russa, Eckersley, and the rest of the A's, and La Russa made it clear he did not want to go through another season like that.

"Last season, when we realized we couldn't finish first, we thought the best thing would be to get something positive out of the season, and I think we did," he said. "We wanted to give our young pitchers innings and our young hitters at-bats. They showed they could compete right away and hopefully it will pay off this year.

"I can see getting back to where we were. One reason we had such a good run is that we separated the opportunities. We didn't look around and say, 'Hey, we can be good for five or six years.' We paid attention and focused on what we had to do each year. I think that's what we'll be able to do this year."

Despite his confidence, most of the media members, including the beat writers who covered the A's, picked the A's to finish no higher than third in the new AL West. "He asked us all one day where we were picking the team and nobody said higher than third," said reporter Mike Lefkow, the beat writer for the *Contra Costa Times*. "He was steaming. He didn't say anything, but you could tell."

The *Times* was La Russa's local paper and he read it every day. La Russa read Lefkow's preview once the A's returned home for the start of the regular season. As soon as he saw the writer at the stadium, he let him have it.

"I was screaming back at him," Lefkow said. "He was telling me they sold most of their season tickets in our circulation area, and the fans were going to be a little reluctant to buy tickets because I had picked them third. I was yelling at him that I was not on the team payroll and I could pick his team where I wanted, and this was the team I saw."

Two weeks later, they got into another screaming match over a story Lefkow had written about pitcher Bobby Witt. Ironically, Lefkow was in the clubhouse chatting with Witt when La Russa confronted him.

"He thought I was too harsh," Lefkow said. "Witt didn't say anything about it. Tony came up yelling and screaming. He told Bobby not to talk to me anymore. As soon as Tony walked away, Witt and I continued our conversation.

"It was always 'us against the world,'" Lefkow said of the manager's philosophy. "He can be the nicest guy in the world until the game starts. One day in spring training he pointed out that the first exhibition game was the next day and he said, 'I'm going to be a different man tomorrow,' and he sure was. That's partially why he is such a good manager. I did have my ups and downs with him, but I will say I learned more baseball from him than any other manager I ever covered."

La Russa may have had a love-hate relationship with the press, but reporters recognized the manager's spirit for what it really was, commitment to his team, and they couldn't ignore his talent.

ATHLETICS

TONY LA RUSSA ss-2b

A superstar athlete in his youth, La Russa caught the attention of a number of major-league scouts. But an early injury would hamper his professional career. (Topps, 1964)

After managing less than three seasons in the minor leagues, La Russa was handed the reins to the Chicago White Sox in 1979. (Getty Images)

Even as a young manager, La Russa was a spirited competitor and defender of his players. (Getty Images)

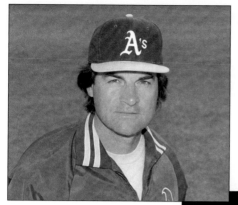

After seven years of managing the White Sox, La Russa was fired. White Sox owner Jerry Reinsdorf would later call that dismissal "the biggest mistake I've ever made." Eleven days later, La Russa was in the dugout as the manager of the Oakland A's. (AP Images)

It didn't take La Russa long to shape the Oakland Athletics into world champions. Not even an earthquake could deter them, as the A's beat the San Francisco Giants in four games in the "Battle of the Bay," the 1989 World Series. (Getty Images)

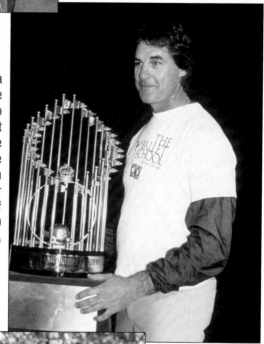

Members of the Oakland Athletics look on as fans rush from the stadium in the wake of an earthquake that struck just before Game 3. (AP Images)

Mark McGwire, Ron Kittle, Tony La Russa, Walt Weiss, Ozzie Guillen and Jose Canseco pose for a photo before a 1991 game between the Oakland Athletics and Chicago White Sox. All five players were Rookies of the Year who were managed by La Russa. (Getty Images)

Rickey Henderson (above) "was unhappy with his contract a week after signing it." Henderson, who was the highest-paid player in baseball until teammate Jose Canseco (left) signed a deal for almost double Henderson's amount. It would be one of many factors that contributed to the team's struggles in the early '90s. (Getty Images)

La Russa was always in search of a competitive edge and sought other coaches' perspectives and philosophies on winning. He asks many of his friends to speak with his players and motivate them. Frequent visitors to the Cardinals' training camp in Jupiter, Florida include basketball coach Bob Knight (top left) and football coaches Bill Belichick (top right) and Bill Parcells (bottom, right, shown with Cardinals owner David Pratt). (AP Images)

Tensions mounted early between La Russa and Ozzie Smith, who believed that his years with the Cardinals guaranteed a starting position at shortstop. (AP Images)

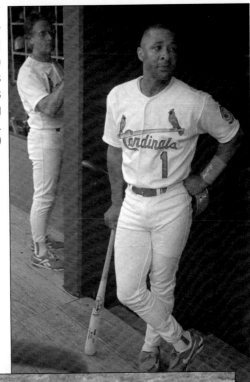

In 1997, La Russa traded three players to the Athletics in exchange for slugger Mark McGwire (left). Shown here, he and third-base coach Rene Lachemann (back center) argue a call with home plate umpire Sam Holbrook (front center). La Russa was fiercely loyal to his players. (AP Images)

A serious student of the game, La Russa studies the numbers and lineups intensely. Former player Walt Weiss described him as "relentless. He never stopped trying to learn or gain an edge." (AP Images)

Albert Pujols is one of the Cardinals' brightest stars in the La Russa era. (AP Images)

La Russa first met pitching coach Dave Duncan (center) as a player in 1964. The two have worked together as manager and coach since 1982. They are shown here with Cardinals senior vice president and general manager Walt Jocketty before a game in 2004. (AP Images)

After a decade managing the St. Louis club, La Russa and the Cardinals win the World Series. (Above) Players storm the field as the Cardinals defeat the Tigers 4–2 to take the series in five games. (Right) The manager celebrates with his wife Elaine as they leave the field after Game 5. (AP Images)

Former St. Louis Cardinals manager Red Schoendienst (left) presents current manager Tony La Russa with a plaque commemorating LaRussa's record-breaking 2,000th game managed as a Cardinal prior to playing the Pittsburgh Pirates on June 1, 2008 at Busch Stadium in St. Louis, Missouri. La Russa is also third on the all-time list of major league games managed, behind Connie Mack and John McGraw. (Getty Images)

CHAPTER 14

Moving On

As incisive and logical a mind as La Russa was, he still had moments when his heart overruled what his brain said. Such a moment came early in the 1994 season, after the A's had signed veteran pitcher Dave Righetti.

Righetti was not pitching well, and when the team was in Boston, La Russa told traveling secretary Mickey Morabito that they would release Righetti after the game. The team was departing for New York after the game, and what Morabito knew that La Russa didn't was that Righetti had made extensive plans for his family to join him in New York for the weekend series.

"I had set the whole thing up," Morabito said. "He had a limo picking up his wife at the airport, he had extra rooms booked, they were going to do a lot of things in the city. I said, 'Tony, I've never really done this before and it's not my job to say this but…,' and I told him the whole story. Tony pounded the desk with his fist and then he put his head down on the desk."

After about a minute, he popped his head up and asked Morabito to get Sandy Alderson on the phone. He told the general manager that the team could not release Righetti, without going into any of the details. "He talked Sandy out of making the move," Morabito said. "It probably was not the best thing to do to help us win games, but he saw the human side of it. He wanted Righetti to enjoy that trip back to New York. We ended up releasing him a couple of weeks later."

Holding onto Righetti for a couple of extra weeks had little impact on the A's. At that point of the season, the team was playing even worse than it had the previous year. In one stretch, the A's lost 21 of 23, and by May 13 their record slid to 9–26. By June, when the team's fortunes had hardly improved, La Russa suggested to Scott Ostler of the *San Francisco Chronicle* that one motivational method could be "for him to lie down on the 880 Freeway today and threaten to stay there until his players play better."

Ostler added, "If La Russa does that, he should bring a lunch, and he should hope his hitters come driving along, because they would either miss, or not hit him hard enough to cause any real damage."

The team's record bottomed out at 16–40 on June 6. Then, as some of the injured players began to get healthy and returned to the lineup, other players began to play better as well. The team started to win, going 20–6 to move into contention in the AL West.

La Russa was pleased by the turnaround, but he also was worried because this season did not promise to be an ordinary year. The players were upset by the lack of a new contract with the team owners, and had set a strike date of August 12. Having endured a strike in 1981, La Russa knew that if the A's were not in first place by that date and they did strike, there was no guarantee of a postseason appearance.

The team fell one game short of that goal, losing the last game before the strike deadline 8–1 to Seattle and landing in second place, one game behind Texas. As his players prepared to scatter around the country, La Russa addressed his team. He wasn't siding with either the players or owners in the dispute, but his biggest concern was a belief that the players were not adequately respecting the game.

"One thing that bothers me and others is a lack of appreciation at how fortunate you are to be a major leaguer at this time," La Russa told them. "I don't know what the right solution is, I really don't. But one thing I do know, however it gets worked out, I get real upset when I see a player who doesn't appreciate being a major leaguer.

"A lot of things had to develop to get to this point, and I think they should be very respectful of the game. They should do their darndest to honor it.... And I want the A's to reflect that attitude."

La Russa knew not every player fell into that category, but he also knew the prime reason why players did believe they were above the game: money, and lots of it, paid to them by the owners.

"One of my pet gripes is players who go after high salaries and then complain if they're criticized," he said. "People have high expectations when they see players getting high salaries. If you don't want to live up to those expectations, take a lower salary. This is the major leagues. Big players have to play big.

"By definition, a professional is someone who is paid for his services. A professional is also supposed to be someone who always does his best. When a player is guaranteed so much money, it takes away some of the edge. I'd rather pay a player $5 million for one year and have him bust his butt to get another contract like that than pay him $2.5 million for two years and have him know that he'll get that second year no matter what he does in the first year."

Despite his strong feelings about salary issues, La Russa felt it was important that he left the subject of money to the front office. When he talked with his players, he wanted their concentration to be on one subject only. "I just try to get them to concentrate on why they're out there, to beat the other team," he said. "That's what the job has always been, and that's what it is now, no matter how much money they're getting."

Since the players' biggest issue in the strike was money, La Russa even offered one creative suggestion that he thought would benefit both sides and perhaps end the strike: the players would receive total free agency every year. No contract would be longer than one year.

"It would be the ultimate climate for Major League Baseball, and in the end the players would make more money," he said. "Instead of signing a five-year contract for $15 million, they may make $15 million in one year. I see no loser in that situation. And just think how fascinating it would be to put a club together every year.... There are some quirks, some details that would have to be worked out, but I'm fascinated by it, how good it can be for the fans, for the players, and for the game."

No one was budging, and the strike languished to the point where the playoffs and World Series was canceled for the first time in history.

La Russa and his family went to England for two weeks, and when he returned he made the decision to come back as manager of the A's with a new three-year contract, turning down opportunities to talk with multiple teams, including the Red Sox and Orioles.

Ironically, when Butch Hobson had been fired in Boston, he had called La Russa to ask him for advice in getting another job.

"Tony called me right back from London," Hobson said. "That shows you what kind of man he is. He interrupted his vacation just to call me back.... To be honest, I've always looked at Tony and watched the way he does things. I think everyone wants to be like him."

La Russa got a chance to express his views on many issues that winter when he agreed to write a weekly column for his hometown newspaper, the *Contra Costa Times*.

"He did it for several weeks," Lefkow said. "I don't think we paid him. He liked being able to express his opinion. He was very hands-on about it, coming into the newspaper and standing around (while the column was edited). He wrote a couple of good ones and a couple were clunkers."

Lefkow said La Russa was always aware of what was being written in the Bay Area newspapers about him and his team. "If you wrote something you would get feedback, especially if he didn't like it," Lefkow said. "He was that way with everybody on the beat."

As the off-season wore on, the biggest question facing La Russa was who the players on his team would be in 1995. The strike wore on, and owners were making plans to open spring training, and possibly the regular season, with replacement "non-union" players. La Russa and other managers openly questioned the idea. In La Russa's case, it was not out of distaste for inferior players, but out of respect and fidelity for his "union" players.

"You have relationships with veteran players," he said. "At some point you think they will be back, and you have to be able to explain why you did what you did. If you told me the game is better served by me sitting it out, then I'd sit out. It's something I'll try to figure out for myself as things develop."

La Russa, like almost everyone in baseball, hoped the situation would not reach that point, but it did. He chose to manage the replacement players.

"I realized the issue isn't who is right," La Russa said. "Putting on the uniform is not a statement for one side or the other, it's a statement for baseball."

What those new players quickly realized about their manager was that if there was a game to be played, and one team was going to win and one was going to lose, La Russa's goal would never change—he wanted his team to be the winner.

"That guy, No. 10, he wants to win every day," said outfielder Kash Beauchamp. "He's not happy if we lose, even though it's spring training."

La Russa realized the ability of the replacement players did not equal the normal major leaguers, but he did appreciate their desire. "I just might video-tape some of these games, and when the regular players get back, show them what it was like when they had the attitude that they really wanted to play," La Russa said.

Baseball was on the verge of opening the regular season with the replacement players when the players' union and owners finally reached a settlement on a new contract. But before La Russa could reintegrate his regulars, however, he had one off-the-field issue to deal with first.

The two daughters from his first marriage, Andrea and Averie, had filed a lawsuit against their father in New York seeking $16 million in damages. They alleged in the lawsuit that La Russa had caused them "embarrassment, humiliation, and ridicule" by refusing to have a relationship with them.

The two girls were five and four when their father and mother divorced in 1973. La Russa's lawyer told the *San Francisco Examiner* that La Russa "had never attempted to seek out his older daughters, saying that two court-appointed counselors recommended as part of La Russa's divorce that his two young children have contact only with their custodial parent, Luzette La Russa."

In accordance with that agreement, La Russa has kept his distance. His biography in the A's media guide in 1995 lists only his two daughters from his second marriage. He made only a brief comment about the lawsuit to reporters, saying, "Obviously there's a lot more to the story—my side, their side. If the story ever comes out, people can form their own opinions."

The story has never come out because neither side will talk about the issue. In a lengthy *Sports Illustrated* profile of La Russa published in 2007, the magazine quoted from an email it said had been sent by the two daughters. "The lawsuit was a plea for attention, for acknowledgment," the magazine quoted the email as saying. "We realize now that that may not have been the best way to handle the situation, but we were so hurt and angry. We guess we never understood how he—who by many accounts is a great dad to our half-sisters, a family man, a rescuer of animals—could have left his first two daughters and never looked back."

La Russa did talk about the divorce with *Sports Illustrated*, one of the very few public comments he has ever made about that marriage.

"If it's a mistake and you stay there, I mean, there was going to be suffering," he said. "And the longer you stay, the more suffering there is for everybody…. I regret that there's three women that I affected. If I hadn't gotten married, that wouldn't be true."

The lawsuit was later dismissed by a New York Supreme Court judge.

Happy to return to baseball and reunite with his regular players, it was business as usual soon enough. He and Rickey Henderson got into a heated shouting match early in training camp. The two spent 30 minutes screaming at each other behind closed doors after the A's returned from a game in Mesa against the Cubs, arguing about whether Henderson should have been on the bus to the game.

"We disagreed on a few things, and when we disagree we get fired up," Henderson told reporters. "I wanted to take some extra hitting today, and he wanted me to go to Mesa. He wanted the team together. It was just him thinking one way and me thinking another. When he wants you to go and you don't want to go, it messes things up."

Henderson said the two hugged at the end of their meeting. "Everything is back on track," he said. "We argue all the time. I think that's what makes him like me."

In an illustration of the kind of control La Russa tries to keep on his team, even in the spring, Lefkow recalled how La Russa even took note of which beat writers made the trips to away games such as in Mesa, a short 20-minute drive from the A's stadium in Phoenix.

"Tony looked up in the press box to see who was there," Lefkow said. "A lot of us begged off on the Tucson trips (a couple of hours from Phoenix) and Tony did not like that. He always said something about it."

There were certain issues that always got La Russa's attention, not to mention his ire, and none fired him up more than a pitcher gunning for one of his batters.

In the first half of the 1995 season, the usual target of those pitches was McGwire, who hit 24 homers before the All-Star break. He also was hit by a pitch eight times. When it happened in the third inning of a game against Toronto on July 8, La Russa and McGwire both exploded. La Russa accused pitcher David Cone of a "gutless cheap shot" by throwing a fastball that hit McGwire's batting helmet, knocking him to his knees. Cone denied that the pitch was intentional.

"I think La Russa has a reputation for thinking everybody throws at his hitter's heads," Cone told reporters. "If anyone has a reputation, it's him."

When Toronto came to bat in the fourth, Oakland pitcher Doug Johns, making his major league debut, delivered his first pitch behind the Blue Jays' John Olerud and was ejected by home plate umpire Dan Morrison. All remained quiet until the seventh inning, when Oakland's Mike Harkey hit Joe Carter with a pitch and was ejected. By then, coaches, players, and the manager of each team were all yelling at each other.

The pitch to McGwire forced him to miss the All-Star Game. It did not matter if the pitch was intentional or not, it still had hit him in the head.

"It's like saying the drunk driver didn't mean to hit those kids crossing the street," McGwire said. "The fact is, it happened. There is no question in my mind, if I wasn't knocked out David Cone would not have finished the game."

Carter also was upset that La Russa brought him into the melee when he had done nothing wrong. "He sits back over there, like the genius manager he is, and orders his pitcher to throw at me," Carter told reporters. "His whole comment was, 'At least it wasn't at your head.' That's his reasoning. Not at my head? So what?"

Carter came up again in the ninth and slammed a three-run homer, which turned out to be the difference in Toronto's victory.

"It's always a revenge thing with Tony. He's been that way all his career." Carter said. "So after a while you just sit back and let it go, and let your bat do the talking. Hit a home run. Oh yeah, that was sweet."

When La Russa was not getting upset with opposing pitchers, he had other targets on his own team for criticism. Having Rickey Henderson around usually gave him an easy outlet, but one day in 1995 he came out firing at Ruben Sierra, who made the mistake of criticizing Sandy Alderson in a Bay Area newspaper by saying he had not been a baseball player. Sierra had not learned the lesson that it would have been much better for him to criticize La Russa than to attack one of La Russa's friends.

"Every time he opens his mouth he makes a fool of himself," La Russa said of Sierra. "You try to protect guys, shade the truth a bit, but there's a term players use, V.I., when a player starts believing fantasy. He's a village idiot.

"The more I think about it the madder I get. In this one case I'm going to say how full of shit he really is. He gets on Sandy because he never played. Here's a guy who went to Vietnam. If Ruben ever went to Vietnam he'd alternate between vomiting and shitting his pants. He's trying to intimidate a guy who did two or three tours in Vietnam."

La Russa's problems with Henderson were different. The A's were struggling to get out of last place, but still had a shot at a wild-card spot in the playoffs, and La Russa felt that Henderson was not always interested and focused on the game.

"I believe that he's got some special talents and he's done some great things in baseball, but he's not a great player," La Russa told reporters. "To be a great player you've got to be interested in the team as you are in yourself. You've got to always be aware of what the team needs. That piece is missing from Rickey."

La Russa told reporters that if Henderson and rookie Jason Giambi could not play during the season-ending series at Anaheim, the team should send them home and "save the hotel bill."

"Is that a chicken shit thing for me to say?" La Russa asked reporters. "I don't think so because I don't think I'm chicken shit. If you're not going to be a part of it, we'll send you a Christmas card. I really detest not sprinting to the end."

Henderson deflected La Russa's criticism. "He's a guy who is so emotionally into it, when things don't go right, he gets upset," Henderson said. "He's just frustrated with the team. He gets frustrated because we're losing."

The A's would end the season with a last-place finish, dropping the final nine games of the year. La Russa also had lost a good friend and boss when Walter Haas Jr. died of prostate cancer on September 20, the day of the final home game—and victory—of the season. The Haas family already had agreed to sell the A's to Steve Schott and Ken Hofmann.

"Walter Haas was an incredible owner. Perfect," La Russa said. "He loved his baseball. He was the nicest man and nobody wanted to disappoint him. When he died, it broke our heart. We were so fond and close to him. Because of the earthquake, we didn't really celebrate winning the World Series in 1989. Every year after that he said, 'Tony, I want to be involved in a parade.' When he died we lost an important edge."

La Russa wondered if his career with the A's was coming to an end. His friend Alderson told him maybe now was the time to look for another job.

"Tony is very competitive," Alderson said in *Champions*. "He wants to know that he has a chance to win every day, as well as cumulatively. It was obvious that we were going to have to tear everything down and rebuild, and it would be some time before we could be competitive again."

La Russa made the decision to leave the A's after a 9½ year run, one world championship, three AL pennants, and four division titles. There was no question he would be a manager in 1996. The only question was where.

CHAPTER 15

Meet Me in St. Louis

After Walt Jocketty graduated from the University of Minnesota in 1974 with a degree in business administration, he withdrew $300 from his and his wife's savings account and headed to baseball's winter meetings in New Orleans. He returned with a job as the assistant general manager of the Triple A Iowa Oaks.

It was in Des Moines two years later when Jocketty's path first crossed that of Tony La Russa, who was a veteran approaching the end of his playing career. In 1979, when La Russa came back to town as the team's manager, Jocketty was still there.

"He really loved the game, and I liked his personality," La Russa said of his early memories about Jocketty. "Guys trusted him. He was very efficient. He got everybody's respect by the way he conducted himself."

After La Russa was promoted to manager of the White Sox, the minor league director's job became available in Oakland. A's owner Charlie Finley called Roland Hemond for a recommendation, and he suggested Jocketty. "Finley called me and I said Walt was terrific," La Russa agreed.

When Jocketty moved to Oakland, La Russa had no idea they would meet up again six years later when La Russa was hired as the A's manager. The two worked together until 1993, when Jocketty took a job with the expansion team, the Colorado Rockies. After the 1994 season, Jocketty was hired by the Cardinals as the team's general manager.

Joe Torre was the Cardinals' manager, and by 1995 the franchise was in the final year of Anheuser-Busch's ownership. Money was tight, and the team was stuck in fourth place. Hoping for a spark, brewery executives instructed Jocketty to fire Torre on June 16 and replace him with Mike Jorgensen, the team's director of player development. The move didn't change the results on the field, and the team limped to a 62–81 finish, 22½ games behind the division champion Cincinnati Reds.

Jocketty was well aware of what was happening in Oakland, and when he sat down to compile a list of candidates to become the next manager of the Cardinals, he stopped after one name: Tony La Russa.

"There was obviously a plan, and the first step in my plan was to hire Tony," Jocketty said in the spring of 1996. "We needed the right guy to run the team on the field and put together a great staff."

There were other manager jobs open at the end of the 1995 season—the Orioles and the expansion team in Arizona, a job that did intrigue La Russa—but the more he thought about the tradition of the Cardinals, the lure of managing in a new league, and the prospect of working again with Jocketty, he decided it was a combination he couldn't refuse. He also remembered advice he had received from Sparky Anderson that at some point in his career he should manage in the National League if he ever had the chance. On October 23, 1995, he was introduced as the Cardinals' new manager.

La Russa knew he had a lot to learn, and he relished the challenge. He talked to his friend Jim Leyland and others about the differences between managing in the American and National Leagues. He tried to familiarize himself with the Cardinals personnel, and he consulted with Jocketty on what moves needed to be made to help improve the team's chances of competing for a division championship in 1996.

One position that La Russa and Jocketty were concerned about was shortstop. Future Hall of Famer Ozzie Smith was going to be 41 years old in 1996.

He had played in only 44 games the previous year because of arthroscopic surgery on his right shoulder and when he returned for 25 games in the final two months of the season, he hit just .199, by far the lowest average in his 14 years in St. Louis.

Not seeing any prospect in the organization who was ready to be Smith's successor and still unsure if Smith would pass a required physical examination in order for his contract to roll over to the next season, Jocketty set out to find another shortstop. He talked to free agents Walt Weiss and Greg Gagne, but both were reluctant to sign with Smith's status undetermined. Jocketty then looked into making a trade, and on December 14 he dealt pitchers Allen Watson, Rich DeLucia, and Doug Creek to San Francisco for Royce Clayton.

"Given Ozzie's injury problems during the 1995 season, we couldn't risk putting ourselves in a situation where we had no proven shortstop," Jocketty said in announcing the trade.

Added La Russa, "I haven't heard anybody tell me he [is] healthy enough to play. He wasn't healthy last year."

One day after the trade for Clayton was made, the Cardinals learned that Smith had passed his required physical exam and been cleared to play in 1996 by an independent physician.

From Smith's perspective, the problem was never a question of health. It was a question of loyalty—in his first two months on the job, the new manager had not bothered to call him and ask how the rehabilitation of his shoulder was progressing. The two did not meet, or even talk, until January, a month after Clayton had been acquired.

It was an uncomfortable situation for all of the parties involved. Clayton had been the Giants' starting shortstop for the past four seasons and at 26 was entering the prime years of his career. Smith was a proven veteran who felt he had earned the right to dictate his own playing schedule. But La Russa only had one consideration: which player would give his team the best chance to win.

As the team reported to spring training, the tension was already mounting. "I've assured Ozzie just as I've assured Royce that all I care about is that the

Cardinals have the best chance to win," La Russa said on the eve of opening camp. "I have no preconceived notions that Royce has taken the job or that Ozzie will come here and prove to be the best. It's open competition, and that makes a lot of sense."

Clayton was not the only newcomer to the Cardinals' camp. Jocketty had a busy winter, signing free agents Ron Gant, Gary Gaetti, and Andy Benes and trading for several ex-Oakland players, including Dennis Eckersley, Todd Stottlemyre, and Rick Honeycutt. He also added Mike Gallego, who joined the former A's coaches who moved from Oakland to stay with La Russa.

"It's great to have all these new players," said pitcher Donovan Osborne, "but I keep wondering if I've been traded to the American League."

Having those former Oakland players and coaches was important to La Russa because he knew they would help ease his transition. They knew his style and his approach, and they would help him convey the messages he wanted to get across.

The first message was the importance of team unity. It was the reason La Russa organized a team dinner the night before camp opened. He wanted the players to have a chance to relax and socialize with their new teammates. The second message concerned learning how it felt to win. At one of his first team meetings, La Russa asked every player who had earned a World Championship ring in his career to stand up and talk about the experience.

"All I know is that the American Leaguers we brought over are guys I personally know are not intimidated by winning," La Russa said. "That's very important. The guys we brought over are used to thinking at the start of the season that they're going to win and playing with that pressure."

The Cardinals had not won since 1987. La Russa was hungry to win again too; his team had not been to the postseason in his last three years in Oakland. Ever since he began managing, he had been motivated by a fear of failure, and that had not changed with his move to St. Louis.

"I don't want the fans and the new ownership and everyone to be embarrassed," he said. "And I don't want to embarrass myself."

La Russa was embarrassed, however, when he saw the cover of the team's media guide, featuring his picture. He wanted the focus on the players, not on himself.

"That was the first thing he said to me," Jocketty said. "When the media guide came out, Tony went crazy. He came to me steaming and said, 'I thought we weren't going to do this'."

The Cardinals' returning players got the first inkling of what life under La Russa would be like at the end of spring training. The team's final exhibition game was in Memphis, against San Diego, who had signed Rickey Henderson as a free agent over the winter.

"He held a big meeting about what Rickey might tell us about him," catcher Tom Pagnozzi recalled. "The only thing I really remember about the meeting was that Ron Gant's beeper went off about 30 times. Everybody was rolling, but Tony got pissed."

La Russa also was upset on Opening Day in New York, when the Cardinals blew a six-run lead and lost 7–6 to the Mets. It was just another sign of the team's early-season struggles. The biggest obstacle facing La Russa was the unresolved question about how the playing time at shortstop would be divided between Smith and Clayton. Smith was upset by the open competition during the spring. He believed that his career longevity and success had earned him the right to be the regular starter as long as he was healthy.

When La Russa said that whoever played the best would play the most, Smith believed him. During spring training, he hit .288 with no errors in 15 exhibition games, and proved that his shoulder was healthy. Clayton hit .190 and made eight errors in 19 games. Smith believed that he had retained his job and would receive the bulk of the playing time when the season started. When that didn't happen, he became openly upset and accused La Russa of lying.

"I think it's fair to say he misunderstood how he compared to Royce in spring training," La Russa said at the time. "He felt like he won the job…. When I and the coaches evaluated the play in spring training—the whole game—Royce started very slowly offensively and you could see him start to get better. By what he was able to do defensively and on the bases, Royce deserved to play the majority of the games. Royce is capable of making more plays."

La Russa refuted Smith's accusations that the decision to play Clayton more often than Smith was personal, and insisted again that he was merely trying to do what he thought gave the team the greatest chance of winning the game that day, the same criterion to which he judged every player on his roster since he had taken over the team.

"You can say I was mistaken in my evaluation, but why would I play Royce and not Ozzie?" La Russa asked. "Because I thought Royce was better to play most of the games. I thought spotting Ozzie was the best way to go. If I was wrong, I was wrong. But I wasn't lying…. [Smith] thought he played the best, so he should play the most. He thought I was being dishonest. If it was a mistake, it was a mistake…. Twice to his face, I told him that the other guy was a better shortstop on an everyday basis."

In La Russa's mind, the issue was never personal. "I'm fighting my ass off to survive," La Russa said. "Why would I penalize the team because of a personal issue with Ozzie?"

The Cardinals were in Montreal when La Russa learned that Smith had told reporters he thought La Russa had lied to him. La Russa immediately pulled Smith off the field during batting practice and confronted him in his office. "That's the last time I want to hear that," La Russa told Smith. "Two things have been true since the day I started managing: I have never lied to a player and I am not afraid of them. The whole issue became a really negative part of trying to build a team."

Smith, of course, knew his career was not going to last forever. He had talked openly in the past about "passing the torch" to the next shortstop. He knew 1996 was probably going to be his final year. Clayton actually seemed a likely successor. He had grown up a fan of Smith's ever since he saw him play against the Dodgers when he was 12 years old.

What was the most upsetting to Smith was that somebody else—and someone brand new to the Cardinals organization, La Russa—was trying to make that transition for him. It was not the way Smith had planned the end of his career. He was hurt, angry and disappointed. La Russa was also upset, as he had been throughout his career when he believed a player was putting his self-interests before those of the ballclub.

La Russa really didn't care about Smith's hurt feelings, but it did bother him that Smith publicly voiced his displeasure and disagreement with his manager whenever he was asked. He had made legions of fans during his career, and many of those fans were choosing to side with him and not with La Russa. It made the manager's transition to the Cardinals even tougher than he had expected. It was an uncomfortable situation for La Russa, whose only chance of emerging unscathed from the episode was by winning—and by having Clayton play well.

In the season's first 40 games, Clayton started 33 times compared to seven starts for Smith, who suffered a hamstring injury in the last week of spring training. The Cardinals were 17–23 at that point in the season.

It was June when Smith announced his decision to retire at the end of the season. He accepted the fact that he and Clayton were going to share playing time for the rest of the year, but just because he accepted it did not mean that he agreed with the decision.

"It wasn't so much about my playing time as the way it was done," Smith said. "I was under the impression I was going to have every opportunity to do what I do. I was told the position would be earned in spring training. I thought I did that. I did everything that was asked of me."

The team's struggle in the beginning of the year did not come as a surprise to La Russa, who had anticipated that it would take some time for all of the new players to jell and begin working together. The situation with Smith and Clayton had not helped either, but La Russa acknowledged his own portion of the blame.

"Paul Richards taught me that the manager is going to be blamed, so you might as well blame yourself and always figure there's something you should be doing different." La Russa said in an interview that year with *Inside Sports* magazine. "We've got to play better, and I've got to blame myself first. I've got to do a better job."

Gradually the wins began to come. After bottoming out with a 17–26 record on May 19, the Cardinals climbed over .500 in a month's time. By the All-Star break, the team was tied for first with Houston, and by September 3 the Cardinals were in first place to stay.

The turnaround began after a 9–0 loss to the Giants in San Francisco on a getaway day in early June. As the team flew to Los Angeles, Pagnozzi, Honeycutt, and Gaetti called a meeting for players only in Pagnozzi's hotel room after the team's plane landed. Everyone was there except Eckersley, who had remained in Oakland.

"It lasted almost two hours," Pagnozzi said. "I took notes, and we had a number of issues we wanted to talk about with Tony. We got to the ballpark the next day and the three of us knocked on his door and said we wanted to talk to him. I told him about the meeting, and he said, 'What players meeting? What coach was there?' Being the smart-ass I am, I said, 'If a coach was there it wouldn't be a players-only meeting, would it?' He got on the defensive right away and said he was the manager and had never had a players-only meeting.

"I was looking at a list of 10 things we wanted to bring up, thinking, 'Which two do I want to talk about the most?' We talked and he was fair, and he said to give him 24 hours to see what he could do. We changed what time the bus left for the ballpark and who could ride on which bus. That's what we got out of it. But we started to grow as a group and played well from that point on."

La Russa was upset when he heard about the meeting. "I knew we were not a cohesive team and there was a lot of distrust of me," he said. "I had not earned their respect. At first I took the meeting very personal, it was a dark day for me. But then we aired out some stuff and started playing better."

Another incident that turned out to be a unifying moment came on July 22, when the Cardinals blew a 5–0 lead and lost to Atlanta 8–6. The target of La Russa's displeasure was first baseman John Mabry, who had made the mistake of laughing at something the Braves' Fred McGriff had said when he reached first after an RBI single that tied the score in the seventh inning.

La Russa and Mabry got into a hearted argument in the clubhouse that Pagnozzi thought might come to blows before other players intervened. "We know John Mabry," Pagnozzi said. "John meant no malice by it. When you're struggling as a team, those kinds of things happen."

Years later, La Russa looked back and considered that incident "my worst moment as a Cardinal."

"That was stuff I should have done in my office," La Russa said. "There are guys who don't give their best all the time and the club knows it. Those are the ones you want to [challenge] in front of everybody. That was a mistake. He [Mabry] is a guy who obviously gives you everything he has every time he puts on a Cardinal uniform. Nobody's better than him."

While La Russa was working to change the attitude of his players, the players were learning about him.

"He didn't know what to expect from the players and we didn't know what to expect from Tony," said outfielder Brian Jordan. "He's a very intense manager. He's deeply into the game and wants to control the game. I think it took the whole first half for the players to get used to him and for him to know what we're capable of doing. Now he knows enough about the players to just let us play."

La Russa has heard other suggestions about his wanting to control the game, and it is a subject he disputes. "To the extent that you have players who really understand how to play the game, there is very little a manager can do to control the game," he said. "But others either don't understand the game well enough or don't care enough about the team competing to the best level possible that if you allow them to go their own way it will hurt the team's chances of competing."

The example La Russa uses is an outfielder who cares about playing defense and understands the score of the game, the count on the hitter, and adjusts where he is playing to fit the situation. Another outfielder, he said, is just out there taking his stance waiting for his next turn to bat. Letting that player do what he wants will impact the team's chances of winning.

La Russa also makes the same example of comparing players when it comes to base running situations, and why some players automatically have a green light to steal and others have to wait for his sign.

"If you have a bunch of guys who can play, you let them play," La Russa said. "When you have others who can't play or won't because of selfish reasons you have to step in."

Some of the players who had experience with La Russa were continually being questioned by those who hadn't played for him.

"Guys didn't know how to take Tony at first," Eckersley said. "They'd come up and ask me what was going on and I'd say, 'Ask him yourself.' There was one game when we had a big inning, maybe in the sixth or seventh, and we were ahead 6–1. Everybody in the dugout was high-fiving like it was over. Tony was still yelling at someone who had failed to advance a base. I could see looks from players that said, 'Give it a rest, La Russa.' Players said to me, 'What's with this guy?' He doesn't give up. He's a grinder."

Infielder Mike Gallego, in his eighth season playing for La Russa, agreed that it took time for the new players to be converted.

"Somehow he makes you learn to appreciate the game his way," Gallego said. "Your first part of your relationship with Tony—and believe me it is a relationship—you may not always agree with him, you may not see it his way, but by October, when you're still playing and the rest of the teams are home, I guarantee you will be a true believer.

"It's been a love-hate relationship—I haven't exactly asked him out to dinner—but when I look at a manager, I'm looking for someone who can lead you to victory. That's why I play for him."

Added pitcher Andy Benes, "I've never been around anyone more prepared than he is. Every pitch of every game, regardless of the score, he's really dialed into what is going on."

That attitude was no different with the Cardinals than it had been for La Russa in Oakland. He still took great issue with pitchers throwing at hitters, and disputes arose during the season with the Expos and Marlins.

On April 23, Montreal manager Felipe Alou and pitcher Kirk Reuter were ejected in a battle of beanballs. Alou later claimed it was started by La Russa ordering pitcher Todd Stottlemyre to hit Shane Andrews after Rondell White had hit a home run, and one night after another Montreal batter was hit in a game in which the Expos hit two homers.

The *Boston Globe's* Peter Gammons reported that Alou said he received phone calls from seven or eight managers and coaches after the episode, thanking him for standing up to what they perceived as an act of intimidation from La Russa.

Another vocal attack against La Russa was launched by Florida's Gary Sheffield after he was hit on the elbow by an Andy Benes pitch on May 13. "I've watched Tony and I played against him in the American League," Sheffield told reporters. "I'm not calling him a beanball specialist, it's just unfortunate his teams are always in brawls. There has to be a reason. I don't think it's a coincidence."

La Russa was steamed when he learned what Sheffield had said. "I suggest he check with every pitcher who ever pitched for me—ever," La Russa said. "Ask them what my philosophy is. And then he can just shut up."

La Russa responded to someone's comment that "La Russa is all about revenge."

"Good comment," he said. "If somebody takes a shot at us, we absolutely come back with one. In this game, if you allow your club to be intimidated, you're beat. Just don't take cheap shots, that's all."

La Russa got into another heated battle—this time of words—in September with the Giants' Barry Bonds, who had hit two home runs in a game to beat the Cardinals. Afterward, he told reporters, "It's fun playing against big egos like La Russa," and suggested that the manager had erred in not bringing in a left-hander when he came up to bat.

"Is he good enough to play left field and manage the other club?" La Russa responded. "He ain't that good.... I'm surprised he knows I manage the club. Really. He's so into himself I'm surprised he knows.... If he cared more for his team and hustled all the time, we'd have a better feeling for him. I take [crit-icism] individually. If somebody like Kirby [Puckett] comes out and rips me, or Paul Molitor, guys I really know and respect, it would have an impact on me."

While La Russa was accustomed to similar battles in his years in the American League, there were differences created by his move, primarily on a personal level. Because his daughters were so active in ballet and other activi-ties, and because of the family's year-round work with ARF, the family decided Elaine and the two girls would remain in the Bay Area. During the baseball season, he would stay in a St. Louis hotel.

The change was harder on La Russa than it was on his family. "It's like being married to a Merchant Marine," Elaine told the *St. Louis Post-Dispatch*. "It really is not that different, with Tony managing in St. Louis. During the baseball season, Tony is on a road trip all season long. Even if he's home, his body shows up but his mind isn't there."

By the time the Cardinals were on the verge of clinching the NL Central title, La Russa had a good feeling about his team and believed they were equipped to make a deep run into the playoffs. While he thought the team had improved competitively, however, he still had a lingering feeling that he was not as close with the club as he had been in Chicago and Oakland.

When a friend telephoned La Russa shortly before the team clinched the division, La Russa related his opinion that during the ensuing celebration, he expected the coaches and he would be celebrating with each other but not with the players. He was wrong. During the party, La Russa was mobbed by the players. "I was overwhelmed with the response the coaches and I got," he said. "It surprised the heck out of me and really was an overwhelming feeling."

A three-game sweep of San Diego in the first round of the playoffs con-firmed La Russa's feeling that the club had come together well. When the Cardinals quickly jumped to a 3–1 lead against the Braves in the NLCS, La Russa's team found itself only one win away from a spot in the World Series.

Unfortunately, that win never came—or even came close. The Cardinals were outscored 32–1 in three straight games by Atlanta, their offense shut down by future Hall of Fame pitchers John Smoltz, Greg Maddux, and Tom Glavine.

In all his years of playoff success in the American League, La Russa had never been involved in a Game 7, something he said would be the ultimate experience. He didn't feel the same way after the Braves' 15–0 victory, an embarrassing loss and a huge disappointment that clouded the team's accomplishments.

"It's important to try to put things in perspective," he said 24 hours after that game. "We were one win away from the National League championship, five wins away from being the world champs. To get that close and not get it all hurts. But 'remarkable' is a heck of a word to use for what we did."

La Russa had plenty of time to think about his team and the season as he drove home to California. Overall, there were plenty of high notes, including his winning another Manager of the Year award.

"We did a bunch of things that should give us confidence," he said. "We also got a taste of the real golden moments. But we left something; we missed a couple of steps. It's nice to feel good about what you did and experienced, but you also think about what could have been and how much you've got to improve. We can use that experience to get us fired up."

CHAPTER 16

The McGwire–Sosa Show

Standing at the podium before a festive audience at the St. Louis Baseball Writers dinner in January 1997, La Russa told the nearly 2,000 people in the hotel ballroom exactly what they wanted to hear.

"I guarantee you we will not relinquish the central division," La Russa said, a pronouncement that received a standing ovation.

The problem with such bold promises, of course, is that they sometimes don't work out. By the start of spring training, La Russa's statement was pasted on bulletin boards in every NL Central clubhouse and he knew he had made a move that might come back to haunt him. "Bottom line, it was stupid on my part," he admitted six weeks after the fact.

At the time, it did not seem like a crazy, off-the-cuff prediction at all. La Russa thought the Cardinals would be improved in 1997 and he thought coming off the near-miss against the Braves would provide an extra spark of motivation. He also believed Ozzie Smith's retirement had removed the biggest distraction that the team had endured through 1996.

"We know we can win if we stay healthy," La Russa said. "If we stay healthy, we're a good club. We've got a good balance with our starting pitching, our bullpen, power, speed. We have all the elements to be successful."

He also felt more comfortable now that he was more familiar not only with his own personnel, but with the differences in National League play and with the Cardinals' opponents.

"When I came over," he said that spring, "I was real, real concerned about not being familiar with personnel—ours and the people we played against. To some extent, that is still true and it's an edge we give up for now. But we should be all right."

The returning players also had a year's experience under La Russa's leadership and knew better what to expect from their manager. "The camaraderie is going to be there this year," Brian Jordan said. "Last year it took us awhile to get there. There's no more putting a lot of pressure on yourself to let him know what you're doing. Take care of your business, work together, do the little things, and now you find yourself winning more games. That happened in the second half last year."

It didn't take long for all of those lofty expectations to begin unraveling. The Cardinals opened the season with a six-game losing streak and lost 10 of their first 14 games.

The team finally climbed back to the .500 mark on July 2, then quickly lost four games in a row. They did not make it back to that plateau for the rest of the season, eventually finishing in fourth place, 16 games under .500.

The biggest problem, as had been one of La Russa's concerns, was health. The team used the disabled list 22 times during the season with a variety of injuries to starting pitchers, relievers, regulars, and extra men. It seemed that nobody was immune.

La Russa had reason to believe that the team might be healthier. At the start of the season, they hired their first strength coach, Mike Gibbons. But as it turned out, that might have been part of the reason for so many injuries. Gibbons reportedly encouraged the players to use creatine, a muscle-building supplement that also requires users to drink plenty of liquids for it to be effective. A lack of hydration increases muscle strains and pulls, which affected many of the players.

"We could not figure out why we had seven calf injuries," said athletic trainer Gene Gieselmann during the season. "When you have mass numbers of a certain kind of injury, you always wonder why."

Gibbons was hired by Jocketty without the knowledge or participation of Gieselmann, who was in his 29th season with the organization and 27th as head athletic trainer. The two were frequently at odds during the season.

"The right arm has to know what the left arm is doing," Gieselmann now says. "You can't have a division there, and we definitely had a division. He kept giving them the stuff [creatine] and the training staff had to keep cleaning up his mess. We basically got along like cats and dogs."

Gieselmann's problems with Gibbons and rehabilitating the injured players were not his only concerns. His relationship with La Russa had not started well and had never improved.

Having worked with managers such as Red Schoendienst, Ken Boyer, Whitey Herzog, and Joe Torre, Gieselmann was used to dealing with different personalities, but one fact he was proud of was that throughout his career, he always had a close relationship, both working and personal, with all of those managers. He never developed that connection with La Russa.

"In two years together he never once invited me to lunch or dinner or never once sent a drink over to me at the bar," Gieselmann said. "All of the other managers always included me and my assistant, Brad Henderson, like we were part of the coaching staff."

Gieselmann had been excited when La Russa was hired. His wife, Roseanna, was friends with him and Elaine. In 1974, her first husband, Phil Bushman, had been a teammate of La Russa's in Charleston, West Virginia. Over his first winter with the Cardinals, Gieselmann estimated that he called La Russa at his home in California 10 times, first to congratulate him on getting the job and second to update him on the team's injuries and rehab schedules from the previous year. He never received a return call. La Russa admits it is one of his personal faults that he always vows to work to improve, but every year he believes he falls short. "What I ended up doing that year was to get a bunker mentality, and I've done it a whole bunch of times since, too," he said.

The two finally met in person in January, when La Russa was in St. Louis filming a television commercial.

"I walked into his office and asked if he had received my phone calls," Gieselmann said. "He said yes, but added that he was very busy in the off-season and that he was up to speed on all of the injuries. I thought it was interesting that he didn't want to hear that information from me."

The next sign came in spring training, when Gieselmann handed La Russa a personal check for $500 from him and his wife for ARF. The Gieselmanns share a love of animals with the La Russas. "It wasn't a bribe. I hadn't even worked with him yet," Gieselmann said. "I thought it would show I was a fairly decent person. He was very appreciative of the check."

The gesture did not change their business-only relationship, however, and soon Gieselmann had another reason why. When the Cardinals flew to San Francisco for the first time that season, landing around 2:00 AM, he found Oakland trainer Barry Weinberg waiting for La Russa.

"Later I questioned Barry about why he would show up like that, and he said he was giving Tony a ride home," Gieselmann said. "He said he had a lot of friends on the staff besides Tony that he wanted to see."

The Cardinals' success in 1996 masked many of their problems, but Gieselmann had no such camouflage in 1997. He remembered he and La Russa had one particular disagreement when pitcher Todd Stottlemyre was hit in the head by a line drive during a game in Montreal in August. Stottlemyre was only two outs away from qualifying for a victory, and the Cardinals led 9–1. Gieselmann advised La Russa that he thought the pitcher should come out of the game as a precautionary move.

"He was not unconscious, but he was somewhat disoriented," Gieselmann said. "I talked to him and he seemed fairly normal, but he took a pretty good blow to the forehead. Trainers are always taught to caution on the wrong side of head injuries. After I told Tony I didn't think Todd should pitch, he asked Todd if he could pitch and he said yes.

"Todd was the wrong person to ask. He was a bulldog, and a good pitcher, and a strong person. Tony said he was going to leave him in, and when we got back to the dugout I went up to Brad [Henderson] and told him to come with me. I wanted him to hear what I had to say to Tony. I said, 'Tony, I want to say this on the record that I disagree with you keeping Todd in the game. If something happens I don't want to be responsible for it. He could feel fine now, but go to sleep tonight and not wake up.'

"We were lucky, nothing happened. Todd got the two outs, qualified for the win, and came out of the game. The fact is, we dodged a bullet."

Gieselmann had no doubt that he was going to be fired at the end of the season. The multitude of injuries would be an easy excuse. The real reason, however, was that after two years of trying, La Russa had finally convinced Weinberg to leave Oakland and move to St. Louis.

"Tony has a lot of good qualities and one of them is loyalty," Gieselmann said. "I was an outsider. I was never on his radar screen; nothing that I did was going to matter. He wanted Barry here from the get-go. Tony is a very complex person. He always wants to have the last word. A lot of people swear by the guy. He can put the biggest charm in the world on to someone he likes. He never warmed up to me or gave me the time of day.

"I said one time that Walt [Jocketty] and Tony were from Oakland, which is earthquake country. There is no warning about earthquakes until the house starts shaking. I'm a Kansas boy, which is tornado country. You get a warning that a tornado is coming when the siren goes off. The siren started going off as soon as he got to St. Louis; I just didn't know when the tornado was going to hit."

La Russa admits that the most important reason for changing trainers was because of Weinberg's past history in working with Mark McGwire, who had been aquired in a trade with Oakland. "Mark was going to be such an important part of how we were going to compete, and he had a lot of physical issues," La Russa said. "Walt felt that to maximize the asset Mark was Barry would be better at the job."

When he was fired after the season, Gieselmann made a few phone calls to let some of his colleagues know. One call was to the Atlanta trainer, Dave

Pursley. A couple of hours later, shortly before the Braves were about to start a playoff game, Gieselmann's phone rang. The caller ID indicated the call was from the Atlanta Braves. When he answered, he found manager Bobby Cox on the line. Cox said he had been told what had happened by his trainer, and wanted to tell Gieselmann, who he didn't really know, how sorry he was that he had lost his job.

"I said to him, 'Bobby, why are you calling? You've got a playoff game in a couple of hours. You've got more important things to worry about.' He said to me, 'Baseball is a game. When you're dealing with human beings that's far more important.' From that day on I have really respected Bobby Cox."

The news that Gieselmann and Gibbons had been fired, and that long-time team doctor Dr. Stan London had been reassigned, was not met with much reaction among Cardinals fans. Since the end of July, they had been mesmerized by a new slugger who arrived in town from Oakland: Mark McGwire.

Jocketty had been talking with the A's since June about McGwire, but would not agree to trading top prospects Eli Marrero and Manny Aybar to get him. McGwire, who had to approve any deal, also had concerns about changing leagues in the middle of the season. Jocketty also had talked with Toronto about acquiring Joe Carter, but they wanted John Mabry.

Oakland came off its demand for Marrero and Aybar, however, and just hours before the trading deadline, McGwire was reunited with La Russa in a trade for pitchers T.J. Mathews, Eric Ludwick, and Blake Stein.

The Cardinals did not know at the time whether they would be able to re-sign McGwire, a free agent at the end of the 1997 season, but they hoped the presence of La Russa in the dugout would give them an advantage over other teams.

McGwire warmed to the city and its fans quickly, and on September 16 he agreed to a new three-year contract, giving up his pursuit of free agency. It was a marriage that would blossom even more in 1998, when McGwire rewrote baseball's history book with his 70-home-run season, taking his manager and everyone else along for the ride.

Ten days after McGwire re-signed with the Cardinals, so did La Russa, agreeing to a two-year extension. La Russa hoped that having McGwire for a full season would improve the team's fortune in 1998.

Except for McGwire's homers, however—and it was a big exception because it took away attention from everything else—1998 was indeed much like the previous season. The team's best record was seven games above .500—in April. By the seventh week of the season they had used 11 starting pitchers. The Cardinals fell below .500 shortly before the All-Star break and didn't reach that mark again until September 18. They eventually finished third in the NL Central, four games above .500.

The best part of the season for La Russa was that the Cardinals' fans were so mesmerized by McGwire's homers that nobody cared whether the team won or lost. It only mattered if McGwire hit a home run. It was a magical summer, and it would be years before anybody talked about steroids or congressional hearings. All people cared about was watching McGwire and Sammy Sosa hit balls out of the ballpark, and almost no one questioned how it was happening.

The lone exception was a writer from the Associated Press, Steve Wilstein, who noticed a strange bottle in McGwire's locker one day. It was androstenedione, a legal testosterone-producing strength enhancer. Suddenly there were allegations that perhaps McGwire's home-run binge was tainted, even though andro, at the time, had not been banned by Major League Baseball. It had been, however, by the NFL, the NCAA, and the International Olympic Committee.

What upset La Russa was the fact that Wilstein discovered the bottle in McGwire's locker and wrote about it, an act the Cardinals considered an invasion of McGwire's privacy. As a result, La Russa wanted to ban all Associated Press reporters from the Cardinals' clubhouse.

"A player's locker isn't something that you should snoop around and see what you can find out," La Russa said. "That's a clear invasion of privacy and it's causing some real garbage here, that's taking away from what Mark's accomplishing."

After McGwire's 61st home run of the season tied Roger Maris' record, La Russa said, "What's happening here these two days is bigger than the game that's being played. What these two guys [McGwire and Sosa] have done for six months…. I can't believe I'm saying it, but that's what I believe…. I think these two individuals are bigger than the game that's being played today and tomorrow night."

What McGwire and Sosa had done in restoring fan interest in baseball, La Russa thought, had really transcended the importance of the results of the game itself.

La Russa would have been able to enjoy McGwire's special moment even more except that he was personally grieving. On September 4, La Russa's mother Oliva died in Tampa at the age of 84. He stayed with the team through the game on Monday, September 7, when McGwire tied the record, then flew to Tampa for his mother's funeral and returned afterward, arriving at Busch Stadium about an hour before the game on September 8 when McGwire hit the record-breaking homer.

Even though McGwire did not need much help, La Russa tried to give it to him by coming up with a plan after the All-Star break of batting the pitcher eighth in the order. His reasoning was that McGwire could then stay in the third spot and be guaranteed to bat in the first inning, but after that he would in effect be the cleanup hitter. The ninth place hitter would act as a second leadoff man as was the case in the American League.

La Russa did not anticipate the furor that arose from his move. It was just one more example, his critics said, of how he was acting like he was smarter than any of the previous managers in the game's history. It was the first time a National League pitcher had hit anywhere except ninth in the lineup since Steve Carlton batted eighth for the Phillies in 1979.

"What I would expect from the guys that know me—and there's quite a few of them—is that they would give me the benefit of the doubt as far as what you're thinking about," La Russa said.

What he was thinking about, of course, was a way to generate more offense and help McGwire in the process.

"The idea is to get guys on base in front of him and protection behind him," La Russa said. "I talked about it with Red Schoendienst and George Kissell. I had tremendous respect for them and I trusted them to tell me what they believed. Both of them said they were not sure they would do it, but why not try it? I held a team meeting and explained my thinking. I knew some people would say to whoever was hitting ninth, 'Tony thinks the pitcher's a better hitter than you,' but I explained to them that was not the case."

The third game in which La Russa sent out his revised lineup, his ninth-spot hitter was Pagnozzi. "I had been forewarned by a writer about it when Tony called me into his office," Pagnozzi said. "I think he thought because I was a veteran I was going to be upset. I just told him that hitting ninth was better than hitting 10th. I said I was really excited about being in the second leadoff spot, because I knew that meant I would have a green light to steal when I got on base. He just said, 'Absolutely not.'"

Pagnozzi's 11-year run with the Cardinals ended when he was released a month later to make room for a pitcher coming off the disabled list. He had no regrets, except that he would have liked to have developed a better relationship with La Russa.

"We had trouble from the get-go," Pagnozzi said. "Do I respect him as a manager? To the utmost. He knows how to win and he's very intense. Do I wish I had done some things differently? Yes. Would I play for him again? In a heart-beat."

Another player who left the Cardinals that season was the would-be short-stop-of the-future, Royce Clayton, who was traded to Texas on July 31 with pitcher Todd Stottlemyre for pitcher Darren Oliver and third baseman Fernando Tatis. Clayton finished his Cardinal career with a .262 average in his 2½ years in St. Louis.

That was only the beginning of changes the Cardinals made before the 1999 season. Jocketty delivered many new additions—including shortstop Edgar Renteria, outfielder Eric Davis, and pitchers Ricky Bottalico and Garrett Stephenson.

Perhaps more important to the chemistry inside the team's clubhouse, La Russa believed, was the absence of some of the players who left it, including Gant, who was traded to the Phillies, and Jordan, who signed as a free agent with the Braves.

Neither had been gone long before both started firing verbal shots at La Russa and making allegations about how he had managed the team the previous couple of seasons. Gant was upset about what he perceived to be preferential treatment of McGwire, who he felt should have hit fourth in the order. He thought it had affected the rest of the team. He also criticized the manager's decision to hit his pitcher eighth in the second half of the year.

La Russa responded by saying Gant had underachieved during his years in St. Louis, which no doubt left him frustrated and trying to place the blame for his poor performance on others.

"If he can't control you, if you're not a 'yes' player, he doesn't want you around," Gant told the *Philadelphia Inquirer* when asked about La Russa. "We were the laughing stock of the league. Guys from every team came up to me and said, 'What's [La Russa] thinking about?' All I could say was, 'No one knows.'"

La Russa responded by telling reporters, "I wonder if Ron got ticked off last year when I called him in and told him he came across as being lazy and rich. I told him, 'You'll be the richest pinch-hitter in the league next year.' … I really hope he goes to Philly and whiffs for them like he whiffed for us, and we'll see what excuses he makes."

La Russa thought the Cardinals had done all they could to help make Gant a better player, like moving him to different spots in the batting order.

"We got him to be a team leader and he just kind of sat there," La Russa said. "We paid him $5 million a year for five years. We did everything to try to help him. Then he came out and said I was a racist."

Just as that storm started to subside, another verbal attack came from Jordan, who spoke to reporters at the Braves' spring training camp. Jordan said his biggest problem with La Russa was that he thought the manager had put McGwire's pursuit of the home-run record ahead of the team's goal of winning games.

"It wasn't about winning," Jordan said about the 1998 Cardinals. "It was about one man making history.... If you're going to win, it's a team effort. Everybody has to be equal. If everything is focused on one man, it changes the strategy of ballgames."

Like Gant, Jordan had issues about McGwire batting third instead of fourth, and about the decision to bat the pitcher eighth.

"As for the lineup, it was about protecting McGwire," Jordan said. "If it was any other team, I'm not sure that Mark McGwire would be hitting third. He'd be the cleanup hitter." About batting the pitcher eighth, he said, "That changes the whole scheme of baseball. You're out on a limb there. I don't think many managers would agree with that, nor players. But once Tony does something, you're not going to change it. You just stick with it and suck it up. I never thought a pitcher would hit eighth. I respect the man. I never said, 'What are you doing?' But I'd scratch my head a little at some of the decisions he made."

La Russa denied that any of the moves he made during 1998 were done solely for the purpose of protecting McGwire. "Those are real unfortunate comments," La Russa said. "What he's saying is, we don't preach winning here. It's just like I told the club before, how much of a distraction is Michael Jordan? He's got six rings on his fingers. Last year, when McGwire mania was at its height in September, check out our September record (18–6). It was the winningest September" since 1966.

As disappointed as he was by Jordan's comments, La Russa still valued the contributions Jordan had made to the Cardinals. "He was a talented clutch player who liked to compete," La Russa said. "He sparked the club in a very positive way."

The accusations by Gant and Jordan were soon forgotten, but La Russa still had reason to feel uneasy. Two disappointing years had left him wondering about his future.

"This year I feel a tremendous amount of pressure," he said during spring training. "I think we have a good possibility of playing into October. So the pressure is definitely here to do everything the staff can, the manager can, to give the guys what they need so it happens. So yeah, I feel tremendous pressure. But I like that pressure.

"If I want to win as much or more than any of the people that are watching our ballclub, then you can't touch me.... I'm already motivated. I can't get more motivated than I am. One of the realities of the big leagues is, if somebody has an expectation and the club doesn't deliver, then there's a consequence. And if that consequence comes to the manager, well, this is 20 years I've lived with that. This year isn't any different."

Unfortunately for La Russa and Cardinals fans, he was right about that—1999 was not much different than the previous two seasons. The team reached a season-high six games over .500 in April and finished fourth in the NL Central, 21½ games behind Houston.

The 75–86 season gave the Cardinals a combined record of 231–254 in the last three years under La Russa, as disappointing to him as it was to the team's fans. It might even have been one of the reasons La Russa found himself in the hospital for several days in July, suffering from an ulcer.

"He's the first to cowboy up and toughen up and shrug off the minor things, but this isn't minor. He's in a lot of pain," said trainer Barry Weinberg. It was only the second time in La Russa's career as a manager that he had missed a game. The first time came in 1997, when La Russa sought permission from Jocketty to miss a game to be home in California when his then 17-year-old daughter Bianca completed a wilderness training camp.

"This is the first time in 18 years that I've missed a game," La Russa said then. "I'm not even proud to say that. It tells me that I've missed some things with my family that I shouldn't have. I've ashamed that it was the first time."

Said Eckersley, "For once in his life, he took a stand for his family. He finally put family over baseball."

The ulcer was no doubt caused in part by stress over his team. In addition to watching his team perform more poorly than he had expected, La Russa was in the middle of deciding whether he should sign a two-year extension of his contract, which had been placed on the table by the Cardinals' owners in spring training.

Weighing on his decision was the fact that La Russa had certain unnamed enemies in town who were trying to drive him out of St. Louis. To give in to their pressure and not come back as manager would, in essence, be to surrender. Then again, he did not want to manage where he was not wanted.

"I've got some very powerful enemies in this place," La Russa said. "I'm not sure how good a situation it is…. I think a lot of fans can figure out whether I should be here or not. Some fans would say yes, some no, some maybe. But I've got some powerful enemies, and I never forget that. That makes it a bit of an unfair contest. It doesn't change what I do, but I'm aware of it."

Some of the criticism of La Russa also was coming from the media, even though St. Louis—unlike either Chicago or San Francisco—had only one major newspaper with one primary columnist. Bernie Miklasz of the *Post-Dispatch* wrote columns that were critical of La Russa, but he also was one of the first to praise him in years when the team was doing well.

La Russa had been labeled an outsider ever since his arrival in St. Louis. He was from California, not the Midwest. He was a vegetarian. He drank wine instead of beer. His family remained in California instead of moving to St. Louis, and he spent his off-season in the Bay Area. La Russa understood that all of those reasons and more contributed to why the team's fans had not warmed up to him.

He also had to fight his dual status as a lawyer, and the George Will-created label that he was a "baseball genius," a title La Russa never wanted, never asked for, and couldn't get rid of.

It just so happened that 1999 was not a good year, the team's third consecutive poor season. By August, La Russa was quoted as saying whether he returned as manager or not should be determined by how well the team played for the remainder of the season.

"I want to come back, but you have to earn the right to come back," La Russa was quoted as saying. "The opportunity to manage a major league team is a special opportunity and you have to prove that you should keep it."

After making that statement, the Cardinals finished the year with a 16–29 record in their final 45 games. Less than a week after the season ended, however, the team announced that La Russa had signed the contract extension.

La Russa said the extension, plus the team's performance in 1999, left him more determined to succeed in 2000. "I wasn't embarrassed this year, but I was disappointed," he said. "A team can play hard baseball and play good, fundamental baseball. This team played hard, but I think, for whatever reason, this team didn't always play good baseball."

That was something La Russa did not intend to let happen again. Among the reasons for his optimism was the arrival of a young pitching phenom, Rick Ankiel, who had burst onto the scene.

CHAPTER 17

A Championship Run

On August 23, 1999, just one month and four days after he turned 20 years old, Rick Ankiel made his major league debut for the Cardinals. The pitcher, who had gone 25–9 in 52 minor league games as a teenager, pitched five innings in the game at Montreal, allowing three runs and not receiving a decision in the game.

Before the game, La Russa knew the spotlight was on the left-handed Ankiel, the kind of pitching prospect who does not come along very often. He also knew, however, that Ankiel's future had been placed in his hands, along with those of pitching coach Dave Duncan.

"It's up to us to do all that we can to make sure he can do the job," La Russa said before that game. "Part of that is having tunnel vision and being oblivious to what people think. We have to take care of this pitcher."

Part of La Russa's concern was Ankiel's age. Also, the Cardinals had seen two young potential pitching aces, Matt Morris and Alan Benes, fall victim to injuries and surgery in the previous two years.

"I don't know what we did to deserve what happened to Alan and Matt, but because of that, you want to be even more careful with Ankiel," La Russa said.

In the remaining six weeks of the disappointing season, Ankiel pitched in eight additional games, including four starts, and finished the year with a 0–1 record, one save, and a 3.27 ERA. He struck out 39 batters in 33 innings, and showed La Russa and Duncan enough that they quickly began counting on him as part of the team's starting rotation in 2000.

The addition of veteran starters Pat Hentgen, Darryl Kile, and Andy Benes over the winter lessened the pressure on Ankiel to deliver as a rookie, but it did not decrease La Russa's opinions about the young left-hander's credentials.

"He's got a special arm," La Russa said in spring training. "But one of the qualities that has impressed everybody is that ever since he came into pro ball he's had a lot of attention, but he just goes on the mound and competes. He puts as much pressure on himself as anybody else, and he just competes. That's special. He has a lot of toughness.

"The second game he pitched for us was an ESPN Sunday night game against the Braves. He probably had the worst stuff and command he had in the whole last month with us, but he gave up just two runs in six innings. He never gave into it; he kept battling."

La Russa knew, as did everyone else, that while he was competing for a spot in the Cardinals' rotation, Ankiel was facing some personal problems. His father had a lengthy legal history, and in March was sentenced to five years in prison after pleading guilty to drug charges. The fact that Ankiel, at such a young age, was mentally tough enough to block out his personal troubles when he was pitching was another attribute that La Russa considered extraordinary. The manager's admiration for Ankiel only increased as the season went on.

While keeping a special eye on Ankiel, La Russa still had to focus his attention on many other areas, including his own job status. The three disappointing seasons since 1996 had left many people wondering if the Cardinals needed to change managers, and La Russa knew he might not survive another poor season. He did, however, get upset when critics suggested that he needed to manage better in 2000, an attack he took personally.

"You get ticked off," La Russa said. "It's insulting, really, for somebody to say you've got something to prove. What's the inference there? Be on your toes more, try and do a better job…. If you only feel urgency when you feel like you're vulnerable or in jeopardy, that says you're unprofessional the rest of the time. I don't feel any extra urgency this year. I put a hundred percent pressure on myself as a manager to make the contribution."

La Russa applied that same logic to evaluating players, which is why many people said it takes a "certain kind" of player to be successful under La Russa.

"The minute somebody comes up and says, 'I need you to kick me in the butt to get me going,' I say, 'Get rid of him.'" La Russa said. "You think I'm going to try harder because Bill DeWitt [Cardinals chairman] or Walt Jocketty says, 'You know, if you don't get off to a good start, it's going to prove you can't do this job anymore.' That's nonsense.

"There are managers who worry about being on the hot seat. They're not around too long. First of all, they'll hurt their chances to win and get beat. Secondly, they won't have the respect of the people in uniform, because they'll smell it out first."

Luckily for La Russa and the Cardinals, the off-season changes—plus the spring training trade for Jim Edmonds—seemed to energize the team and the season began with a 17–8 April. The team was 10 games over .500 before the end of May, spent only three days out of first place all season, and never had less than a four-game lead after June 14. The team's 95 wins were the most since the 1987 pennant-winning club.

Edmonds slammed 42 homers and drove in 108 runs while McGwire, limited to just 70 starts because of knee and back injuries, still hit 32 homers. Kile won 20 games to lead the pitching staff, which also got a boost from Ankiel's 11 wins and 194 strikeouts, breaking Dizzy Dean's franchise record for most strikeouts by a rookie pitcher.

Along with Ankiel, the Cardinals had another blossoming young star, 24-year-old outfielder J.D. Drew, demonstrate to La Russa what he could do as he spent his first full season in the major leagues. Drew hit .295 with 18 homers and 57 RBIs. As with Ankiel, the manager was trying to bring Drew along slowly, realizing his talent but also knowing his limitations because of age and experience.

"If you turn him loose and he struggles, then people say, 'He's being thrown to the wolves,'" La Russa said. "J.D. is still a learning player. So it will be a lot better for J.D. and the Cardinals if he can play when things are working well for him, and if not, he doesn't have to get buried. Last year, he took some at-bats that I wish we didn't have to give him."

Part of the learning process included La Russa trying to correct Drew's mistakes, such as throwing to the wrong base or committing base-running miscues. It was the start of an unusual relationship between the two that would last until Drew was traded to the Braves after the 2003 season.

The problem any manager faces with any talented young player is the knowledge of how to motivate him to achieve the greatest possible success. But in La Russa's case, it had been well established throughout his career that his desire was to have players who reflected his attitude and intense style. Drew, a soft-spoken, quiet kid from very rural south Georgia, was such a gifted athlete that it often appeared to La Russa and others that he was not playing at a hundred percent, almost always a fatal flaw in trying to earn the manager's respect.

"J.D. is a plus, gifted athlete," La Russa said. "He's got to always remind himself that real success doesn't come easy, and he's going to have to really keep pushing to improve and get to be the player he can be because he can settle in at .270 with 75 RBIs, 15 home runs. But J.D. should not be a .270 hitter. He could settle and be a little above average defensively, a little above average as a base runner. I just hope he realizes he's got to keep pushing.

"I'm sure sometimes he probably thinks that I'm rougher on him than the other guys. But there isn't a time when he does something good that the coaches and I don't walk up and pat him on the back. J.D. has to understand something. He's got a responsibility to be as great as he can be."

Drew said publicly that he understood, but privately it was apparent that the manager's criticism bothered him. "I don't think they pick on me," he said. "It's part of the game. Play the game, play the game hard, and hopefully help the team win games. I don't want to let the guys down out there."

In much the same way, La Russa did not believe he would be doing his job the best way he knew how if he *wasn't* constantly riding Drew, telling him what he did wrong, and imploring him to do better.

"I don't know that our relationship could be any better than it is," La Russa said. "There are times when I've been honest and told him, 'If this was all about you, you would play today. But it's not about you, it's about us.' And knowing that doesn't change anything about how he is."

Even though their personalities were very different, the situation was very similar to the way La Russa felt about Ankiel—how the manager did his best to protect him and bring him along at a certain speed, tried not to expect too much too soon, or be disappointed if there were occasional setbacks.

By the end of the season, La Russa considered Ankiel, unbeaten in his last 10 starts, to be the team's second-best starter, trailing only Kile. As the playoffs approached, La Russa and Duncan tried to set up their rotation to maximize the number of starts each could make.

What no one could have expected, however, was that none of the starters would be able to pitch to starting catcher Mike Matheny. On the eve of the playoffs, Matheny was opening a belated birthday gift, a hunting knife, when he accidentally severed two flexor tendons and sliced a nerve in his right ring finger. Could Matheny's presence behind the plate possibly have changed what was to occur in the next couple of weeks? It is a question La Russa has pondered many times over the last several years, but it is a question that nobody will ever be able to answer.

With or without Matheny, La Russa and Duncan decided the best order for their rotation was to go with Ankiel in the first game with Kile pitching Game 2, even though he was the team's ace. If the series went to a deciding fifth game, Kile would be able to pitch that game on three days' rest instead of pushing Ankiel into that role. The lineup also would have Kile and Ankiel available to pitch four of the potential five games.

Even though most managers likely would still have followed the traditional approach and started Kile in Game 1, there was logic behind La Russa and

Duncan's decision. It was a decision that has been debated, analyzed, and second guessed for years.

Duncan, in particular, was worried about placing all of the attention and focus that falls on the Game 1 starter on the young Ankiel. He was worried that reporters would ask him questions about his family situation and might somehow distract the pitcher and take him off his game.

"We've got to do everything we can to get him as under control as he can be," Duncan said before the playoffs. "All that attention is a distraction and the more you can keep attention away from the young guys, the less distracted they get. The older guys can deal with it. The younger guys haven't learned to deal with it yet."

The decision La Russa and Duncan made was basically to lie to the media about who would be starting the first game of the playoffs. The Cardinals announced Kile as the Game 1 starter and sent him to the interview room to answer the media's questions about the game coming up the following day.

Kile knew that La Russa and Duncan were playing a bait-and-switch game with the media, and he dutifully went along with the plan. He carried out his assignment of convincing the media that he was pitching the next day.

It wasn't until La Russa spoke to the media, and after Ankiel and Kile had both had time to finish their workouts and leave Busch Stadium, that La Russa admitted Ankiel was starting the opener and not Kile. His plan of deception was designed expressly to keep the media away from Ankiel. At the time, he thought it had worked.

La Russa didn't care that the media members were understandably upset. It was one more decision he had made looking for that extra little edge, trying to give his team an unexpected advantage.

"Why put him through answering a lot of questions about how he thinks and he feels when he's never been there before to know how he thinks and feels?" La Russa said in trying to rationalize his decision.

Columnist Bernie Miklasz, writing in the *Post-Dispatch* the following day, was almost prophetic.

"The Cardinals have a chance," Miklasz wrote. "But if Ankiel gets blown up in Game 1, La Russa will be second-guessed for, oh, forever. If Ankiel wins Game 1, and the Cardinals go on to eliminate Atlanta, La Russa will be a genius again."

It did not take long for the second-guessing to begin. After the Braves' Rafael Furcal singled to lead off the game, Ankiel struck out Andruw Jones and Furcal was thrown out attempting to steal second. The first signs of trouble then appeared with back-to-back walks, before Ankiel got out of the inning on a foul pop-up.

Most observers thought Ankiel's spurt of wildness was the result of nerves, and after the Cardinals unloaded on Greg Maddux for six runs in the bottom of the first, they were certain the youngster would settle down. Indeed, despite allowing a one-out double to Walt Weiss in the bottom of the second, Ankiel got out of the inning by getting Javier Lopez to line into a double play.

It was after Ankiel went back to the mound for the third inning that the trouble really began. After a leadoff walk to Maddux, Ankiel retired Furcal before unleashing two wild pitches. Following a walk came the third wild pitch of the inning, but then Ankiel moved one out away from getting out of the inning by striking out Chipper Jones on a called third strike. He never got that out. First came another walk, then another wild pitch, an RBI single, another wild pitch, another walk, and a two-run single before La Russa came to the mound to get him.

The five wild pitches in one inning had only happened one time before in major league history, in 1890. Even though the Cardinals came out on top and won the game, Ankiel's performance was the only topic of conversation after the game.

Various theories were advanced, including the fact that Carlos Hernandez was catching Ankiel instead of Matheny. Others attributed his performance to stage fright or nerves. Nobody was seriously concerned, believing the problems would be corrected when Ankiel made his next start.

A day later, Ankiel asked a philosophical question to a reporter, "You can't get any worse, I don't think," he said. "Can you?"

The answer did not come until Game 2 of the National League Championship Series against the Mets. Thanks to the Cardinals' sweep of the Braves, Ankiel did not have to pitch again in that series so he had a nine-day layoff before taking the ball again.

La Russa did not shield Ankiel from the media before this start, nor did he play any cloak-and-dagger games. Ankiel answered all of the reporters' questions, albeit with boring responses, and didn't seem any worse for having gone through the experience.

"Have you ever experienced anything quite like that in your life?" he was asked. "Not that I can remember," he said. "How supportive were your teammates?" was another question. "Very" was the answer. "Did any of their comments stick in your head?" "No," he said. He had to answer one question about why, despite growing up in Port St. Lucie, where the Mets conduct spring training, he was never a Mets fan. "I just didn't like them too much, I guess," Ankiel said.

The whole interview session lasted only a few minutes, with the only real notable sound bite being Ankiel's admission that, "I am trying to forget about that day as much as I can."

Twenty-four hours later, Ankiel had another day he would have liked to forget. This time, he did not get out of the first inning. He threw 34 pitches, the first of which went over leadoff hitter Timo Perez's head and hit the backstop screen. Three more pitches hit the screen later in the inning, even though he was only officially charged with two wild pitches.

Changing catchers, to Eli Marrero, made no difference. Only 13 of the 34 pitches were strikes and he walked three of the eight batters he faced and recorded only two outs before being lifted from the game.

The Mets scored a run in the ninth to win the game 6–5, but all anybody wanted to talk about afterward was Ankiel.

"Before anybody starts kicking Rick around," La Russa said, "I think the blame is on me for putting him there. There's where it ought to end."

Then La Russa offered a statement that, in the retrospect made available by a span of eight years, proved significant.

"The kid's going to be all right," La Russa said then. "If we're all going to have Rick's problems, the rest of our life is made."

Neither La Russa nor anybody else, of course, had any idea that the postseason meltdown was the beginning of the end of Ankiel's pitching career. His final appearance of the playoffs came in relief in Game 5, with the Cardinals only nine outs away from losing the series to the Mets and trailing in the game 6–0.

La Russa was hoping that a positive appearance would give Ankiel something to build on for the winter, but the plan once again backfired. His first warmup pitch went to the backstop and fans at Shea Stadium began chanting "wild pitch" as leadoff hitter Mike Bordick walked. Ankiel did get two outs, on a sacrifice and a strikeout, but then came two more wild pitches and a walk before he left the game.

La Russa's plan might have worked had he taken Ankiel out of the game following the strikeout of Perez, but instead he stayed in one batter too long. The fact that the Cardinals lost the series and the pennant in five games to the Mets was almost an afterthought.

At the time, La Russa expressed no doubts that Ankiel would be able to come back and pitch effectively in 2001. "Absolutely," he said. "Ankiel is going to move forward. He had a terrific year of experience. It was mostly great, with a couple of hiccups. I'll think he'll use both of them."

La Russa still felt that way the following spring. He still believed Ankiel, now all of 21 years old, would restart his career and everybody involved would one day be able to joke and laugh about what happened in those four playoff innings in 2000.

As always, La Russa's first obligation that spring was to his team, and his second was to his players as individuals. As much as he wanted Ankiel to succeed, he had to first concentrate on getting his entire roster ready for the start of the season.

As much as the media focus had been on Ankiel in the playoffs, it was even more intense in the Florida spring. All the national writers and television crews coming through the Cardinals' camp wanted to interview Ankiel and write again about what had happened in October. The scene quickly grew tiring. Ankiel began turning down almost all media requests, and the Cardinals had him work out at sunrise on a back field so photographers could not observe him.

After one mass press conference, Ankiel said he would not talk again about what had happened and La Russa said, "Anybody who wants to try to mess with Rick, we're going to treat them like the unwanted."

When the regular season began, the Cardinals even resorted to having Ankiel warm up in a tunnel under the stadium instead of in the bullpen. He made his first start of the season on April 8 at Arizona, and beat Randy Johnson. He stuck out eight in five innings.

That turned out to be Ankiel's only highlight of the season, however, and by mid-May he found himself back in Triple A. By the end of the year, he was back in rookie ball in Johnson City, Tennessee, trying to start his long road back at the beginning. He would not wear a major league uniform again in the regular season until September 2004.

After several years to think about what had happened over those fateful two weeks, La Russa said in an interview with Fox Sports Midwest in 2008, "I'm absolutely convinced that if Mike Matheny had caught that first game Rick would not have had the problems with the wildness. He would have speared a couple of those balls. The confidence factor was not there for a young pitcher pitching in the bright lights of the postseason."

La Russa later added, "Carlos Hernandez had a bad back, and his mobility was restricted. Mike would have gotten Rick back in the groove."

As much time as he spent worrying about Ankiel in the spring of 2001, La Russa also had other concerns that filled up much of his days in Jupiter, Florida.

Mark McGwire had undergone knee surgery in October, and La Russa needed to see if he was healthy. A youngster who had played only one year in the minors, Albert Pujols, was making quite an impression but La Russa was not certain he could make the jump from Single A ball to the majors.

La Russa experienced a new first that spring—finding himself ejected from a game during spring training. Minor league umpire Matt Hollowell ejected

La Russa for arguing whether Mets' runner Rey Ordonez had gone out of the base line while trying to elude a tag.

That same game was historical for another reason. Veteran Bobby Bonilla, signed as a free agent, felt a twinge in his left hamstring during the game. That injury put Bonilla on the disabled list at the start of the season, and opened a roster spot for Pujols. At the time, La Russa had no idea how significant that would be.

Even with Pujols' unexpected contributions, the Cardinals found themselves limping along for much of the first half of the season. On May 6, the team was 14-15 before opening a 10-game winning streak. By July 3, the record had dropped below .500 at 40-41 and the team stayed within a few games of the break-even point until August.

The headline on Bernie Miklasz's column in the *Post-Dispatch* on June 30 read, "With a big payroll, La Russa has no excuses—he must deliver." The Cardinals lost their fifth game in a row the next day, prompting a postgame meeting between La Russa and Jocketty and a promise that if the losing continued, some kind of move would be made "to shake it up."

That move would not be a change in managers, even though La Russa was once again in the last year of his contract. Ownership had placed a new two-year offer on the table during spring training, but La Russa had made no attempt to sign it, believing as he had throughout his career that those decisions needed to be made at the end of the season.

Two moves did materialize: the Cardinals reassigned hitting coach Mike Easler at the end of July, and the team traded veteran outfielder Ray Lankford to San Diego for pitcher Woody Williams.

Only 13 players had worn a Cardinal uniform longer than Lankford, who had been with the club since 1989. Lankford later said his final months in that uniform were among the most disappointing of his career and he believed the organization tried to place the blame for losing on his shoulders, specifically pointing to La Russa.

"I never did get along with [La Russa]," Lankford told the *Sacramento Bee* after the trade. "When things were going well for me, there was nothing he could do. But when I struggled, he always singled me out. I lost respect for him.

"We didn't even talk for the last month. It was like I was grounded. He wouldn't even put me in the lineup against right-handers, then he would put me in against a lefty, like he wanted me to fail. I just wanted him to let me know what was going on, at least communicate with me. I'm not a kid. My problem was that I had an opinion."

Said La Russa, "I told him he had the talent to be a great player but he had to be more into the game. He had some very productive years, but toward the end he was in the 'if it happens, it happens' category. That's where we had problems. I never saw Ray not try, but to be really special he had to do it as part of a team effort."

La Russa thought that the trade would help Lankford get a fresh start in San Diego, and that the addition of Williams would be a positive move for the Cardinals. It seemed to bear fruit quickly as the team began an 11-game winning streak on August 9, surging to 68–55. Still, the team trailed first-place Houston by 3½ games.

The Cardinals would spend the rest of the season trying to chase down the Astros, but they—and everybody else in the United States—experienced some unexpected interruptions in their daily life on September 11.

The Cardinals were in Milwaukee when the terrorists attacks occurred in New York and Washington, and because all air travel was grounded, the team had to take a 6½ hour bus ride back to St. Louis. La Russa, like many, was shocked by the attacks and said it definitely put baseball in perspective.

"Sometimes people get on me for being too serious, but [baseball] is just a game," La Russa said. "I never like it when we're included in essential things. We're not essential. I don't care how intense or serious I get about the Cardinals playing in October. I'm not nuts…. You can do without what we do for a living."

When the major leagues resumed play on September 17, the Cardinals were five games behind Houston. They overcame that gap to move into a tie with six games left to play, the final three scheduled against the Astros. St. Louis took the first two games of the series and was up by one game with the third and final game to play, but a 9–2 Houston victory left both teams with a 93–69 record. Houston had the season's edge in head-to-head competition, so the Astros were awarded the division championship and the Cardinals took the wild-card spot. La Russa considered the Cardinals "co-champions" of the division, a stance that angered the Astros throughout the winter and into 2002.

As the wild-card entry, the Cardinals traveled to Phoenix to open the postseason against the Diamondbacks. Curt Schilling outdueled Matt Morris for a 1–0 victory in Game 1, but the Cardinals came back behind Williams to win Game 2. After the two teams split the two games in St. Louis, the fifth and deciding game was played in Phoenix.

The score was 1–1 going into the bottom of the ninth when the Diamondbacks won the game and the series on an RBI single by Tony Womack.

More notable perhaps than the final result was what turned out to be the final career appearance for Mark McGwire, who announced his retirement in November via a fax to ESPN. In the top of the ninth inning, in a sacrifice situation, La Russa sent rookie Kerry Robinson up to pinch-hit for McGwire.

"One of my lowest moments as a manager was pinch-hitting for Mark," La Russa said. "But you've got to try to win the game. Pinch-hitting for Mark is not something I am going to remember fondly."

As talk of McGwire's retirement stirred, so did the talk about La Russa's future, and the expected debate about whether he should or should not return, a topic that divided Cardinal Nation.

The headline on Miklasz's column in the October 18 *Post-Dispatch* read, "Ugly La Russa debate still is divisive issue for Cardinal Nation." Miklasz wrote, "Oh no, another column on Tony La Russa. I'll be deleting all of my email today. If there's anything I've come to dislike more than writing about La Russa, it's reading the responses to the columns. I've never covered such a prominent hot-button personality as La Russa; people start foaming at the mouth at the mere mention of his name. The opinions tend to be extreme. There's very little middle ground...."

"If Tony comes back, fine, Good luck to him. But I won't be broken-hearted if La Russa decides to quit. I just get tired of the constant sniping about La Russa among various factions. La Russa has become a divisive figure. I look forward to the day when we can all follow this proud baseball franchise again and engage in civil debate over routine baseball matters without taking such antagonistic, immovable positions on La Russa."

Later that day, La Russa informed Jocketty he wanted to return as the Cardinals manager for 2002.

"There's probably mixed emotions over the job that has been done," La Russa said. "How do you rate the success we've had when we haven't won the world championship? There is a mix there. But there is one certainty. The certainty is that [the fans] don't want a world championship any worse than I do. We both can be unhappy and disappointed at the same time."

Unhappy and disappointed, La Russa and the Cardinals hoped there would be better moments and more positive emotions in 2002. What couldn't be predicted was a unifying moment produced by tears and tragedy in a season no Cardinals fan would ever forget.

CHAPTER 18

Tragedy Strikes

The reasons for optimism filled Roger Dean Stadium in Jupiter, Florida, during March of 2002. La Russa thought the nature of the clubhouse had changed, becoming more like the atmosphere he was used to in Chicago and Oakland. He thought he had earned the trust and respect of the players, and that the team now had more of a "family" atmosphere because of the presence of players such as Matheny, Kile, Edmonds, and Edgar Renteria.

Even though McGwire had retired, Jocketty had lured Tino Martinez away from the Yankees to play first base. La Russa had gone to high school with Martinez's father. Jocketty had also given La Russa a new closer, Jason Isringhausen, fulfilling one of the team's major needs. Albert Pujols had come out of nowhere to win the Rookie of the Year award with one of the best inaugural seasons in history, and every indication was that he would not be a one-year wonder.

La Russa himself was working under a new three-year contract, instead of an anticipated two-year deal, because he felt that St. Louis was where he was supposed to manage. "I was always sincere that if at the end of the season, they [the owners] didn't want me, I wouldn't be here," La Russa said. "And if I didn't have a good relationship in the clubhouse, I wouldn't be here."

There were some distractions during spring training, of course, like the day the Dodgers changed starting pitchers at the last minute, sending La Russa into a frenzy because his well-detailed schedule had a lineup ready for a right-handed starter, not a left-hander. He also had to deal with the death of his godfather, and went back-and-forth on whether to play Pujols at third base or left field, finally settling on the outfield.

The regular season was a week old when La Russa, preparing for a game against Milwaukee, received a phone call with the news that his father, Anthony Sr., had died in Tampa at the age of 90.

Devastated, La Russa filled out the lineup card and left the stadium. He later returned, spending much of the game in his office, watching on television, as the Cardinals beat Milwaukee 6–5.

"I just couldn't handle it," La Russa said. "I would have done a disservice to the people I'm responsible to. I just couldn't have done it. I just put up the lineup and got out of the way."

La Russa was back in the dugout the next day, after spending part of the day on the telephone, helping to complete the funeral arrangements. The Cardinals once again won 6–5, this time in extra innings.

"I was thinking about him all game," La Russa said in a quavering voice and fighting back tears, as he talked about his father, who followed all of the Cardinals' games very closely. "He was there all game."

The death of his father, naturally, would continue to affect him. The team also received another emotional jolt when La Russa and several of his players took a tour of the site of the terrorist attacks in New York during an off-day in late April.

"We were given a unique opportunity to have an escort from the New York Police Department and we went into some buildings across the street from the destruction and got a bird's eye view," said catcher Mike Matheny. "If it wasn't real enough already, coming that close and seeing it made it that much more real. We also went to some of the rescue sites and saw the work that was being done. They were already a couple of levels down and to see all of that debris was just amazing.

"We saw a lot of memorials and photos of missing people. There were still people searching, hoping they were going to find their loved ones. We realized just how that event had changed the course of everyone's lives forever."

It was an experience that put baseball into perspective; suddenly issues such as using 10 starting pitchers in the opening month of the season did not seem as important.

Despite that, most fans tended to care most about what happened in the last game, and whether their team won or lost. After every Cardinals loss, fans were quick to jump on La Russa. The phone lines lit up on the local sports-talk radio stations, and more comments filled the Internet forums.

One questionable move came in a game against the Braves on May 3, when La Russa had the option of intentionally walking Chipper Jones with a runner on third and two outs in a scoreless game in the eleventh. Gary Sheffield, mired in a one-for-31 slump, was on deck.

Even when the count on Jones reached 3–0, La Russa made no sign for reliever Gene Stechschulte to intentionally throw ball four. Stechschulte didn't, and Jones slammed a home run 411 feet over the center-field wall.

That was not what was supposed to happen. La Russa, standing in the dugout, literally reeled backward after Jones's homer and pulled the cap off his head. When he had composed himself, he wrote one word on the back of the lineup card he keeps in his pants pocket: "unbelievable."

Stechschulte was not ordered to walk Jones intentionally because La Russa has long believed that an intentional walk is a sign of disrespect for the hitter waiting on deck. It is the reason his teams rank perennially among the major league clubs that issue the least intentional walks. Sometimes the strategy dictates the move and he can't avoid it. In this situation, his instruction to the pitcher was not to throw a pitch that Jones could hit.

"The problem with sticking the hand out [for an intentional walk] is there's a guy on deck who you're insulting," La Russa explained to reporters. "And I'm not going to insult Gary Sheffield. You don't have to. I wrote it on my card. It's unbelievable that that 3–0 pitch is in the zone. In the end, we walked the wrong guy and pitched to the wrong guy."

The loss was the Cardinals' 12th in 17 games, coming at a time when injuries were wracking the team's pitching staff. One of the new starters was Jason Simontacchi, a 28-year-old rookie and a former tow-truck driver who had been pitching in Italy only two years earlier. He pitched the night after the Jones homer, and held the Braves to two runs in seven innings in a 3–2 win, his first major league victory.

The Cardinals went to Chicago after the Braves' series, and when those two teams play, it doesn't really matter who is pitching; the games are likely to be memorable. In this series, the biggest matchup was between La Russa and Cubs' manager Don Baylor, who had played his final season for La Russa in Oakland in 1988.

La Russa and the Cardinals thought the Cubs were stealing signs while Sammy Sosa was at bat, and were letting him know ahead of time what pitch was coming, or its location. (La Russa, of course, had been on the other side of stealing signs during his career.) He just didn't like it when *his* signs were the ones that he thought were being stolen. He and Baylor quickly got into a war of words.

"I warned our team the first day these are some of the things [La Russa's teams] try to do," Baylor said. "They're not going to intimidate this club."

La Russa is not easily intimidated either, especially by accusations that his pitchers sometimes took "cheap shots" at opposing hitters or that he tried to play mind games with opponents.

"I've been around a long time," La Russa said. "You can take all the players who have played for me and I'll take my chances on what they say about how we compete, whether we take cheap shots, whether we play mind games.

"When you've been around for 20 years, there are going to be incidents once in a while. Over time, they pile up. 'Tony's a headhunter,' you will never find one pitcher who ever played for me who says it. In fact, they've been told the opposite. If you throw at somebody's head you will not pitch for our team."

A more staggering and lingering blow came on June 18, which kept La Russa from enjoying Darryl Kile's 7–2 win over the Angels that moved the Cardinals into first place. Hall of Fame broadcaster Jack Buck, one of the icons of the franchise, died at age 77 after a long illness. Buck had been one of the people who had helped La Russa adjust when he arrived in St. Louis and the two had developed a close bond and friendship. Even though he knew Buck's illness was serious, the news that he had died—just two months after his own father's death—hit La Russa hard.

"I thought Jack was a genius. I really mean that," La Russa said. "The man had so many talents. I don't think a lot of people have a full understanding of how gifted he was, not just as a broadcaster.... I think in whatever he would have wanted to do, Jack would have been the best."

La Russa considered his relationship with Buck and wife Carole to be "tied for first among my very best memories of my time in St. Louis."

Specifically, La Russa credited his friendship with Buck and fellow broadcaster Mike Shannon as a major factor in his continuing as manager of the Cardinals past the first three or four years in the job.

"I'm not sure I would have survived past 2000 had it not been for Jack and Mike," La Russa said. "I was getting heat from a lot of different places but I think Jack and Mike believed in me. They were on the radio every day, and I think had a lot of credibility with the fans. On some of my darkest days, when the jury was out on me, people would come up and tell me things Jack and Mike were saying on the radio. If those guys had not believed in me I think the outcry would have been so great I don't think I would have survived.

"Sometimes a manager gets fired for not doing his job, or for losing the team, but sometimes a manager gets fired because the fans don't think he is worth a shit. Jack and Mike's support gave me a fighting chance."

The team held a public memorial service for Buck two days after his death at Busch Stadium, and La Russa, Jocketty, the team owners, and other executives attended a private funeral on June 21, then flew to Chicago, arriving just in time for the start of a weekend series against the Cubs. Jon Leiber outpitched Woody Williams in a 2–1 Chicago victory.

Saturday's game was scheduled to be on national television, and the stands at Wrigley were packed with almost as many red-clad Cardinal fans as blue-clad Cubs fans, one of the special perks that has made the matchup arguably the best rivalry in baseball, if not in all of sports.

The Cardinal players were on the field, stretching and getting in their pregame workouts, when a couple of players noticed that Kile was not there. It was not his day to pitch so he didn't need to report early, but he was almost always one of the first players in the clubhouse even on his days off.

"Dave Veres came up to me and said, 'Darryl's not here yet,'" Matheny said. "I felt kind of panicked at that point. There are some guys that, if you told me they weren't there for stretching, I would have laughed, thinking, 'They will be surprised when they wake up and realize it was a day game.' But not Darryl Kile; the first thing that came to my mind was that something was wrong."

Matheny ran off the field and into the clubhouse, where he attempted to call Kile on his cell phone. There was no answer. Matheny ran into trainer Barry Weinberg and told him about Kile's absence and the fact he did not answer his phone. Matheny did not know then that Veres, another close friend of Kile's, had begun a search for him as well. Veres's wife, Robin, was on the trip and was at the Westin Hotel, so he called her to see if he was still at the hotel.

Kile's wife, Flynn, was in San Diego and about the same time became concerned when she was unable to reach her husband by phone. Her phone call to Robin Veres was another sign that something was wrong.

The Cardinals contacted hotel security, and when there was no answer to knocks on the door of Kile's 11th-floor room, they entered the room. They found Kile dead in his bed. An autopsy later revealed that Kile died of coronary arteriosclerosis; two of the arteries in his heart were 80 to 90 percent blocked.

Word began to spread around the clubhouse that something was wrong with Kile. Robin Veres had called her husband with the news that people were in Kile's room but would not tell her anything.

Matheny called the players together and he and Williams led the team in prayer. As they finished the prayer, they saw La Russa had joined the group. As the players looked to their manager, he struggled to make the news official. "Guys, I just got off the phone with Walt, and they went to Darryl's room and found him dead," La Russa said.

So many thoughts filled La Russa's mind. Nothing could ever prepare a manager for dealing with such a tragedy. Kile was 33 years old, the father of three young children. He had passed a physical exam in spring training and showed no signs of health problems. He had been with the team a day earlier.

Matt Morris had talked to him later that evening, asking if he wanted to come down to the hotel bar for a drink. Kile declined, saying he was tired and was going to bed.

As players openly wept or silently mourned, La Russa retreated to his office, alone in his thoughts. Cubs President Andy MacPhail walked through the Cardinals' locker room and agreed with La Russa that his team could not play a baseball game that day. The game was canceled. La Russa gave a brief interview to Fox television, but canceled a news conference. The team solemnly filed onto its bus and returned to the hotel, where the players, coaches, staff, and La Russa assembled later in the evening.

"The news devastated our club," La Russa later said. "There was no bigger leader on our ballclub in every way…. You see so many strong men, and you're seeing them break down."

At the team meeting, La Russa opened up the floor to let the players speak and express their emotions and feelings. The decision was made to play on Sunday night, which would have been Kile's turn to pitch, because "that's what Darryl would have wanted." In his 11 years in the major leagues, Kile had never missed a turn in the rotation and had never been on the disabled list.

The team got together again on Sunday morning at the hotel. Several players spoke, as did Kile's widow, who encouraged the team to play the game that evening.

At the ballpark, La Russa recalled how the team had come together to overcome other obstacles in the past. He said that the best way for them to honor their teammate was by playing the game the way Kile had always played it. Even if it was not verbalized, a slogan was adopted as the team's mantra for the remainder of the season, "For Darryl."

The Cardinals played the game, and lost 8–3, but there was no exuberance among the Cardinals, the Cubs, or the crowd. La Russa recalled a somewhat similar experience. Only days into his first managerial assignment with the White Sox, his team had gone to Yankee Stadium to play the first game there since the death of catcher Thurman Munson. The Yankees had attended the memorial service earlier that day.

"Billy Martin likened it to his having been run over by a truck," La Russa said. "It was almost embarrassing to win that game because [the Yankees] had no chance." La Russa understood the feeling.

Kile's absence echoed through the dugout, the playing field, the clubhouse. "You're used to hearing him," La Russa said. "You know where he would sit on the bench. You miss him. And it's going to happen over and over again."

The Cardinals stumbled through the next several games, and through more memorials and remembrances of Kile. La Russa and his coaches admitted they really did not know what to do, how to balance the emotional needs of the players with the goal of winning games.

Then La Russa read in the *Post-Dispatch* some comments that Kile himself had made after his own father had died at the age of 44. La Russa decided it helped him put Kile's death into focus, and perhaps it would do the same for his players. He called a meeting before a game, and said he wanted to read those comments to the players.

"I don't think I'll ever get over it," Kile had said. "My father was my best friend. But in order to be a man, you've got to separate your personal life from your work life. It may sound cold, but I've got work to do. I'll never forget my father, but I'm sure he'd want me to keep on working and try to do the best I can do."

One manager who knew a little of what La Russa was going through was Mike Hargrove. He was the manager of the Indians when the team lost two of its pitchers, Steve Olin and Tim Crews, to a boating accident. After he read about Kile's death and the hard times the Cardinals were going through, several times he picked up the telephone to call La Russa. Each time he hung up before the call went through; he didn't know what to say and he didn't want to intrude.

"I don't know if our players have ever heard it, but among our coaches we always called Darryl 'John Wayne,'" La Russa said. "This is a very, very tough-minded competitor, a conscientious teammate, a wonderful friend and family man. Be like Darryl."

The Cardinals won four in a row, and when they closed out the first half of the season with a 12–6 win over the Dodgers, the emotions finally got to La Russa. He sat at his desk and cried, for all of the reasons imaginable.

"I don't really have a feel for how much understanding the majority of fans have about what this has been like," La Russa said. "I know we're judged on winning and losing. I've lived with that principle, and I think our players should live with it too. But in measuring this team, to look at this list of things that this club had to deal with…and they kept on playing hard. I have so much admiration for them.

"There's an old saying about how the strong get tested. I told them they must be pretty strong, because this has really been a test, and I think they really passed it. Nothing deters them. Sure, there have been games we could have won and didn't. But in my opinion, to be plus-nine [games over .500] after what we've been through, that's a hell of a number.

"It's been really hard for these guys. There's been a lot of sadness. There have been so many punches to the gut and punches to the jaw…. But it's a wonderful team in the clubhouse."

La Russa went home to California to be with his family for the All-Star break, as well-deserved a rest as could have been possible.

For the rest of the season, the Cardinals continued to honor Kile by winning, and made aggressive moves to improve their ballclub. The biggest was a trade with the Phillies for All-Star third baseman Scott Rolen.

Even La Russa's critics had to admire his performance and response to tragedy in leading the Cardinals. Wrote Miklasz in the *Post-Dispatch* on September 8, "No NL manager has had to deal with so much adversity this season. And no manager's team has played harder than this one. The Cardinals have 36 come-from-behind victories this season. It's a team of character, harmony, and grace and La Russa has been a constant source of strength."

Even apart from the deaths of Buck and Kile, the challenges for La Russa were immense. The team used 26 pitchers during the season, including 14 starters. Eighteen players spent at least part of the season in the minor leagues.

La Russa juggled the lineups as usual, trying to keep the bench players sharp and looking for advantages wherever he could find them.

The players needed a leader, and they found one in La Russa. "Our guys had to search for new ways to get themselves ready," La Russa said. "After we lost Darryl, there were a lot of days where they probably didn't feel like playing. It's tough to play with a hole in your heart, when you're sad as hell. There guys helped each other out. As a result, this club is like glue. There isn't anything someone could do to us, or we could do to ourselves, that would break us apart."

The team's strength in unity helped the Cardinals clinch the division title on September 20. Jocketty took in the clubhouse celebration and marveled at what he had witnessed.

"If you had seen this team that Saturday [when they learned of Kile's death] and the next two days, you wouldn't have known if this team was ever going to recover," Jocketty said.

Along the way, they picked up the respect and admiration of every player in the league. In Colorado, former Kile teammate Larry Walker told several Cardinals, "You've got to win this for DK, because that's what he was all about, winning and helping people. You've got to do it."

When the Cardinals finished the regular season with a 4–0 victory over Milwaukee, it was their 97th win. On June 22, the day Kile died, the team had 40 victories; they won 57 games after Kile's death. Kile also wore uniform number 57. A superstitious person like La Russa could not help but notice that symbolism.

The Cardinals first-round opponent was Arizona, the team that had eliminated them in 2001. The Cardinals made sure that it would not happen again, and despite a freak injury to Rolen, pulled off a three-game sweep that placed them in the league championship series for the third time in La Russa's seven years in St. Louis.

La Russa heard the celebration of his players from his office, and once again his emotions overtook him. The tears flowed as he was hugged by one of the team's owners, Drew Baur. At that moment, he and the players really believed that this was a team of destiny, and that they were meant to win, "For Darryl."

Their opponent in the league championship series was the San Francisco Giants, managed by Dusty Baker. La Russa's relationship with Baker dated back to 1971, when they were teammates trying to stick with the Atlanta Braves. Baker's playing career ended in Oakland in 1986, with La Russa as his manager. At the time, Baker had no plans of becoming a manager.

"I was going to be a stockbroker," Baker said. "I was for one summer, then the market crashed and Al Rosen asked me if I was interested in coaching. My dad told me it was something I should consider, so I did.

"I was only with Tony for half a year but we talked baseball all the time. I always noticed and paid attention to what all of my managers did, and what the opposing manager was doing. When I started managing, I called Tony and asked if he had any advice for me. He said the biggest thing was to get your team prepared before it went out on the field. He told me that one of the biggest mistakes he made was that at the end of my career he should have made me part of his coaching staff in Oakland."

La Russa did have a great deal of respect for Baker, and because he lived in the Bay Area, he perhaps paid a little more attention to the Giants than he did to other clubs. He was home on an off day during the 2002 season, in fact, when he was listening to a sports-talk radio show and Baker's future as the manager of the Giants was being discussed. La Russa became so upset by what he heard that he had to fight the urge to pick up the telephone and call in to the show.

La Russa was irritated by callers saying Baker "needed to prove himself in the playoffs" before he should get a new contract.

"He's proved it year after year," La Russa said of Baker's managing ability. "The guy is really good. He's managed so well, he's taken for granted. He's underappreciated. Nobody does a better job than Dusty Baker."

The matchup between La Russa and Baker was one that observers wanted to watch during this series, knowing that whichever manager made the proper moves likely would be the one to come out on top, since the two teams were so evenly matched.

The series did not get off to a good start for La Russa and the Cardinals. The Giants won the first two games in St. Louis, putting the team in a big hole. The Cardinals flew to San Francisco, knowing they had to win two of three games there to get the series back to St. Louis.

Waiting for them in San Francisco was Kannon Kile, Darryl's five-year-old son. He wore a child-sized Cardinals uniform and sat on the bench during the game. The players were happy to see him, and it gave the team an emotional lift that carried over onto the field, as the Cardinals won 5–4.

While Kannon Kile no doubt wanted the Cardinals to win, he did not know the importance of the game. When Matheny, who had homered earlier in the game, later made a key out and came back to the bench, Kannon was waiting for him.

"He came up to me and asked if I wanted part of his peanut butter and jelly sandwich," Matheny said. "I almost fell off the bench because I was laughing so hard. Moments like that help you keep things in perspective."

Unfortunately for Matheny, La Russa, and the Cardinals, that was their last victory of the year. The Giants pulled out a 4–3 win in Game 4 and clinched the series with a dramatic 2–1 win in the bottom of the ninth in Game 5, winning the pennant and the trip to the World Series.

As is usual in those situations, there was a lot of second-guessing going on, debates about moves that were made or not made. For La Russa, the biggest question in his mind was why his team hit .077 with runners in scoring position. He needed to come up with an answer to why his team always seemed to come up short in October. In the three NLCS appearances as Cardinal manager, the team was 0-for-3 and had won just five of 17 games, and only two of the last 13.

Those numbers were especially incongruous with the team's success in the first round best-of-five division series. In seven trips to that round in St. Louis, La Russa's teams were a combined 20–5, winning six of the seven series.

"Most players and managers look at the first round as being the most pressure you will face anytime in October," La Russa said. "You lose three and you're out. If you get beat in the division series there is a tendency to disrespect the regular season."

There was a long winter ahead, with plenty of time for introspection. All that La Russa wanted to do at this moment was reflect on what his team had accomplished. He was mad that the team had lost, and many of the players felt the same way.

"We came to play every day," Matheny told reporters. "We never made excuses, even when fans and media in St. Louis and around the nation were willing to put those excuses on a platter for us. We never ran from what happened to us. Our response was to compete as hard as we could. We leaned on each other a lot away from the field. We became very close as a team.

"The World Series was just sitting there for us. It was there to be taken and we didn't do it. That's why I feel sick.... Maybe we will look back on this and realize that we can feel proud about some of the things we accomplished this season, but right now I feel that we let a lot of people down. I know we had a good enough team to win this series and the next series and make it the most special year this organization ever had. We were too close to settle for this."

La Russa acknowledged that he had made some critical decisions that had not turned out the way he wanted—taking one pitcher out too early and leaving another in too long.

"They say that if a decision works, it's a good decision," La Russa said. "If it doesn't work, it's a bad decision. I don't judge decisions on whether they work or not. But where I would look at myself when you're talking about a club failing in the championship series is, what could I have done to get them more prepared to have done it better? How could we have made our hitters more productive? How could we have made our pitchers more productive?"

He didn't have immediate answers, which upset him a great deal. Those close to La Russa said he was at his lowest point of the season since Kile's death. He told majority owner Bill DeWitt that if the club thought another manager could get the team past that final step he would walk away from his contract, which had two years remaining. The loss to the Giants still ranks as the most disappointing loss in La Russa's managerial career. DeWitt and the team's other owners all told La Russa they had no intention of changing managers.

"It's going to eat at him," Jocketty said. "He wants to win as much, if not more, than anybody. I told him several times, he brought us through a period this year that most guys wouldn't have been able to endure. It certainly was, for him, a trying year. It really was a highly emotional season. To be able to contain all that and take this club where he did, it was a major accomplishment."

The season still ended short of the ultimate goal. La Russa's pursuit of that prize would have to start all over again in the spring.

CHAPTER 19

The Struggles Continue

Baseball's off-season has always been a time for physical healing and for mental rest and recovery. But for La Russa and the Cardinals, the effects of the 2002 season were not easily forgotten.

At the end of January 2003, three months after his team had been eliminated from the playoffs by the Giants and two weeks before the start of spring training, La Russa still was talking about the NLCS. It was simply his most profound disappointment as a manager, he said, not being able to lead his team to the World Series and a championship.

For some teams, just being able to carry out their daily business after a teammate's death would have been a major accomplishment, but La Russa felt the Cardinals were not like most clubs.

"There were 10, 12 days after Darryl died, I didn't just wonder, but doubted whether we would come out of it," La Russa told the *Post-Dispatch*. "Not just for professional reasons, but all the personal reasons. You see guys looking around, wondering about things way beyond a pennant race. They were sad and totally distracted. But they were still playing games that counted."

The team then reached a point where La Russa thought it could play all the way through October, which was why falling short became such a disappointment.

"There was a point where you could see their determination kick in," La Russa said. "The guys decided to keep playing. You go through something like that where you're really worried about the season getting away, then see the club decide to go for it. People were going to judge this team on whether or not we finished first. We ended up finishing first. I knew in my heart our club would come to grips with it and be admired. But most people would only admire them if they finished first. We finished first, but it got away from us."

La Russa knew that for the Cardinals to succeed in 2003, they needed closure on 2002. Very few teams had endured such a season, and it was highly unlikely that whatever obstacles were to come in the new year could be worse. Any year has its ups and downs, its injuries and sub-par performances. It is the team that is able to make adjustments to those common occurrences that is usually successful. One thing La Russa knew about his team was that nobody could question its mental toughness.

"Tony talks about this all the time," Matheny said. "If you think about it, when is the team's overall health really good? When everyone is healthy, that's rare. So adversity is normal around here. And the guys who play are good. So why worry about who isn't there, or who's not at a hundred percent? Just go out and play hard and play the right way. That's a healthy mentality to have. There's always going to be adversity. How you handle it is what makes the difference. And we aren't the type of team to reach for excuses."

There really were not many excuses the Cardinals could make for not qualifying for the playoffs in 2003, ending a three-year run. They had three players drive in 100 or more runs. Three players hit 28 or more homers. Four starting pitchers made at least 27 starts. They were never more than four games out of first place until September 13.

In the end, however, the Cubs were just the better team and won the division title, three games better than the Cardinals' 85–77 record.

It was a much more normal season in that sense than 2002 had been. La Russa was happy when his team won and upset when they lost. On September 10, he became just the eighth manager in history to reach 2,000 career wins with a 10–2 victory over Colorado.

La Russa admitted he did become sentimental as the end of that game drew near, with the victory assured. "There's no doubt that in the ninth, thoughts about my dad were prominent," La Russa said. "I also thought about Tino [Martinez] because I knew his dad. I thought about his dad never being able to share in all the wonderful moments that man's had."

Pitcher Brett Tomko presented La Russa with the baseball after the final out of the game. "The response I got in the dugout and the clubhouse…I'll never forget it," La Russa said.

As in a "normal" year, there were players on the team, including reserve outfielder Kerry Robinson, who had issues with La Russa. Jose Canseco once publicly criticized La Russa for playing mind games with players and jumping guys when they made mistakes, usually in front of other teammates. Robinson said he had the same opinion as Canseco.

"That's not the way I manage," La Russa responded. "I jumped Canseco one time about not hustling. You have to establish trust with players: if they don't trust you, you have no chance. If I am going to confront a player I do so privately. I don't play mind games. I pay attention to their minds."

La Russa said his issues with Robinson concerned playing time. Robinson wanted to be a regular and play every day, and La Russa thought Robinson could make a more valuable contribution to the team in a reserve role.

"When I talk to football or basketball coaches, what we talk about more than anything is how to get a player's attention," La Russa said. "Kerry was dying to be an everyday player. He had been an outstanding athlete in high school, but I didn't see him in that role. We had Jim Edmonds playing center field. I had no personal dislike for Kerry Robinson but he didn't want to accept a reserve role. It ate his heart out that he wasn't playing."

Canseco's description of La Russa was "the most accurate I have ever heard anybody say about him," said Robinson, who played in 116 games for the

Cardinals in 2003. "I know he played mind games with players because he did it with me."

Robinson recalled one particular incident in a game at Pittsburgh. Only a couple of days earlier, La Russa had told Robinson that he was going to be his top pinch-hitter off the bench, which meant he would be used in late-inning situations.

So early in the game, Robinson was hitting in the batting cage behind the dugout when coach Jose Oquendo came running up to him, saying La Russa wanted him in the dugout ready to pinch-hit. By the time Robinson switched into his jersey and headed for the dugout, Oquendo was back, telling him not to bother.

"At the end of the inning, I was in the tunnel and La Russa came up to me and started cursing and yelling at me," Robinson said. "I stood up to him and asked him what he was talking about. 'If you thought you were going to use me early in the game why didn't you tell me? I would have been ready.' Later in the game Miguel Cairo and Eduardo Perez were doing the same thing I was doing, and he didn't say a word to them about it. There are a whole bunch of guys who played for him who don't have good things to say about him."

Whether players liked him or not, La Russa's personal mood was dictated more by the results of the game than a personal issue with a player. He just could not stand losing under any circumstance, and he took his feelings to a new level after a game in Atlanta.

The bullpen had blown a lead late in the game, but several players were talking and laughing on the team bus back to the hotel. La Russa couldn't stand it. He ordered the bus driver to stop, got off the bus, and went out to dinner by himself. He later walked back to the team hotel.

La Russa evaluated every day based on a simple statistic: a win or a loss. "The bottom line is, in this league, you either get it done or you don't," La Russa said.

When the Cardinals did not get it done in 2003, La Russa, Jocketty, and the team's ownership huddled to see what could be done to improve the club. A big trade came in December when the organization sent J.D. Drew to

Atlanta in a multiplayer trade. Ever since he had made his major league debut for the Cardinals the night Mark McGwire hit his 62nd home run in 1998, Drew had been an awkward fit on the team.

As *Sports Illustrated* wrote after the trade, during his five full seasons in St. Louis, Drew had developed a reputation of having "the passion of a lamppost, a guy with Mantle-esque talents and Randall Simonesque desire, a man who would sit out a week with the slightest toothache or muscle pull. In short, a guy who's softer than a roll of Charmin."

Part of the reputation was built on the multiple injuries that Drew suffered during his Cardinal career, and part was attributable to the fact that Drew was a devout Christian, a soft-spoken guy from south Georgia who didn't drink, smoke, use drugs, or curse.

During his years in St. Louis, Drew never played more than 135 games in a season and was on the disabled list six times. He once twisted his ankle climbing the dugout steps. The 2003 season was a typical Drew year; he played in just 100 games but displayed his talent by hitting 15 homers and driving in 42 runs in just 287 at-bats.

"I can't control a label," Drew said during the season. "You look in the paper and somebody says, 'Aww, he's hurt his side again.' But it's not easy for me to call everybody who reads the paper and say, 'Listen, I'm hurt.' I'm doing everything I can to get back in the lineup. But if I go out there now and check my swing or something like that, I'm done for the rest of the season."

Drew might have had an easier time convincing the fans that he could not play hurt if he had been able to convince his manager of the same thing.

"Nobody can ever know what I was going through," Drew said in a 2005 interview with the *Post-Dispatch*. "I always thought St. Louis fans were great. I wouldn't be in the lineup and they've got to wonder, but the fans can't know. I was dying. When you watched me on a daily basis, you knew what I could do, and then you saw me limping around. That's not a way to play baseball. I couldn't play baseball at a competitive, major league level, the way my knee felt. It's hard to play a game and then take two days off. You never build that rhythm."

Drew knew his manager was frustrated, but not any more so than Drew himself.

"I can understand how it would be frustrating from a managerial standpoint," Drew said. "You see comments that were made. I knew what I was going through, and it was hard to relay that kind of information. They'd look at the MRIs and it didn't look that bad, and then Dr. Paletta opens it up and goes, 'My gosh, this is terrible.' That makes me feel like I'm not going crazy."

La Russa made some very critical comments about Drew in the book *Three Nights in August*, portraying Drew as an underachieving player who did not have the fire to play up to his potential. He was the type of player, La Russa said, who was merely satisfied with being good instead of great.

Drew, who found himself in La Russa's office many times during his Cardinal career, said he has never talked with La Russa about his comments in *Three Nights in August*.

"I never have read it," Drew said of the book. "[La Russa] is entitled to his opinion. I've kind of heard things about it, but it's something I can't focus on. I can only control what I do out there on the field on a daily basis, and I try to take it a game at a time and an at-bat at a time."

La Russa knew Drew wanted to play; his frustration came from wanting him in the lineup because he knew his presence would improve the Cardinals' chances of winning. The manager wanted Drew to go to spring training and follow McGwire and later Albert Pujols around, to see how they approached their job and how hard they worked on an everyday basis.

"Those were guys who pushed themselves to be all they can be," La Russa said. "J.D. didn't want to dig in and do that. It was just part of the times. It was nothing personal."

Even when he was healthy and playing, Drew was such a naturally gifted athlete that at times he appeared to be doing things so easily that it did not look as if he was giving a hundred percent effort. On a La Russa team, that is a major sin. "People don't think I care enough, which couldn't be further from the truth," Drew said in a 2006 interview. "I care very deeply about the game and whatever team I've been on and how to help the team win games. I'm just quiet. I'm the type of person who keeps things inside. It's just the way I am.

"I'm not a rah-rah guy and never have been. That's not who I am. I've never been a showboat or thrown my helmet or my bat or tried to upstage anyone. Maybe sometimes those types of players get the attention and I don't. I'm not going to try to be something I'm not."

The Cardinals also traded Eli Marrero to the Braves, acquiring pitchers Jason Marquis, Adam Wainwright, and Ray King in a deal that seemed—on paper, at least—as if it would benefit both clubs.

As the 2003 season came to a close, La Russa met with several of his veteran players, trying to assess where they had come up short. There was a belief in some corners that La Russa had lost his control of the team, an opinion that was quickly shot down by Matheny.

"To say Tony has lost respect in this clubhouse is just a generalization that questions the character of all of us," Matheny said. "It looks like there's a mutiny going on in here, and there's not. It's just not true. You go up to any of these guys and talk about Tony and you'll see respect. We respect him as our leader and our manager."

There was no doubt, however, that another season without a trip to the World Series left Cardinal fans frustrated. Bernie Miklasz, writing in the *Post-Dispatch*, expressed what many fans believed.

"Two thousand four should be an ultimatum year for La Russa," Miklasz wrote. "His contract expires after 2004. It will be his ninth season. If La Russa can't get the Cardinals to a World Series in nine seasons, with all of the power and resources that he's been granted, then it's time for him to move on."

One of his goals for the season, La Russa admitted, was to have a more cohesive team than had been the case the year before. How to do that was one of the topics he broached in his individual discussions.

"I think there's a closeness, a trust, with Tony that has developed over a number of years," Matheny said. "He's a very intelligent man, and that can be intimidating to people. But I've seen him put up with a lot and deal with it with class. Unfortunately, I don't think a lot of people have the opportunity to know him that way."

Third baseman Scott Rolen also met privately with La Russa. "He's a very smart and very creative man who's constantly rolling things around in his head, looking for an edge," Rolen said. "I think with someone like that, there is the possibility players can sometimes see things differently than he intends them. Tony might be trying to win a game. A player might look at the move more personally. 'Why is he doing that? Has he lost confidence in me?' It might have nothing to do with that, but sometimes it's difficult for the player to know."

Rolen's comments spoke to the issue of communication between La Russa and his players, something the manager hoped would not be a problem in the new season.

In January, La Russa emerged uninjured after a small jet in which he was riding skidded off a snowy Colorado runway. He considered it a good omen for the remainder of the year. La Russa joked, "After you have one-run leads in the ninth inning for 20 years, a minor landing issue gets easier to brush off."

Most prognosticators had failed to include the Cardinals as a favorite along with the Cubs and Astros in the NL Central race. It was not an easy thing for the manager to swallow. Despite the fact that the Cardinals projected five-man rotation won a combined 42 games in 2003, compared to 75 and 72 wins for the Cubs' and Astros' rotations, La Russa did not believe the critics were taking the Cardinals seriously as a pennant contender.

"By the time we play some games this summer, people will be talking about our rotation like they're talking about others now," La Russa said in March. "It doesn't make any difference what people think right now. In the end, we feel this is a game where if you have a good, competitive attitude and you execute the game, you have a chance to win."

He also felt like the lines of communication with his veteran players, which had started to open up in 2003, were strengthened after another round of meetings during spring training. The players involved included Rolen, Morris, Matheny, Edmonds, and Renteria. "We talked about all of the things we could do to make us a more competitive club," La Russa said. "I told them if there were things we should do differently to tell me and I would listen. I said, 'This club is yours.' And they've taken it. The only thing I said is, 'If you come up with something like "We never want to practice," forget it.' But if they have concerns, let's talk about them. If I have issues, we'll talk about them. The first meeting was supposed to be 30 minutes and it went an hour and 15 minutes. It was really good. A lot of concerns were aired. Those sessions were good because we all had the chance to make some points and understand each other."

The players agreed. "He made a conscious effort to throw it back to the ballplayers," Rolen said. "That's not necessarily his style. But he talked to me and a couple of other guys about it and we kind of said, 'Hey, we're all accountable.' We've got a nice veteran corps here. We also thought Tony was being too hard on himself. A veteran team with veteran players can police itself. Things are taken care of, in house, from player to player. It doesn't always have to be from manager to player.

"Tony really went out of his way to make a strong effort to say, 'Here you go, guys. What do you guys think, what do you want to do, how do you want to handle this situation?'"

Some of the changes the players sought were minor, such as banning jeans on the team's charter flights. That change personally affected La Russa, who was used to wearing jeans on trips, but the players felt they were dressing for success.

The Cardinals' improved attitude began to take hold. After a slow start, the Cardinals found themselves at 24–22 on May 27, then won 30 of their next 41 games, giving them a record of 54–33 at the All-Star break. The team won 12 of its first 15 games after the break, and was 30 games over .500 by July 30. After moving into first place to stay on June 11, the Cardinals had at least a 10½ game lead every day after August 6. They won the division by 13 games, and their 105 wins equaled the second-highest total in franchise history and was the best record in the major leagues that year.

Along the way, there were the usual scrapes between La Russa and opposing managers over brushback pitches, but La Russa was correct in his spring training assessment that the team's mental outlook was going to be to the key to its success. They had everyday star players in Pujols, Edmonds, and Rolen; steady starters in Morris, Jeff Suppan, Chris Carpenter, and Jason Marquis, all of whom won 15 or more games; and a healthy Isringhausen in the bullpen, earning 47 saves. They also had the spare parts necessary for a championship club.

"What's made this team different than some others we've had is our approach, which is the same day in and day out," Matheny said. "We're used to playing hard every day. We just don't let up. We did see a little lull [in early September]. In a way, it was beneficial. We didn't like losing. Winning isn't automatic. We were reminded that it takes a consistent effort to go out there and play with intensity."

La Russa refused to let his players celebrate the division championship after a 3–2 loss to Arizona on September 19. Even though the magic number was officially still one, the Cardinals knew they had clinched the division because of the complicated tiebreaker system. It was good enough for the team to begin selling division champions merchandise outside Busch Stadium after the game, but not good enough to pop the corks on the chilled champagne in the clubhouse.

La Russa erupted after the game when asked if the team had begun to celebrate.

"What the hell kind of question is that?" he snapped. "Before we clinch? Does anybody else have a question? Didn't I explain before the game that that's not a clinch? How do you figure that? That's a rule for the thing when it's tied at the end of the season. We've got another 14 games to go. Why'd you ask that? I answered that before the game."

Said pitcher Woody Williams, "Losing, to Tony, is not winning."

Driving home that point to his players, the message on the clubhouse blackboard was "Magic number is 1. Championships won on field, not some formula." La Russa admitted that he wrote the message.

"I wanted our team to be able to celebrate with the fans," La Russa said, "but you don't celebrate tiebreakers. You celebrate winning."

The celebration came the next night, in Milwaukee, after a 7–4 win over the Brewers. It was a wild scene. When reliever Ray King dumped a bucket of ice on La Russsa, the manager chased him around the clubhouse. When he caught him, he jumped on King's back and rode him piggyback, pumping his fists in the air.

"I told him he's been riding me all year, why stop now?" King said later.

After getting tired of celebrating in the clubhouse, several players scrambled to the upper deck at Miller Park and took turns sliding down Bernie Brewer's slide, how the home team celebrated home runs. It was, Larry Walker said, one of the joys of winning in baseball that grown men got the chance to "act like a complete idiot for a minute, and get away with it."

Officially clinching the division title did not bring about a drop in La Russa's intensity level during the final week of the season. Walking back to the dugout after making some lineup changes, the manager was so focused on the card that he didn't see the famous Sausage Race going on around the edge of the playing field. If he had not looked up at the last minute, La Russa would have run head-on into the race-leading bratwurst. He also was not ready to celebrate the team's 100th win of the season because he was frantically searching his office for a missing set of rental car keys. Perhaps, also, La Russa was distracted from enjoying the team's final wins of the regular season because his mind was already on the playoffs. After all, he simply had to draw on past personal experiences to know that a great regular season did not guarantee success in the postseason.

The biggest question was the makeup of his starting rotation, and he was worried that the team's ace, Chris Carpenter, would not be available. The 15-game winner had been forced to leave a game on September 18 with what was called a "right biceps strain" and had not pitched since. Later tests revealed a nerve irritation in his right arm. Carpenter, who had undergone two operations on his shoulder in two years, said there was no way to predict whether or not he would be able to pitch.

"I can wake up tomorrow and everything would be fine," he said, "or it could not be fine for a month. I'm trying to stay as positive as I can."

So was La Russa, but he knew that if Carpenter was unable to pitch, the Cardinals' chance of making a run deep into the playoffs would be much more difficult.

The players also realized it would give their critics another chance to attack their success, but, in an odd way, perhaps that also could serve as another motivating tool.

"It's the same thing we heard in spring training," Matheny said. "People said, 'I don't know how good they'll be.' So why should it be different now? We don't need to concern ourselves with that. All we need to do is look around this room, and everybody is excited by what we have here. All we have to do is believe in each other."

Their first-round opponent was the Los Angeles Dodgers, managed by Jim Tracy, who admitted that one of his biggest challenges in the best-of-five series was matching wits against the manager in the opposing dugout.

"I have a special appreciation for Tony," Tracy said. "Strategically he's a tremendous challenge for any manager. Through all the time he's put into this game, and after all he's won, the passion is there and it's so strong. You can feel it as you manage against this man, pitch to pitch. The pressure is still overwhelmingly there. He loves the game. He loves his job. I have gained the utmost respect for this guy."

When the Cardinals had played in Los Angeles in September, La Russa had gotten his veteran players together in a hotel room and relayed a story he had been told by Bill Russell and Don Nelson, talking about the glory days of the NBA's Boston Celtics. "If they were excited the rest of the club would get excited," La Russa said. "I told them how important it was for them to push as hard as they could and how they had to set the right tempo for the team, just as Russell and Nelson had done for the Celtics."

Tracy earned more respect for the Cardinals after La Russa's team brushed aside the Dodgers in four games to win the first round and move into the league championship series once again, the fourth time in La Russa's nine seasons in St. Louis. Their three previous trips had all ended in defeat, one stop short of the World Series. References to those failures were rampant as the series against the Astros began.

Some of those stories began to change after the Cardinals quickly grabbed a 2–0 lead in the series, but it only took three days in Houston for the naysayers to once again become dominant. The Cardinals lost all three games in Houston, the third a grueling 3–0 loss when Jeff Kent's walk-off homer in the bottom of the ninth ended a scoreless battle.

The Cardinals suddenly found themselves coming back to Busch Stadium down three games to two in the series. They would have to win both Game 6 and Game 7 to not fall short one more time.

La Russa was not about to let his team believe for a moment that they were doomed to fail. "There hasn't been one situation this team faced where I haven't liked our chances," La Russa said moments after Kent's homer stunned his team. "I know we'll be ready Wednesday.… I like our chances and I love our club."

The tension is always greater than normal any time a team is playing an elimination game, and that was the situation the Cardinals found themselves in during Game 6. One slipup could mean the difference between forcing a Game 7 showdown or going home for the winter. The only advantage the Cardinals had was getting the final at-bat.

In one of the best games ever played at 38-year-old Busch Stadium, the Cardinals were one out away from victory when Jeff Bagwell's RBI single tied the game. It stayed tied until the twelfth, when Edmonds launched a two-run homer that allowed the Cardinals to reach Game 7.

As they prepared to decide the NL pennant and league representative in the World Series with a one-game showdown, how even was the series between the Cardinals and Astros? In addition to each having three wins, they had each scored 29 runs. Each team's batting average was .246. Each team had a 4.80 ERA. One edge the Astros possessed was that Roger Clemens was their starting pitcher for Game 7.

"We had a hitters meeting and I told them a story Jim Leyland had told me," La Russa said. "I said we were getting ready to face one of the game's greatest competitors, and that our best chance was for each guy hitting against him to compete as hard as Roger was competing against us. We needed to have eight guys fighting during every at-bat. That would give us a chance to break through."

In the game, a diving catch by Edmonds in the second inning likely saved two runs, and when Pujols came through with an RBI double in the sixth and Rolen followed with a home run, the Cardinals were ready to close out the 5–2 victory.

La Russa was even more nervous than normal as he watched his team get the final three outs in the ninth inning.

"My biggest feeling was that I didn't want to let people down," he said. "And we didn't let anyone down."

While the Cardinals were celebrating, La Russa got word that Clemens was waiting outside the Cardinals' locker room and wanted to talk to him.

"He said he had heard what I told our hitters and wanted me to know how much he appreciated the compliment," La Russa said.

Having won a seventh game for the first time in his career, La Russa found himself back in the World Series for the first time since 1990. "It's an indescribable feeling," he said.

Just getting back to the Series for the first time since 1987 made the season a great accomplishment for the Cardinals and their fans, who didn't know as the celebration wound through city streets until well past midnight that it would be their last night of partying for the year.

After holding out hope that Carpenter would be able to pitch again if the Cardinals advanced to the Series, La Russa reluctantly had to leave him off the roster. Whether Carpenter's presence would have made any difference in the results will never be known.

The Red Sox swept the Cardinals in four games, exorcising their well-known curse by winning the World Series for the first time since 1918. The Cardinals never led during the 36 innings the Series lasted, and hit just .190 as a team. They scored a combined three runs in the final three games and the three middle-of-the-order batters—Pujols, Edmonds, and Rolen—were a combined six-for-46, five of the hits by Pujols.

The loss left La Russa numb, almost speechless. The fact that he had been the losing manager twice before in the World Series did not make this loss any easier to accept or explain.

"The most important message to send is, the Cardinals got beat," La Russa said. "We could have pitched better, but we didn't pitch so bad that we couldn't hit well enough to win. We should all share."

La Russa also was disappointed that baseball fans who had not seen his team perform during the first 173 games they played in 2004 did not see his club at its best. He also knew that in the minds of at least a few Cardinals' fans, failing to win the World Series still meant he personally had something left to prove.

If La Russa needed any additional motivation to propel him into 2005, he had found it.

CHAPTER 20

Vindicated

When La Russa arrived in Jupiter, Florida, for the start of spring training in 2005, he was prepared to be questioned about the Cardinals' disappointing performance in the World Series and how his personal record managing in the Series had fallen to 5–12, with losses in the last eight consecutive games.

There was another topic on the minds of reporters that spring, however. Steroids was the buzz in baseball, and several former and current players were summoned to appear at a congressional hearing in Washington, D.C., about the use of steroids in the game.

One of the players was Mark McGwire, whom La Russa had steadfastly defended over the years. Another player called before Congress was Canseco, who had written in his book *Juiced* that he had introduced McGwire to steroids when they were Oakland teammates.

La Russa's comments about the issue had not changed. He "suspected" Canseco was taking steroids but he had no such questions about McGwire. He said he had confronted Canseco about the issue but that the player "just laughed it off."

"For a lot of good reasons, I believe in Mark," La Russa said on March 16. "What's closing in on him? A couple of criminals that talked with the FBI? I'm surprised members of the media give those guys and Canseco—who everybody kind of dismisses as a buffoon for the last 10 years—all of a sudden they get credibility.

"I saw [McGwire] build up gradually in everything. Knowledge of the strike zone, of his stroke, of his training, the effort he put into all that. All the time in the cage. He just kept getting bigger and better. Finally, record-breaking. Our coach, Dave McKay, was in the gym all the time with him. Dave said he'd swear on a stack of Bibles."

Two days later, La Russa sat in his office at Roger Dean Stadium glued to his television, watching the testimony at the congressional hearings, like almost everyone in baseball. And like almost everybody in the game, and all Cardinal fans, he came away disappointed by McGwire's testimony and said he thought McGwire had missed an opportunity to publicly state that he had not used steroids.

"I was surprised by it," La Russa said. "He's made a statement where he's denied it. I think it was a great time for him to make that same statement. I think he was coached on the one thing about making it about the future and not the past. I was surprised he didn't just repeat what he had said in his earlier statement.

"It's impossible for me to separate myself from what I know and how hard he worked and how he developed. Would I have an opinion about it if I was just a fan? Yeah, [McGwire] looked uncomfortable the whole time.… It looked like he had been coached in the other direction and he came off uncomfortable."

While he was tired about having to constantly answer questions about the steroid issue, La Russa felt worse for McGwire, because he knew the player's public image suffered a major blow during the hearings. He knew that with that testimony most likely went McGwire's chances for election into the Hall of Fame.

What La Russa *really* wanted to talk about was baseball, specifically why he thought the 2005 Cardinals could be an even better team than the NL champions of the previous year. First, though, one more unpleasant subject reared its head.

The former pitching phenom, Rick Ankiel, had finally worked his way back to the major leagues the previous September, making five relief appearances, and La Russa was encouraged about his progress. Ankiel had gone to the Dominican Republic to pitch winter ball, but left the team and returned to Florida because he was worried about his mechanics.

Ankiel was still concerned when he reported to spring training, and one day walked into La Russa's office and announced that he was quitting baseball.

The manager was not prepared for that decision. Jocketty asked La Russa what he thought about suggesting that Ankiel try to learn to play the outfield. La Russa told Ankiel to think about it for 24 hours before doing anything.

"The feelings for him are so strong, this is almost all about Rick's career and his struggles and what's ahead for him," La Russa said. "That overwhelms the impact on what the organization has put into him. It's really, really a concern that this comes out right for him."

One element that La Russa enjoyed about spring training perhaps as much as anything was that the Cardinals' stadium, and particularly the manager's office, seemed to attract many celebrities, including high-profile coaches from other sports.

Among the regulars in the Cardinals' camp were college basketball coach Bob Knight and pro football coaches Bill Parcells and Bill Belichick. The group often shared laughs, but they also had many serious discussions about coaching problems and the philosophy of coaching, a discipline that transcends their sport.

"That's one reason coaches in all sports talk to each other," La Russa said. "A lot of what you're trying to get accomplished is getting a lot of effort and execution."

Parcells admitted that he saw a lot of similarities between himself and La Russa, especially after reading *Three Nights in August.*

"The stuff about Tony walking the streets alone after a bad loss really hit home to me," Parcells said. "I don't know how many times I walked out of Giants Stadium on a Sunday night, drove down to the Jersey shore by myself, and just sat on the boardwalk looking out into the ocean, reliving the game in my mind all night long."

The other conversations La Russa had that he enjoyed that spring were with his veteran players, following up on his decisions a year earlier to let the team have more input and authority in decisionmaking. Bolstered by a new three-year contract and his ongoing tenure with the Cardinals, La Russa had a increased feeling of confidence. Although he still got irritated when told he had become more "laid-back" than before.

"I don't like it, because it might give off the impression I'm comfortable," La Russa said. "That's not true. I don't think I've changed my approach. You do this a long time, and sure, everyone tweaks here and there. Nobody here is on cruise control."

New players arriving in the Cardinals camp certainly found out that was a correct statement.

"You look at him from across the field and it's easy not to like him," said new outfielder Reggie Sanders. "He'll do things to try to get inside your head. It can be distracting if you let it. But when you get here, you realize what he's all about. He's very prepared, he cares for his players, and he wants to win. You can't have a problem with that."

To La Russa, that was a great compliment. "I've heard too often from players we've competed against who have come to our club that we're different from what they perceived," La Russa said. "Our coaches and myself remember the essence of what we're here for—the competition against the other side. We're all for our side, not their side. That's your family. We reinforce a very strong *our team vs. you.* If I find somebody who's a real hard competitor, somewhere in there I'll have a grudging respect for him. But he'll bother and upset me unless we get him."

The Cardinals' success in 2004 allowed La Russa to feel more confident in letting the players set some of the team rules.

"He's willing to listen to what we have to say," said pitcher Matt Morris. "He can take criticism. Guys have told him, 'Hey, Tony, it's spring training, just chill out.' He might not be crazy about it, but he weighs what we say.

"Sometimes it seems like he looks at spring training games like it's a playoff game. His intensity is amazing. But I think with some of the other stuff he's allowed his players to be happier off the field, which as a result helps on the field.... I think he's allowed players to go about their business more and police themselves. But it's still obvious he's going to be in charge."

Added Edmonds, "I think there have been years when Tony had a more difficult time trusting his team. He trusted our team last year. I have the same feeling this spring."

La Russa admitted his trust was greatly determined by how well the team performed on the field.

"People talk about a 'players' manager,'" he said. "I'm a players' manager if the players are committed to caring for their teammates and winning by playing the game properly. If either one of those isn't in place, there's an issue. Last year's team was great about both."

La Russa expected, or at least hoped, that would be the same in 2005 and it turned out he was not disappointed. By April 16, the Cardinals were in first place, and would remain there for the rest of the season, building as much as a 16-game lead over the second-place club. The team never lost more than three games in a row and reached the 100-victory mark for the second consecutive season for the first time in franchise history since 1943–44.

Despite the Cardinals' success, there still were intriguing contests along the way, including the April 29 matchup of La Russa against Bobby Cox's Braves, the first time since 1950 that two managers with 2,000 or more wins in the major leagues had faced each other in a game. (The last such matchup came between Connie Mack of the Philadelphia A's and Joe McCarthy of the Red Sox.) En route to that milestone, Cox had managed against La Russa on multiple occasions and was quick to praise the Cardinals' manager.

"Tony is one of the most organized guys in baseball, there's no doubt about that," Cox said. "He's been a great manager for a long time. One of his keys, I think, is that he gets the most out of every little piece of talent he has. We always seem to have good battles against him.

"He can manage different types of personalities, which is important, because people are different. You had better be able to identify with each person if you want to be a success. The game has changed quite a bit over the years, and managers have had to change, too. You have to have a passion for it to last this long, and I know Tony has it."

Cox puts La Russa in a class with the best managers in the history of the game, including Sparky Anderson and Gene Mauch. "Those were the guys I thought were tough," Cox said. "They could catch you with your pants down. They were really ahead of the game. They were thinkers, and not afraid to try things."

There was perhaps no manager whom La Russa respects more than Anderson, which made the 6–3 win over Pittsburgh on August 25 so significant. It was the 2,195[th] victory of his career, moving him past Anderson and into third place on the all-time list for games won by a manager.

Edmonds spoke to his teammates in a closed clubhouse after the game to emphasis the importance of La Russa's milestone. "To have the most wins in the modern era, I think, is pretty special," Edmonds said.

The win was commemorated by some of La Russa's closest friends. Jim Leyland and his family presented La Russa with a check for $2,194 to ARF, and Walt Jocketty flew Roland Hemond to Pittsburgh to personally congratulate La Russa.

The players greeted La Russa with a beer shower, and Pujols dumped a tub of ice water on his manager. The Cardinals also bought a case of Dom Perignon champagne to help toast their manager.

La Russa could not help but think back to the early days of his career, and all of the advice and help he had received from Anderson. "Those messages increased in value over the years," La Russa said.

"One thing he always told me was that you—and the coaches'—major responsibility is to try to figure out what your guys do well and where they struggle, and try to play one away from the other," La Russa said. "For example, if a guy can't bunt, don't put him in a position to bunt. If someone is a bad base runner, don't give him a green light to run. If a guy has trouble going back on the ball but can come in, play him deeper. If a guy can go better to his right, shade him to the left. All of that crystallized the idea to play to strengths and away from weaknesses."

There were not many weaknesses on the Cardinals that season. The term "relentless" was the word that was used the most often to describe the team, but it was also the word Jocketty used to describe La Russa's personal approach to the game.

"Sometimes I want to say to him, 'Tony, ease up,' but that's not who he is," Jocketty said. "He's always in that intense, competitive mode. It's who he is, and it's reflected in how his teams play."

And La Russa was enjoying how the team was playing. "[The team] plays consistently hard every day, no matter what the score," he said. "I really thought that was the mark of last year's team beyond just playing well. It didn't celebrate too soon. It went about it the right way, day in and day out."

The only major obstacle the Cardinals faced was another shoulder injury to Scott Rolen. He suffered a torn labrum in a first-base collision with Hee Seop Choi of the Dodgers on May 10. He had surgery and was on the disabled list for a month, but still was hurting when he returned. He sat out the All-Star Game, and tried to come back and play, but by August realized the shoulder was not going to improve without more surgery, which sidelined him for the rest of the season. The question of whether Rolen was healthy or not would become a constant issue in his relationship with La Russa for the next two years.

Rolen's injury did not slow down the Cardinals, however, who clinched their second consecutive division title—and fourth in six years—with two weeks left to play in the season. In a scene repeated from the previous year, the Cardinals mathematically clinched the title two days before La Russa allowed them to celebrate.

Writing in the *Post-Dispatch* on September 18, the day after the champagne party, beat writer Joe Strauss said the 2005 Cardinals had definitely become an extension of La Russa's personality.

"Hardly the best-liked manager within his fraternity, La Russa is highly respected," Strauss wrote. "The highest compliment he receives from scouts, executives, and rival managers is his ability to have high-visibility players do blue-collar things. La Russa deflects praise by pointing to a system rather than a cult of personality."

"What they buy into more than anything else is a commitment to play hard every day, win every series, and since you're playing hard, the game should be played right," La Russa told Strauss.

Pujols said that he, and the other players, had come to appreciate what La Russa's presence meant to the team. "You know to respect the manager and do things right or you're not going to be here very long," Pujols said. "That goes for everybody. You look at what he has done, the fact that he's a Hall of Fame manager when he's done, and there's nothing to argue with. He knows what it takes to win. You listen."

The 2005 season marked the final year at Busch Stadium, which opened in 1966, and part of the uncertainty of postseason play is that a team is never certain what could turn out to be the final game. The team celebrated the final regular-season game on October 2 with a 7–5 win over Cincinnati.

Their first-round opponent was San Diego, and the Cardinals swept the Padres to set up a rematch of the dramatic 2004 NLCS against Houston. The two teams split the first two games in St. Louis before the series moved south.

La Russa knew the Cardinals needed to win at least one of the three games in Houston, and he hoped they could win two. With Roger Clemens on the mound for Game 3, he used a pregame conversation to try to send a message to home-plate umpire Wally Bell.

"I have to tell you, a concern is [Bell]," La Russa said. "Clemens has so much command, he's like [Greg] Maddux. He's going to pitch the edges. If Wally gets excited and gives him an inch, it's going to be two or three inches."

When told what La Russa had said, Clemens laughed. Houston catcher Brad Ausmus took the matter more seriously. "That's Tony," Ausmus said. "If he thinks that's going to help his team.... I just can't see necessarily any reason to do that other than to try to help your team win."

It didn't help. Clemens won 4–3, which was one of the reasons La Russa knew that the fourth game of the series was going to be so crucial—and it didn't take long for him and the Cardinals to get upset about home-plate umpire Phil Cuzzi's strike zone.

Pujols told La Russa that Cuzzi had threatened to eject him in the first inning when he questioned a called strike, and more disputes arose during the game. By the seventh inning in the 1–1 game, La Russa could not stand it any longer. He went onto the field to complain to Cuzzi, who promptly ejected him from the game in what turned out to be a 2–1 Houston win.

"I would never do it any different," La Russa said, given a day to reflect on the situation. "I know our attitude about playing the umpires is not how we compete. We play the other side. It just reached a point where it had gone too far. The players had made too much of a commitment. Somebody had to stand up, and it was my job."

The win left Houston a game away from the World Series, a spot they occupied in 2004. By the top of the ninth inning, they had built a 4–2 lead. The first two Cardinals were retired, and it looked as if the St. Louis season was almost over.

A high-ranking White Sox official called La Russa during the inning to express regret that the season was over "barring some kind of miracle."

That miracle was set up by a single by David Eckstein and a walk to Jim Edmonds, which brought Pujols to the plate. He delivered a 412-foot blast that punctured the heart of the Astros and their fans, wiping out their victory celebration. The home run and 5–4 victory was one of the most dramatic in Cardinals' history and while La Russa and his team celebrated, the manager also knew its true significance would only be measured by what happened in the rest of the series.

The blast brought the series back to St. Louis, but the Astros still led three games to two. Roy Oswalt went to the mound in Game 6, and he made certain there was no Game 7 with a workmanlike 5–1 victory, the final game at Busch Stadium.

The dual sentiments of losing the game and the closing of the stadium lingered for La Russa and his players. By the time the start of the 2006 season arrived, and the players and manager got their first look at their new home, however, they were re-energized.

"If you didn't feel something, then you don't have a heartbeat," La Russa said of the first game at the new Busch Stadium, a 6–4 win over Milwaukee.

The 2006 regular season would turn out to be another successful one for La Russa and the Cardinals, but not in the manner the previous two years had been. The team moved into first place on May 12 and remained there for all but one day the rest of the season, but there a lot of doubts were raised along the way.

The team endured two separate eight-game losing streaks during the year—though they didn't drop out of first place during either of them. During the second streak, in early August, the Cardinals lost a 16–8 game to the Phillies.

An obviously steaming La Russa appeared before reporters after the game. "This won't take long," said La Russa, who normally answers questions for several minutes after games. "No part of our team was good enough, including the manager. And I don't have anything more to say."

La Russa left the interview room, and in the safety of his office later, he still refused to answer media inquiries. A couple of days later, La Russa had calmed down enough to talk, but he still didn't have answers about why his team was not playing better. "One of my pet peeves is to see a coach or manager say, 'I'm doing all I can. It's really them. They've got to fix it.' That's never true," La Russa said. "We have a responsibility to find something that will improve them. There's always something we can do to help put those guys in a better position."

By September, however, the situation had improved slightly—due as much to the failures of other clubs in the division as to what the Cardinals were doing. They had increased the division lead to seven games with 14 to play and then began to lose again, threatening to join the ranks of the 1964 Phillies as a team that collapsed down the stretch.

Their season came down to the final day, when a Houston loss clinched the division title despite an 83-win season. La Russa made a decision to hold ace Chris Carpenter back from that game, making him available to potentially start two games in the first round of the playoffs, and luckily that strategy proved correct.

One of the beauties of baseball, of course, is that when postseason play begins, what happened in the regular season means nothing. La Russa used that statement to encourage the Cardinals as they opened the playoffs in San Diego.

La Russa told his players that what he had learned over the years was that eight teams qualify for the playoffs, and any of those teams is good enough to win the World Series. "It's a brand-new three series challenge, and the first team to win 11 games wins," La Russa said. "This is all about getting hot and staying hot. I was working on the lineup last night, and if you look at it, we are going to be a very dangerous club to play."

The Cardinals dispatched the Padres in four games in the first round, returning the Cardinals to the NLCS again, this time to face the New York Mets, who won 97 games in the regular season.

La Russa once again played the underdog card to full effect, and had the Cardinals in front three games to two as the series moved back to New York. A 4–2 Mets win in Game 6 forced a deciding Game 7, the second time in three years La Russa and the Cardinals had found themselves in that position.

It is always easier playing a deciding game at home, because you know your team always will have the last at-bat. It was just one more obstacle the Cardinals had to overcome. The game was tied at 1–1 when the Cardinals thought they had gone ahead, only to see Endy Chavez reach over the left-field wall, pulling back a would-be home run by Scott Rolen, who was in the middle of his own personal test of wills with La Russa.

The game remained tied until the ninth, when Yadier Molina's homer stayed over the wall and when rookie Adam Wainwright struck out Carlos Beltran, the game was over and the Cardinals had a 3–1 victory. La Russa's club found itself once more on its way to the World Series.

Waiting to face the Cardinals were the Detroit Tigers and La Russa's long-time friend, Jim Leyland, who now was their manager. During spring training, the two had gotten together for dinner in Florida and each told the other that his club was good enough to reach the World Series.

Perhaps the only negatives about the matchup were that there could be no late-night phone calls to discuss what was happening with their teams and that one of the two was going to come out of it as the loser.

"You lose a couple of tough games, you lay in bed thinking, 'Could I have done something different?'" Leyland said. "Tony is even more that way than I am. That's why we get phone calls from each other at 2:00 or 3:00 in the morning."

Luckily, there were not many moments during the Series where either manager was left second-guessing. La Russa was criticized for not making a bigger issue out of Kenny Rogers perhaps smudging baseballs during Game 2. Some critics said that the only reason he did not challenge Rogers was because Leyland was in the other dugout.

La Russa insisted those claims could not have been further from the truth. It was Anderson and Paul Richards who taught him the difference between having a strategy and a philosophy, and those thoughts filled his head as he watched Rogers pitch.

"In that situation, I have about five minutes to make the call," La Russa said. "I was thinking, I had the luxury and good fortune of teachers who taught me the difference between philosophy and strategy. In that situation, I might have strategized, 'Hey, I can get this guy thrown out of the game.'

"Strategies have their place, but they don't replace philosophy, because philosophy is what you represent, and what you want your team to represent. You're talking about the most prestigious and highlighted competition you can have in Major League Baseball. This is the World Series.

"What if I say something? What if I say nothing? What if I ask the umpires to go to the mound? What if I do nothing? What if I do something in between? I really was weighing everything against this: when it's over, which of those responses fits what you've been taught and what you try to teach a ballclub about the way we're supposed to compete?

"We want to win within our philosophy. Part of that philosophy is abhorring BS baseball. I don't like it.... I believe in the beauty of the competition.

Let's play the game. We get ready, they get ready. You play as hard as you can, and there's a winner and a loser."

Reflecting back on that moment, La Russa acknowledges it was the toughest strategic decision he has ever encountered during a game in his career. Ultimately he decided to ask the umpires to tell Rogers to clean off his hand, which he did before the next inning.

"Five minutes is a long time when you are thinking, and I had to think about all of the consequences," La Russa said. "In the end you just have to do what you think is right, even if there is a bad result. When I called home later after the game Elaine told me callers on the radio and on the Internet were all over me for not trying to get Rogers thrown out of the game."

La Russa's heart, however, told him he had made the right decision. "I was so appreciative of all the teachers I had over the years, and in the end you just have to believe in the lessons you have learned about their philosophies. I knew however it turned out, it was the right thing to do."

Rogers's win was the only Detroit victory in the series. The Cardinals took advantage of sloppy defense by the Tigers and won the next three games, capped by Wainwright's strikeout of Brandon Inge that clinched a 4–2 victory in Game 5. It was the 10th world championship in Cardinals history, matching the uniform number on La Russa's back and making La Russa only the second manager, behind Anderson, to win a World Series in both the American and National Leagues. The victory came 17 long years after his 1989 championship in Oakland.

As expected, the win left La Russa emotional and he admitted, "I'm having a hard time holding it together."

All of the skeptics, and critics, who had attacked La Russa over the years had to hand it to him, even if some did so reluctantly.

"You have to give Tony La Russa credit," Bob Elliott wrote in the *Toronto Sun*. "Wow, that wasn't as painful to type as we thought it would be."

The win gave La Russa the parade he never had in Oakland. It also gave him the respect of many of the Cardinals' fans that he never had. For a manager consumed by winning, nothing can take away the satisfaction that comes from winning the World Series.

Reflecting on the moment a couple of months later, La Russa said, "If my time in St. Louis finished at year 10, I would have been disappointed because they wouldn't have gotten that 10th World Series," he said. "I wouldn't have apologized because they got my best shot every day of every year. The six losses were frustrating and disappointing but not embarrassing. The difference is, there was an 11th year. I feel like that we got the prize. There's a certain fullness to what that means."

The victory meant that La Russa no longer had to live with the irritating thought that his teams were good enough to make the postseason but not good enough to win the World Series. He now had his championship. And nobody could ever take it away from him.

CHAPTER 21

The Road Ahead

If finally winning the World Series was supposed to make La Russa's life easier and less stressful, somebody forgot to give him that memo. He didn't even make it out of the following spring training before once again becoming the center of a firestorm.

The first signs of controversy came as the Cardinals opened camp in Jupiter. Instead of stories about how the team was preparing to defend its championship, reporters concerned themselves with La Russa's future. His contract was up at the end of 2007, and La Russa himself was hinting that maybe it would be his final season in St. Louis.

"I'll keep saying it until people get it right, because it's the truth," La Russa said. "If the players, the fans, or the organization want somebody different—whatever the contract says—the person shouldn't hang around. Whether it's the first, second, or third of three years, I feel no different.

"This is 12 years [in St. Louis]. That's one issue.... At the end of the year, you just check and see how you feel. I don't know if they'll still want me. One of these years the players will have had enough of me, don't you think? Unless we keep enough of the young guys here."

What motivated La Russa more than worrying about his own situation, however, was what was gong to happen to his team in 2007. As in any other year, the canvas was empty and the picture was yet to be painted.

"It's really a turn-on everybody can use," La Russa said. "There's no crystal ball about what might happen in '07. That's the fascination."

La Russa relied on his famous friends to come into camp and help motivate his players. Knight and Parcells were returning visitors, and so were Bill Belichick of the New England Patriots, Billy Donovan, the basketball coach at Florida, and former Notre Dame football coach Lou Holtz.

"Lou said to me, 'You're not trying to defend a championship, you're trying to win the championship again,'" La Russa said. "'Look, common sense tells you it was a great thing you accomplished—and that it's a terrific memory, a great achievement, all those things. The problem is human nature.'... We're going to be congratulated by people every day this spring, told what we did was great. Now, the key is we have to make that work for us and not against us."

As he was seeking that outside assistance to motivate his players, La Russa also had one lingering issue to settle himself: making peace with third baseman Scott Rolen after the two had been on the outs since the previous postseason. The two had not spoken all winter, even when they attended a charity banquet together. A truce was established, but that would ultimately prove to only be temporary.

If La Russa thought any of those issues were not challenging enough, he found himself in the middle of his most serious incident early on the morning of March 22. After enjoying a late dinner with singer Vic Damone, former Cardinal manager Red Schoendienst, Hall of Fame player Mike Schmidt and his wife, La Russa was driving his rental SUV back to his spring home when he fell asleep behind the wheel.

Police officers found La Russa slumped over the steering wheel of his Ford Expedition, stopped in the middle of an intersection several blocks from where La Russa was staying. The car was in drive, but La Russa's foot was on the brake. Loud music was playing on the stereo, and officers finally awakened La Russa with repeated pounds on the window.

La Russa consented to two alcohol tests and they came back with a reading of .093, above the Florida legal limit of .08. He was booked at the jail on a charge of driving under the influence and spent the night in jail. When he reported to Roger Dean Stadium, La Russa apologized for the incident, expressed his regret, and pledged to take full responsibility.

La Russa's critics, of course, used the incident and the decision by the Cardinals' ownership not to discipline La Russa against him, but his friends rallied behind him and continued to offer support.

Knight, Parcells, and former Saint Louis U. coach Charlie Spoonhour spent the first full day with La Russa and Knight joked that La Russa was "lucky he's got his expert consultant on controversy here now."

Media critics, including Bernie Miklasz of the *Post-Dispatch*, also weighed in and offered their opinion.

"La Russa is all about control, and this time he lost it," Miklasz wrote. "La Russa has always tried to be a strong leader and set the right example for his players. He realizes in this instance, he failed. He's a proud man, conscious of his image and protective of it. This collective loss of control, reputation, and respect must be humiliating for La Russa."

What only a few people—both those critical of La Russa or supportive of the manager—pointed out, however, was how lucky La Russa had been that his vehicle had not gone out of control while he was driving and struck another car, injuring himself or others.

Most people, of course, realized that La Russa made a mistake and he was the first to admit that fact. "I'm sorry," La Russa said. "I'm embarrassed, I made a mistake, I was at fault. There's nothing to say in explanation that wouldn't sound like an excuse, and there is no excuse."

La Russa, the fans and the media were ready to move forward as the regular season began, and it didn't look before another incident gave everybody something new to talk about. In late April, the Chicago Cubs were coming to St. Louis for the first time with La Russa's childhood buddy Lou Piniella now as their manager. The mere presence or mention of the Cubs seems to always raise La Russa's intensity meter a few inches higher.

The previous year, La Russa had demanded to know what Cardinals employee was responsible for running a condescending cartoon about a Cubs-related video game on the stadium's jumbo-tron. The cartoon did not run again.

In advance of this series, one of the *Post-Dispatch's* baseball writers, Derrick Goold, was assigned to write a story "about the five, 10, or however many reasons why the Cubs will never win a World Series."

"In all candor, I didn't feel comfortable doing that because I thought the Cubs were a really good team," Goold said. "I thought there was maybe a better, more creative way to do it. I had always been a big fan of the 'Tinker to Evers to Chance' poem. I had a poster of it when I was a kid. I thought maybe I could have a little fun with it."

Goold's story was a parody of the famous poem, concluding there was "no chance" the Cubs could win. He wrote the story from a St. Louis hospital room, where he was spending the night with his young son, who was ill.

La Russa had told the newspaper's beat writers that he did not want anything written before the series that was "disrespectful" of the Cubs. In his mind, Goold had crossed that line. During La Russa's pregame session with the media, he told Goold he was not going to take questions from the *Post-Dispatch* all weekend. "He said he didn't think the newspaper should have printed what it did," Goold said.

After the game, won 5–3 by the Cubs, another *Post-Dispatch* writer, Joe Strauss, asked La Russa a question during his news conference. When La Russa again said he wasn't talking to the newspaper, Miklasz—physically a much bigger man than La Russa—spoke up in defense of his fellow reporter and the two engaged in a heated debate, which was televised live by Fox Sports Midwest as part of its postgame show. Miklasz accused La Russa of "grandstanding," which upset the manager even more.

"It was very much a satire that pokes fun at itself more than it pokes fun at any team," Goold said. "Piniella said he thought it was funny. Tony made a bigger deal out of it than did Chicago radio stations, which is impossible to do. It was like we had been bad so he was putting us in time out."

By the following day, La Russa had called off his vendetta against the newspaper. Only a few hours later, both sides were drawn together by another tragedy striking the Cardinals' family.

Relief pitcher Josh Hancock was killed in an early-morning traffic accident on April 29. He was on his way to meet several teammates at a local restaurant when the SUV he was driving crashed into the back of a parked tow truck on the highway. Hancock was killed instantly. Tests later revealed that he had been legally intoxicated.

La Russa received the terrible news in an early-morning telephone call, and then completed the horrible task of calling Hancock's father in Mississippi to deliver the news that his son had been killed.

"You sit there for 15 minutes thinking about it," La Russa said. "It doesn't help."

For the second time in five years, La Russa and his team had to face the reality that a member of their family was dead. In a somewhat twisted way, La Russa said, maybe the club was more prepared to deal with it having gone through the death of Darryl Kile in 2002.

Enduring that experience did make the situation easier, especially since many players on this team were on the 2002 club. The situation also was different because of the circumstances involved in Hancock's death.

Before all of the facts were known, La Russa warned his players to be on the lookout for the "insincerity" of media members. The team had flown to Milwaukee for a series against the Brewers and as he faced the media on the field before the game, La Russa threatened to swing a fungo bat at any reporter who he thought asked an insincere question.

La Russa later apologized for his remarks, but when it was revealed that Hancock had been drunk, more issues were raised. It also was reported that La Russa had met twice with Hancock in the previous few days to discuss the issue of drinking and driving.

"I did have a very serious heart-to-heart with Josh on that Thursday, and here on Saturday, he still drank and crashed," La Russa said. "Maybe I can do a better job in my conversation, but I pulled out all the stops."

Hancock apparently had another vehicle accident a few days before his death, which made him late to arrive for the Cardinals' day game that day, but he told La Russa he simply had overslept.

La Russa now had a challenge of allowing his team time to grieve, while also getting the players back on the field and focused on the task of trying to win games. The Cardinals had only a 10–13 record at the time of Hancock's death. It unfortunately was an early indication that there would be no championship repeat.

As the team continued to struggle to reach the .500 mark, more questions were raised about La Russa's future. The fact he would not commit to returning to the team in 2008 was cited by Miklasz as at least a contributing factor to the team's performance.

"Just about everyone assumes La Russa is moving on after the season, and that lame-duck status only damages his ability to lead," Miklasz wrote in his column on May 17. "In years past, whenever La Russa has entered the final year of his contract, the overwhelming feeling around the ballclub was that he would return. So the players knew they would have to deal with La Russa again—in the following season and into the future. The fear factor was in place."

Without that fear factor, Miklasz went on to say, players did not risk getting on La Russa's bad side. If La Russa was not going to be the manager in 2008, the players did not have to worry about trying to please him in order to keep their jobs.

Miklasz wrote that La Russa needed to make the first move and announce that he would be returning in 2008 to end the uncertainty, but the manager was not ready to make that statement. He thought back to something Anderson had once told him: never announce that it will be your last season until after that season. Do not make up your mind too quickly.

In all honesty, La Russa still had not made up his mind about returning. He once again took the stance that he wanted to make sure the owners wanted him and the majority of the players wanted him back. His feeling of insecurity was still strong, 12 years into his Cardinal tenure and 28 years into his major league managing career.

Some observers thought La Russa had lost his zest for the job, but he insisted that was not the case.

"There are still times when you've got a five-run lead, when it's tense and I can't swallow," La Russa said. "I've got a headache, and I'm afraid I'm going to throw up. You only feel that stuff because you're anxious about the outcome."

It just seemed to be one of those seasons where almost every high was immediately followed by a low, beginning on opening night when Cy Young winner Chris Carpenter was forced to leave the game against the Mets with pain in his elbow. He underwent surgery and missed the rest of the season.

Rick Ankiel completed his minor league odyssey as an outfielder and returned to the Cardinals on August 9, when he hit a three-run homer in his first game. In the dugout, La Russa reacted with a glee he had never displayed, smiling, yelling, and clapping his hands. He admitted afterward the only moment that had exceeded Ankiel's home run for him, since he had been wearing a Cardinal uniform, was the final out of the 2006 World Series.

The same day, it was revealed that reserve Scott Spiezio had entered a drug rehab program.

As his lame-duck status continued, La Russa won the 1,042nd game as Cardinals manager on August 31, passing Red Schoendienst for the most career wins by a Cardinal manager. In that same game, a 6–5 victory over Cincinnati, outfielder Juan Encarnacion was struck in the left eye by a foul ball while standing in the on-deck circle. Encarnacion suffered permanent eye damage that ended his career.

As the season ended, La Russa still had not made up his mind about returning. His decision became more complicated when his longtime confidant, Walt Jocketty, lost a front-office power struggle and was fired.

Two weeks later, La Russa announced that he would be back in St. Louis, agreeing to a two-year extension of his contract running through 2009. He also cleaned up one other piece of unfinished business from the long year by pleading guilty to driving under the influence from the spring training incident. The plea agreement called for La Russa's driver's license to be suspended for six months and required him to pay a $678 fine (including court costs), complete DUI school and any recommended treatment, and perform 25 hours of community service.

La Russa was happy to put the incident behind him; he felt he could now concentrate on baseball again. One matter he told new general manager John Mozeliak that he wanted resolved before the team began spring training in 2008 was trading Scott Rolen. La Russa told Mozeliak, however, that he did not want Rolen traded merely because of their personal differences. "Do it only if it will improve the club," the manager said.

Even though La Russa and Rolen had worked out a truce after their prior disagreements during spring training of 2007, their relationship had deteriorated even further during the season and had now reached a point where La Russa did not believe it could continue.

It was an odd relationship, because on the surface, Rolen appeared to be the kind of player La Russa admired and wanted on his team. Additionally, Rolen was a major animal lover, even naming his charity foundation after his two dogs. Those elements were not enough, however, to help Rolen. He was the only veteran player who told La Russa at the end of the season that he thought the manager should move on and not return to St. Louis in 2008.

The La Russa–Rolen relationship had been strained since the third baseman's shoulder injury in 2005, and subsequent disagreements over his treatment/surgery and whether he was healthy enough to play. Rolen did not appreciate being benched in the 2006 playoffs, and was upset that he found out he was not playing by looking at the lineup card instead of being told personally by La Russa.

The truce evaporated over the 2007 season as Rolen had more problems with his shoulder, which eventually resulted in a third operation. The manager said he did not know if the injury was still affecting Rolen's performance.

After the season, La Russa went public with his anger at Rolen, first in a chat with reporters and then again at baseball's winter meetings after Rolen became upset with a four-page letter La Russa sent to him in October.

The letter contained "stuff he should know to give him the chance to be the player he needs to be," La Russa said. Rolen's reaction, however, was quite different. He informed general manager John Mozeliak that he would agree to waive his no-trade clause to move on to another team.

"It's very clear that he's unhappy, and I'm making it clear that I don't know why he is unhappy," La Russa said in December. "I can make a list of 50 respect points that this man has been given by our organization. It's time for him to give back.... If he plays hard and he plays as well as he can, he plays. And if he doesn't he can sit. If he doesn't like it, he can quit."

It was obvious to all parties after that attack by La Russa that Rolen had to be traded. Mozeliak finally found a willing partner in Toronto, and Rolen was dealt to the Blue Jays in January 2008 for fellow third baseman Troy Glaus.

Rolen has refused to say much about his problems with La Russa or the unknown reasons behind their friction. In turn, La Russa still is very guarded in his public comments about Rolen other than to say, "It was the toughest personnel situation I've ever been in, tougher even than the situation with Ozzie."

After he joined the Blue Jays, Rolen told the *New York Times* in February, 2008, "We're different people with different morals. You can write that if you want, I don't care.... That's as politically correct as I can say it, I guess."

Rolen also told the *Post-Dispatch* that it became "a personal issue...there was nothing professional about it. It came to a point where [a trade] had to happen. It's unreasonable to think the competition was going to stay on the field. It hadn't been on the field, really, for the last year and a half. The energy, the focus and the competition were off the field. That's not good for me, it's not good for the team, it's not good for the fans. It's not good for anything."

Rolen was not the only veteran player missing when the Cardinals opened spring training. Center fielder Jim Edmonds also had moved on via a trade to San Diego. Edmonds and La Russa also had an interesting relationship during the outfielder's final couple of seasons in St. Louis, and he also had requested a trade after learning he was going to have to compete in the spring for a starting position. Shortstop David Eckstein also was gone, having signed as a free agent with Toronto.

Virtually no one was predicting more than a middle-of-the-pack season for the Cardinals, always irritating to La Russa. Before he could confront that issue, however, La Russa had more salient matters on his mind.

He thought the team needed another bat in the lineup to protect Albert Pujols, and for the second consecutive year he openly campaigned for the Cardinals to sign Barry Bonds. After all, he would fit right in with all of the other Cardinals named in the Mitchell Report, the record of the long investigation into steroid use in baseball.

"When you look at somebody dangerous to hit behind Albert, Barry was the guy I thought of," La Russa said. "For whatever reason, at the general manager or ownership level, they didn't agree."

The Mitchell Report included information on five players in the Cardinals' camp —Ankiel, Glaus, Ryan Franklin, Ron Villone, and Juan Gonzalez, a non-roster invitee. While La Russa said he resented the fact so many Cardinal players were named, as well as former Cardinal Mark McGwire, he refused to criticize those players.

"One way I was taught to survive, is my number one accountability factor is myself," he told *Post-Dispatch* columnist Bryan Burwell. "This is my 30th year doing this at the major league level. There isn't anybody—the commissioner, our owner, the fans, you—there isn't any person, man or woman, who can make me any more accountable than I am right now because of myself. And I know there isn't anything we've done in all those years that was, with one small exception where we stole signs—a little hiccup—there isn't anything else that has happened on our ballclubs in Oakland or St. Louis that there's a hint of illegality. There isn't anything that we didn't actively and proactively attempt to do it right."

Three days after La Russa made that comment, the Cardinals learned that reserve Scott Spiezio—who had undergone drug and alcohol treatment in 2007—was named in an arrest warrant stemming from a December auto accident in California. The Cardinals promptly released him, and La Russa was involved in making that decision.

A few lighter moments came during the spring when La Russa was surrounded by his friends Knight and Parcells.

La Russa recalled the first time he and Knight met, when he was managing the White Sox. "He was by the batting cage, and I shook his hand and he told me to get out of the way," La Russa said. "He said when I had enough time in the league I could come back and say hello to him."

After he moved on to Oakland, where Weinberg was the trainer, La Russa frequently mentioned Knight in his talks with his players. Weinberg had been at Indiana with Knight, and called Knight and told him La Russa was referencing things that Knight had said during his player meetings.

"One day the phone rings and I pick it up, and I'm thinking, 'Who the heck is this guy? It sounds like Bob Knight," La Russa said. "He said, 'I take it very personal when someone is quoting me, and I want to make sure that if someone's quoting me they're quoting me correctly,' He said he would be in Yuma, Arizona, [for spring training] in 1988. Ever since then, I don't think he's missed one spring."

La Russa's hopes to leave Florida after spring training and rebuke the critics who predicted the Cardinals would not be a contending club did not pan out. By the end of May, the team had settled into second place and never got closer than two games to first place, eventually finishing with an 86–76 record, in fourth place and 12½ games behind the Cubs.

It was a July series against the Cubs that provided the biggest fireworks of the season, involving the former Cardinal, Edmonds, who signed with the Cubs after being released by San Diego.

When Edmonds said he did not know what kind of greeting he would get from Cardinal fans in his return to Busch Stadium because he now played for the Cubs, La Russa got involved and called on St. Louis fans "to ignore him." La Russa said the difference between Edmonds and all of the other former Cardinals who had left for other teams was that none of those players wanted to forget their St. Louis years.

"None of those players said anything about 'wanting to put those days' behind them," La Russa said. "Edmonds said he didn't want to talk about his Cardinal years. None of the other guys discounted what happened in St. Louis. I just said if that was his attitude, then we ought to ignore him. I thought he had disrespected the family we had in St. Louis and all of the adulation he had received from the fans. He can't have it both ways."

Edmonds was upset by La Russa's reaction, igniting a war of words between the two. The Cardinal fans ignored La Russa's advice, giving Edmonds a prolonged standing ovation when he came to bat for the first time.

"I think he's just trying to stir it up," Edmonds said. "He gets a little excited about this rivalry. This is always a tense time."

It does seem La Russa, despite his long tenure in the game, does get extra motivation and satisfaction out of beating the Cubs. He has almost the same attitude about beating Milwaukee or Houston—whichever team he believes happens to be the one standing between the Cardinals and playing in October.

La Russa, nearly 30 years after becoming a major league manager, has not lost his love or appreciation for baseball, and especially for the history of the game. It was why, on an off-day in late September, he made a special pilgrimage to Yankee Stadium to see the most famous stadium in all of sports one last time.

As he sat in the stands with Jerry Reinsdorf and watched the Yankees play the White Sox, La Russa came up with his own personal top 10 list of the moments he had witnessed at Yankee Stadium, including seeing Mickey Mantle's long home run off the A's Bill Fischer in 1963, La Russa's rookie season.

"I have so many memories from that place," La Russa said.

During his playing career, La Russa appeared in seven games at Yankee Stadium, going a collective 1-for-11. His only hit was a single to left off Stan Bahnsen in the second game of a doubleheader on July 16, 1970.

More important to La Russa, however, were the many games he managed in that stadium, and whether his team won or lost.

For nearly 30 years, that really is all that has mattered to La Russa. Winning or losing dictates whether he had a good day or a bad day. It dictates whether his team will be good enough to play October baseball, his goal as a manager during every season.

Now 64 years old, La Russa suspects the day will come when he loses that edge, when winning or losing doesn't mean that much to him. He doesn't know when it will happen, whether it will be after the 2009 season or some time further into the future. He may stick around to win enough games to pass John McGraw and move into second place on the all-time wins list. Then again, he may not. If he does, it won't be because he is just trying to move up one spot in the record books.

"I'll be surprised the day he quits," Jim Leyland said. "Both of us are doing something we absolutely love. He loves the game, he respects it, and he loves his players. When the day comes that he feels he has lost the edge to compete, he won't stick around. I know him too well. The day he thinks he is cheating somebody out of a day's pay, he will move on."

The day will come when La Russa knows the fire no longer burns inside him. You can fool people, he once said, but "you aren't going to fool yourself." Once again, he knows he will rely on advice he received years ago from Sparky Anderson and former NFL coach Bill Walsh, who both told him when the day comes, he will know it in his heart.

All La Russa knows now is, that day is yet to come.

Bibliography

Bissinger, Buzz. *Three Nights in August.* New York: Houghton-Mifflin, 2005.

Canseco, Jose. *Juiced.* New York: ReganBooks, 2005.

Dickey, Glenn, Vida Blue, and Joe Morgan. *Champions: The Story of the First Two Oakland A's Dynasties and the Building of the Third.* Chicago: Triumph Books, 2002.

Freedman, Lew and Billy Pierce. *"Then Ozzie Said to Harold...": The Best Chicago White Sox Ever Told.* Chicago: Triumph Books, 2008.

Kittle, Ron and Bob Logan. *Ron Kittle's Tales from the White Sox Dugout.* Champaign, IL: Sports Publishing, 2005

Koppett, Leonard. *The Man in the Dugout.* New York: Crown, 1993.

Migala, Dan. *Dugout Wisdom.* Self-published, 2008.

Phillips, Dave and Rob Rains. *Center Field on Fire.* Chicago: Triumph Books, 2004.

Piersall, Jimmy. *The Whole Truth.* New York: Chicago: Contemporary Books, 1985.

Rains, Rob. *A Special Season.* Champaign, IL: Sports Publishing, 2003.

Will, George. *Men at Work: The Craft of Baseball.* New York: Harper, 1991.

Index